# Shakespeare and Democracy

# SHAKESPEARE
# AND DEMOCRACY

By

ALWIN THALER

KNOXVILLE, TENNESSEE

## THE UNIVERSITY OF TENNESSEE PRESS

1941

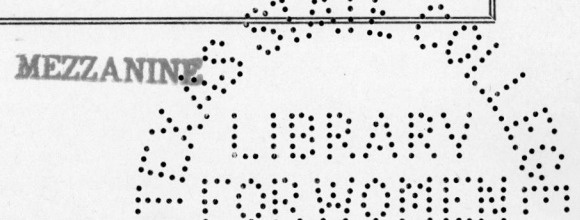

TO MY WIFE

*Harriet Page Thaler*

# Preface

IT IS the privilege—if not the duty—of criticism to look at both the worlds, the now and the everlasting. Scholarship, of course, must try to weigh facts dispassionately in seeking truth. Certainly literary criticism, in our time even more than in Matthew Arnold's, needs sane "disinterestedness" if it is to approximate, however modestly, any valid criticism of life. But critical disinterestedness has never meant mere passivity, and must not now be confounded with pale indifferentism. My readers, at any rate, will observe that the stern form and pressure of contemporary events have left their mark upon this book, especially upon its opening and closing pages. These public addresses—small excerpts from the record of The University of Tennessee's program of public service in critical times—are here printed in their original form: as documents, such as they are, of our day.

Readers who have happened to see earlier work of mine, may notice that I have here put old and new together. In creative art and literature—as I have suggested at the end of this book—the old and the new often gain by being viewed together; and I believe that something of the same principle may hold in humbler fields of endeavor. Therefore I have integrated, in the three sections of this book, materials old and new which, according to friends and scholars whose judgment I trust, belong together. In the opening section, for example, I have put together certain critical and historical "revaluations." Their similarity in approach and method should supply an over-all test of the validity of my conclusions and of my purpose. It is my belief that criticism, in order to keep alive, must, from time to time, pour its old wine into new bottles. It must seek—as I have suggested elsewhere—to brush away some of the dust and cobwebs of tradition: to estimate the real worth of received opinions, rather than their market price.

I have sought to put two and two together also in the second part of this volume, the section devoted to strolling players—the lusty "grass roots" democrats of the theatre. According to good authority dating back to Shakespeare's time (and noticed below, page 157), one difficulty of the strollers has always been that they "never" could "hold together." This has been too true also of most studies attempting to deal with the strollers at large—including my own, till now scattered piecemeal over sundry years and journals. Like others before me, I originally planned to write a comprehensive and definitive book on the subject. Unhappily, I have not been able to command the extra lifetime of leisurely inquiry needed to do justice to this project. I hope, however, that the chapters here (in the parlance of the stage) "revived, with added attractions," will be found to *hold together*, and that they may encourage others to complete the picture.—The reader will note, finally, that this section of the book carries on the "argument" of the last preceding study, and that the last section of the volume, similarly, supplements the matter and method of the preceding chapters.

In preparing this book I have incurred many obligations which I am happy to acknowledge. The editors of various journals—specifically named in the footnotes below—have kindly allowed me to reprint or adapt, for this book, earlier articles of mine first printed in their pages. I am grateful to Professor Mark Van Doren and to Mr. Lynn Landrum for permission to quote from their work; also, for permission to use copyrighted material: to the publishers of *Time*, to Messrs. G. P. Putnam's Sons for the quotations from Walt Whitman's *Complete Writings*, to the Yale University Press for the materials from Professor Tucker Brooke's *Shakespeare of Stratford*, to the Harvard University Press for the quotations from Professor C. J. Furness's *Walt Whitman's Workshop*, and, for quotations more specifically accredited below, to the University of Pennsylvania Press, The Macmillan Company, the Houghton Mifflin Company, the McGraw-Hill Book Company, and to Miss Edna St. Vincent Millay and her publishers, Messrs. Harper & Brothers.

It is pleasant to acknowledge also my very real indebtedness to the John Simon Guggenheim Foundation — for the fellowship award which enabled me, some years ago, to work happily at several of the studies now revised in this book. I am grateful too, for many kindnesses, to the directors of The University of Tennessee Press and to the members of the Committee on University Publications, Mr. F. C. Lowry, Professor Stanley Johnson, and Dr. F. C. Smith; and no less grateful, for good counsel and many valuable suggestions, to my colleagues and tried friends, Professor Charles Bell Burke, Professor John B. Emperor, and Professor John C. Hodges. But I owe most — more, indeed, than the sum of all — to my most exacting critic. To her, my steadfast comrade and good companion in the making of this book, I have inscribed it.

# Contents

# I

## REVALUATIONS:
## CRITICAL AND HISTORICAL

# I

## SHAKESPEARE AND DEMOCRACY

"We must be free or die who speak the tongue
That Shakespeare spake, the faith and morals hold
Which Milton held."

WILLIAM WORDSWORTH published these lines in April,
1803 — barely a month before the renewed outbreak of war
between Britain and Napoleon shattered their uneasy two-year-
old truce, the so-called peace of Amiens. But the cliffs of England
stood firm, though the hearts of England felt the spear-thrust of
threatened invasion from across the Channel. For there, at
Boulogne, flat-bottomed barges were being collected, "and troops
trained to embark and disembark." [1] No wonder that Wordsworth — still in his young manhood then, and always a lover of his
country — rose to the challenge. "It is not to be thought of" — so
opens the sonnet from which I have already quoted —

that the Flood
Of British Freedom, which to the open sea
Of the world's praise, from dark antiquity
Hath flowed with pomp of waters unwithstood . . .
That this most famous stream in bogs and sands
Should perish and to evil and to good
Be lost forever. . . .

In his country's defence, therefore, he invoked unfading
memories of mighty deeds wrought long ago against tyrants at

1. J. H. Robinson, *History of Western Europe* (New York, 1903), p. 610.

home and invaders from abroad. Runnymede and the invincible Armada are a part of that record, and so is the living, undaunted word of England's sages and poets singing her ancient hatred of oppression, her abiding love of liberty. Whether we like it or not, we Americans speak their language; we cannot shut our ears to the echoes of the grand old voices. England's foes, naturally, do not relish this fact. "The German 'news services,' " says a recent commentator,[2]

> complain of British propaganda in the United States. But the greatest propagandist that the British have lies peacefully in his grave. His name is Shakespeare.
>
> No Big Bertha that Hitler's men can contrive can drown out the voice of Big Ben in the ears of American listeners.
>
> No Lord Haw Haw can make us forget the Christmas Carol or Drink to Me Only With Thine Eyes. There's a little bit of the shamrock and the heather in most of us over here, a little of hedgerow and glen which the eyes of the flesh have not seen, a little of blood and dreams of ancestors long since laid beneath sheep-cropped sod.

Propaganda and sentimentality? Perhaps—but, if so, so are the golden rule and the love of a man for a maid. The fact is that the unforgotten echoes of Shakespeare and Milton, of Burns and Shelley, bring no mere British propaganda to American ears. In our halls, too, is "hung the armoury of the invincible knights of old." The shields of our invincible knights—Washington, Franklin, Lincoln—bear good American names! Of course they bear dints of deep wounds struck by English hands—deep scars of old wounds; but also memorials of a great heritage, of noble and priceless gifts.

Our second president, John Adams, had been, in difficult times, a hard-bitten American ambassador in London. He was never an Anglophile. Yet he says flatly that the English nation, for its

> improvements in the theory of government, has . . . more merit with the human race than any other among the moderns.

2. Lynn Landrum, "Thinking Out Loud," *Dallas* (Texas) *News*, June 1, 1940.

The liberal speculations of many [European] writers . . . are manifestly derived from English sources. Americans, too, ought for ever to acknowledge their obligations to English writers, or rather have as good a right to indulge a pride in the recollection of them as the inhabitants of the three kingdoms. The original plantation of our country was occasioned, her continual growth has been promoted, and her present liberties have been established, by these generous theories.[3]

Let us notice especially that debatable passage in the middle of my quotation from Adams: "Americans . . . ought for ever to acknowledge their obligations to English writers." It is pertinent to our inquiry—since we are here concerned with the significance of the greatest of English writers, to us, in our democracy's time of trial. The fathers of this country certainly delighted in remembering Shakespeare. Washington as commander-in-chief quoted him when writing to the presiding officer of Congress from the battlefield.[4] Adams, Jefferson,[5] and even the practical Franklin[6] joined in the chorus of praise and quotation; and Adams[7] in particular hailed the English poet not only as "the great master of nature" but as "a great teacher of morality *and politics*." But we are concerned with later times. One hundred and four years ago, a great American, one who believed that "democracy is good for America," delivered an oration which Oliver Wendell Holmes described as "our intellectual Declaration of Independence." In *The American Scholar*, Ralph Waldo Emerson proclaimed that

Our day of dependence, our long apprenticeship to the learning of other lands, draws to a close. The millions that around us are rushing into life, cannot always be fed on the sere remains of foreign harvests. . . . The English dramatic poets have Shakespearized for two hundred years. . . . We will walk

3. *Works*, ed. C. F. Adams (Boston, 1851), VI, 3 ff.
4. *Writings of George Washington*, ed. J. C. Fitzpatrick (Washington, 1936), XIII, 15 (cf. E. C. Dunn, *Shakespeare in America*, New York, 1939, p. 104).
5. Dunn, *op. cit.*, p. 95.
6. Cf. Thaler, "Franklin and Fulke Greville," PMLA, December, 1941.
7. *Works*, VI, 265-266.

on our own feet; we will work with our own hands; we will speak our own minds.

So we will; so we must. And so, let us recall, did Emerson — in another utterance which is also pertinent to our inquiry. It was published thirteen years after *The American Scholar*, and it suggests that, now and hereafter, Shakespeare may still have much to say not only for England and for all the world, but for our America in particular. Let us hear Emerson speak of Shakespeare again, in *Representative Men* (1850). "Shakespeare's book of life," said Emerson, "wrote the text of modern life: he drew the man of England and Europe, the father of the man in America." — *"The father of the man in America"?* A sentence or two from an exchange of letters between John Adams and Thomas Jefferson in 1811 will help to elucidate Emerson's suggestion. "The same political parties," Jefferson wrote, "which now agitate the United States, have existed through all time." To which Adams replied: "Precisely. While all other sciences have advanced, that of government is still . . . little better understood, little better practiced now, than three or four thousand years ago." [8] Perhaps — but all this was written well over a century ago! Times have changed: new Napoleons, new "representative" men, are rewriting history to-day. Shall we look to the dead past and, with homesick longing, vainly acknowledge bygone obligations to outmoded English writers? All this, while the tidal wave of the future rolls on, threatening to engulf all we cherish? No man knows upon what shores that wave may break, or who, for the moment, may ride its crest. Is old truth false the while, and the past dead indeed, and evil might the only right and reason? Happily, the voices of sages, saints, and prophets may still be heard above the storm. "What is excellent," they answer, "as God lives, is permanent. . . ."

8. *Correspondence of John Adams and Thomas Jefferson*, ed. P. Wilstach (Indianapolis, 1925), p. 20.

> Be not the slave of words: is not the distant, the dead,
> while I love it, and long for it, and mourn for it, Here . . .
> Now? . . . There *is* no Space and no Time: We are—we know
> not what—light-sparkles floating in the aether of Deity. . . .

> O benefit of ill! Now I find true
> That better is by evil still made better;
> And ruined love, when it is built anew,
> Grows fairer than at first. . . .

> Fool! All that is at all
> Lasts ever, past recall.
> Earth changes, but thy soul and God stand sure.[9]

This faith, of course, has no standing to-day in many parts of
our world. It is all the more vital for us because it is, funda-
mentally, the doctrine of Christianity, and, by virtue thereof, the
doctrine of democracy. For democracy, like Christianity, is built
upon the rock: the supreme validity of the individual soul. And
Christianity and democracy are both motivated by faith in the
sacrificial triumph of right over might. Therefore, as James
Russell Lowell reminds us—"Christ was the first true democrat
that ever breathed." [10] Therefore also, and because we are concerned with Shakespeare and democracy, two basic concepts of
his must be underscored at once. (1) Heredity and environment
united to stamp indelibly upon Shakespeare's mind the consequences of the endless misery and terror of civil war—out of which
the Tudors arose. He hated the stupidity and the tyranny of the
mob, and he tended to see in any popular uprising the dangerous
potentiality of mob rule.[11]

> An habitation giddy and unsure
> Hath he that buildeth on the vulgar heart—

9. Emerson, "The Threnody"; Carlyle, *Sartor Resartus;* Shakespeare, Sonnet 119;
Browning, "Rabbi Ben Ezra."
10. "Democracy," 1884.
11. Cf. W. M. MacCallum, *Shakespeare's Roman Plays* (New York, 1910), p. 525.

on the "slippery people," "the still discordant wav'ring multitude." [12]   But, however great Shakespeare's distaste for the mob,
however urgent his sense of the need of order, "degree" [13] and
discipline in the state, he did not forget that a man's a man for a'
that.  Says King Henry V to the soldier Williams at Agincourt,
"the King is but a man . . . all his senses have but human conditions. . . . Every subject's duty is the King's, but every subject's
soul is his own." [14]  The good king in *All's Well* [15] also speaks
plainly on this subject.  "The place," says he, "is dignified by the
doer's deed . . . not by the title. . . ."

> Honors thrive
> When rather from our acts we them derive
> Than our foregoers.

"Here," says Schofield,[16] "we rise to the . . . height of true
democracy." — (2) Shakespeare observes that often "in the corrupted currents of this world" we find "captive good attending
captain ill." [17]  But it is Shakespeare also who proclaims unequivocally the Christian doctrine

> That better is by evil still made better
> And ruined love . . . Grows fairer than at first.

Ruin without end, meanwhile, looms black across the waters.
More than sceptre and crown have tumbled down.  We may hope
that our shores are still relatively secure against military invasion,
but England's cause comes ever nearer home.  Wings across the
sea — winged ships and winged words — bring home to us the
certainty that it is not the flood of *English* freedom only that is
endangered in our time.  A world war is waging, and the world

12. *II Henry IV*, i, iii, 89-90; Induction 19; *Antony and Cleopatra*, I, ii, 192.
13. *Troilus and Cressida*, I, iii, 83-136; see below, p. 38.
14. *Henry V*, IV, i, 105-185.      15. II, iii, 133-144.
16. *Chivalry in English Literature* (Cambridge, 1912), pp. 259-261.
17. Sonnet 66; see also Sonnet 119.

is small today. We may or may not be disposed to grant that the causes of the catastrophe are complex, that the evil is not all on one side. Probably no war, however victorious, can make the world permanently safe for democracy. But, in the face of the program and the might of the authoritarian powers, it can scarcely be denied that this war is likely to test whether any democratic nation can long endure in the present world. Certainly we shall be serving our own cause if, in marshalling our spiritual resources for this struggle, we pause to see what we can gather of aid and comfort, of warning and inspiration, from the man who, of all ancients and moderns, "had the largest and most comprehensive soul." Democracy seeking to build impregnable defenses should find a mighty stronghold in Shakespeare—because he was pre-eminently, as Emerson says, "the man who carried the Saxon race in him," though he was also the "poet of the human race." [18]

On general principles this would surely seem to be a reasonable expectation. It is the more curious, therefore, to note how unqualified a denial of this assumption seems to underlie the views of many commentators, old and new, from both sides of the Atlantic. On general principles, nobody denies that Shakespeare is for all time; but many a distinguished critic, poet, and scholar asserts or implies that Shakespeare's social and political thinking belong primarily and finally to his own Tudor England, or indeed, to the preceding age of feudalism. Therefore, they argue, his writings have no relevance for our democracy and its problems. Let me cite an example. When the biographer of Lincoln, the poet Carl Sandburg, speaks out loud and bold for democracy, few will refuse to listen. I, for one, heard him say recently,[19] and virtually in so many words, that the work of Shakespeare is a document of negligible importance for a democratic people. Without attempting to explore all the whys and wherefores of this

18. *Representative Men.*
19. In a public lecture at the University of Tennessee, October, 1938.

pronouncement, I venture to think that Abraham Lincoln himself would not have subscribed to it, at least not without substantial reservations. It is clear, at all events, that Lincoln was deeply impressed by certain of the histories and tragedies of Shakespeare which have no small bearing upon politics, rule and government. *Macbeth* was Lincoln's especial — but by no means his only — favorite. Those who know their Lincoln may recall that he loved to read Shakespeare aloud to his friends — such speeches, among others, as Richard II's beginning

> For God's sake let us sit upon the ground
> And tell sad stories of the death of kings.

And they may recall also that on one occasion, in the thick of the Civil War, Lincoln read his secretary to sleep with the end of *Henry VI* and the opening of *Richard III* — "till my heavy eyelids caught his considerate notice," John Hay reports, "& he sent me to bed." [20] This was on August 23, 1863. Six days earlier Lincoln himself had written to James H. Hackett to praise that actor's presentation of *King Henry IV*. He is "very anxious," Lincoln writes, to see the play again, and also *Richard III*. And he adds, significantly, I think: "Some of Shakespeare's plays I have never read; while others I have gone over perhaps as frequently as any unprofessional reader. Among the latter are *Lear*, *Richard III*, *Henry VIII*, *Hamlet*, and especially *Macbeth*. I think nothing equals *Macbeth*. It is wonderful." [21]

Even so, Mr. Sandburg is but one of the many writers, English and American, who are in substantial agreement upon the general proposition that Shakespeare has about as little to do with democracy as the great soul — according to the Emersonian doctrine of self-reliance — has to do with consistency; i.e., "simply nothing." I think it will serve our purpose to examine, summarily, the

20. *Lincoln in the Diaries of John Hay*, ed. Tyler Dennett (New York, 1939), p. 82; cf. E. C. Dunn, *op. cit.*, pp. 275, 280.

21. *Works of Abraham Lincoln*, ed. J. G. Nicolay and John Hay (New York, 1920), II, 392-393.

grounds of this opinion, and then the *other* side, as one view or the other has found notable expression in England and America from John Milton's time to Robert Browning's, from John Adams to Walt Whitman and Edwin Arlington Robinson. Besides analyzing the cause of this clash of opinion, we shall have to glance at a few of the plays for ourselves in order to determine whether or not Shakespeare's work is a negligible document for our democracy, to-day.

Among recent American poets, no less authentic a voice than that of Carl Sandburg is that of the late Edwin Arlington Robinson. That these two were not songbirds of a feather is clear enough, but criticism makes strange bedfellows. Of course, it is not strange that Robinson pays notable homage to Shakespeare, the man and the artist—such tribute to his brooding dreams, his gloriously zestful and multitudinous humanity, as Carl Sandburg would certainly be the last to challenge. "Tell me now," says Ben Jonson, in Robinson's poem concerning the man from Stratford—[22]

> Tell me now
> If ever there was anything let loose
> On earth by gods or devils heretofore
> Like this mad, careful, proud, indifferent Shakespeare . . .
> He treads along through time's old wilderness
> As if the tramp of all the centuries
> Had left no roads—and there are none for him.

This is true; not strange. On the other hand I think it is curious that both the poet of *The People—Yes* and the austerely aristocratic Robinson emphasize primarily that side of Shakespeare which tends to date him, to make him peculiarly the mouthpiece of the old order. These modern poets, I believe, see too little of what Shakespeare himself saw when he looked into his heart to write: not only his "own fears," but also "the prophetic

22. "Ben Jonson Entertains A Man From Stratford," *Collected Poems*, quoted by permission of The Macmillan Company, Publishers.

soul of the wide world, dreaming on things to come." [23] Robinson dramatizes sharply—too sharply, I think—Shakespeare's land-hunger and his courtly leanings.  Robinson's Shakespeare—at least according to Robinson's Ben Jonson—"itches, manor-bitten to the bone."  "What he wants most" is "his dukedom down in Warwickshire."  He is "fribbling all the time with that damned House"—"that prodigious grand new House in Stratford."  Or, again, in London

> He sees too many lords.
> They're part of half what ails him . . .
> Albeit he knows himself—yes, yes, he knows—
> The lord of more than England, and of more
> Than all the seas of England in all time
> Shall ever wash.

After all, however, Robinson strikes a partial balance.  The "dust and sweat" of the actor's calling, he writes, was bitter ointment for Shakespeare's spirit, "with his lords looking on and laughing at him."  And yet—

> King as he is, he can't be King *de facto*
> And that's as well, because he wouldn't like it;
> He'd frame a lower rating of men then
> Than he has now; and after that would come
> An abdication. . . .

To which we might add, for our purposes, a prosaic question which Robinson, understandably enough, does not raise.  May not a great man, a poet or a statesman—a Shakespeare, say, or a George Washington—one who is fond of acquiring or upbuilding land and mansions and family honors, an aristocrat by birth or by instinct and association,—may not such an aristocrat so live and so write that aftertimes will not willingly let die what he has wrought *for the common life of the many?*

To raise this question, is not to deny that Shakespeare—like

23. Sonnet 107.

many who in the long run have rendered yeoman service to democracy — had strong conservative leanings. An excellent modern authority puts the case as follows:

> The author of the Shakespearean plays . . . was not the advanced political thinker that Bacon was, or Ralegh, or Spenser, or even Marlowe. He was distinctly a traditionalist in politics and social theory. His attitude toward the state and sovereign was not Tudor but Plantagenet, not renaissance, but feudal. It represents the feeling of Stratford much better than that of London. . . . Shakespeare's loyalty was always that of the Tory country-dweller. . . .[24]

I shall indicate later that I am quite ready to grant almost all of this, except perhaps the two adverbs, *"distinctly* a traditionalist," and *"always* . . . the Tory." But before resuming my summary of the case against Shakespeare, I think it may be in order to observe that history and literature record many examples of constructive services rendered to society and to the body politic by "traditionalists" — practical day-by-day conservatives who hated tyranny and loved liberty, and whose liberal instincts and social conscience made no slight contribution ultimately to the democracy of the human spirit, if not immediately to the cause of political democracy. James Russell Lowell was one of them in comparatively recent times; Dr. Samuel Johnson, in the eighteenth century, was another; and these men had Elizabethan predecessors. Mr. A. H. Bullen describes one of them as follows:

> In practical affairs . . . a strong upholder of the King's prerogatives — his speculative opinions and . . . his views on church matters were of a liberal character. In reading him, we come to regard him rather as a lofty-minded puritan and republican than as a church-and-King man.[25]

24. Tucker Brooke, *Shakespeare of Stratford* (New Haven, 1926), pp. 144-145.
25. *Elizabethans* (London, 1924), p. 206.

This was Fulke Greville, Lord Brooke, counselor to King James and friend to Sir Philip Sidney. Now Shakespeare was neither a puritan nor a republican—but, before we label him finally as an unqualified "traditionalist . . . in social theory" let us recall for the moment but three Shakespearean utterances— one from the *Merchant of Venice* and two from *King Lear*. Take Shylock's *apologia*,[26] "Hath not a Jew eyes . . . ?" The implications of this speech—the recognition of the practical case for tolerance—are *not* merely traditional. Indeed they are altogether missing in at least one of the great Elizabethans whose political and social thinking, we are told, was more "advanced" than Shakespeare's,—witness the unalloyed deviltry of Shylock's prototype, Barabas in Marlowe's *Jew of Malta*. Again, consider King Lear's speech and the Duke of Gloucester's, when suffering has taught them charity and perhaps something of the elements of social justice. Says Lear:

> Poor naked wretches, wheresoe'er you are,
> That bide the pelting of this pitiless storm,
> How shall your houseless heads and unfed sides,
> Your looped and windowed raggedness, defend you
> From seasons such as these? O, I have ta'en
> Too little care of this! Take physic, pomp;
> Expose thyself to feel what wretches feel,
> That thou mayst shake the superflux to them
> And show the heavens more just.

Gloucester, too, speaks pointedly of the problem of distribution—not to say of "sharing the wealth"?—

> Here, take this purse, thou whom the heavens' plagues
> Have humbled to all strokes. That I am wretched
> Makes thee the happier; heavens deal so still;
> Let the superfluous and lust-dieted man
> That slaves your ordinance, that will not see
> Because he does not feel, feel your power quickly:

26. *Merchant of Venice*, III, i, 61.

> *So distribution should undo excess*
> *And each man have enough.*[27]

Have not these speeches some degree of pertinence for a democratic people? I believe that John Milton thought so; that these "Delphic lines" took "deep impression" upon his heart. Certainly he expressed the same idea in almost identical terms. Witness this passage in *Comus:*

> If every just man that now pines with want
> Had but a moderate and beseeming share
> Of that which *lewdly pampered Luxury*
> Now heaps upon some few with vast *excess,*
> Nature's full blessings would be well dispensed
> *In unsuperfluous even proportion. . . .*[28]

It is curious, therefore, that Walt Whitman, the poet of democracy, seems to have ignored these lines, though he was deeply impressed by *King Lear.*[29] For it was Carl Sandburg's master, Walt Whitman, who most roundly attacked Shakespeare — in order to establish the principle that democracy must sing its own songs in its own native key.

This famous frontal attack upon Shakespeare, however familiar, must be quoted in full here. Later we shall have to take account of the fact — less generally known — that the attack was not Walt Whitman's last word upon Shakespeare's uses for America. But the original blast is of first importance for our inquiry. Written in 1888, in the Preface [30] to *November Boughs*, it begins with a series of questions.

> Of the great poems receiv'd from abroad and from the
> ages, and to-day enveloping and penetrating America, is there

27. *King Lear*, III, iv, 28-36; IV, i, 67-74.
28. *Comus*, 768-773; *On Shakespeare*, 10-12; cf. Thaler, *Shakspere's Silences* (Cambridge, 1929), p. 159.
29. See Whitman's *Complete Prose Works* (Boston, 1898), pp. 391, 477; *Uncollected Poetry and Prose*, ed. Emory Holloway (Garden City, New York, 1921), I, 208, II, 108; *Complete Writings* (New York, 1902 — hereafter referred to as *Writings*), Prose, *VI*, 89.
30. "A Backward Glance O'er Travel'd Roads," *Writings*, III, 52 ff.

one that is consistent with these United States, or essentially applicable to them, as they are and are to be? Is there one whose underlying basis is not a denial and insult to democracy?

Whitman "willingly" admits that "the emotional, moral, and aesthetic natures of humanity have not changed." Unlike Jefferson and John Adams he makes no allowance for the slow changes in the *political* nature of humanity. Yet he grants that within the limits he has indicated "the old poems apply to our times and all times." They "are of incalculable value as pictures of the past" and "perhaps . . . the most precious bequest" of that past to "American civilization." As a theatre-goer and reader Whitman enjoyed them keenly, discriminatingly, and yet with a splendid creative fervor, all his life long. *But:*

> Even Shakespeare, who so suffuses current letters and art (which indeed have in most degrees grown out of him,) belongs essentially to the buried past. Only he holds the proud distinction for certain important phases of that past, of being the loftiest of the singers life has yet given voice to. All, however, relate to and rest upon conditions, standards, politics, sociologies, ranges of belief, *that have been quite eliminated from the Eastern Hemisphere, and never existed at all in the Western.* As authoritative types of song they belong in America just about as much as the persons and institutes they depict.[31]

It should be noticed that Whitman here sums up three main aspects of a doctrine he had elaborated long before — notably in the *Democratic Vistas* [32] of 1871. Therein, he had admitted, first, that for *us* no less than for any nation the grand old monuments "stand" —

> For us those beacons burn through all the nights. Unknown Egyptians . . . Hindus . . . Hebrew prophet . . . Christ, with bent head . . . Greek . . . Roman . . . Dante, stalking with lean form . . . Angelo, and the great painters,

31. My italics.
32. For passages quoted, see *Complete Prose*, pp. 233, 200, 209, 202, 218. (My italics.)

architects, musicians; *rich Shakespeare, luxuriant as the sun, artist and singer of feudalism in its sunset, with all the gorgeous colors*, owner thereof, and using them at will. . . .

But — to come to his second point — these, after all, are not for America, — because they are not of our time and because they are against democracy:

> Ye powerful and resplendent ones! Ye were, in your atmospheres, grown not for America, but rather for her foes, the feudal and the old — while our genius is democratic and modern. . . . *Never was anything more wanted than, to-day, and here . . . the poet of the modern.*

For all the *old* poetry, indeed all literature has *discriminated against "the People."* It has glorified the ancient damnation of courts; it has ignored the "ill-bred" masses:

> Taste, intelligence, and culture (so-called) have been against the masses, and remain so. There is plenty of glamour about the most damnable crime and hoggish meannesses . . . of the feudal and dynastic world over there . . . its lords and queens and courts, so well dressed and so handsome. But the people are ungrammatical, untidy, and their sins gaunt and ill-bred.
>
> Literature, strictly consider'd, has never recognized the people, and, whatever may be said, does not to-day. Speaking generally, the tendencies of literature, as hitherto pursued, have been to make mostly critical and querulous men. It seems as if, so far, there were some natural repugnance between a literary and professional life and the rude rank spirit of the democracies. . . . I know nothing more rare, even in this country, than a fit and reverent appreciation of the People — of their measureless wealth of latent power and capacity . . . far surpassing all the vaulted samples of book-heroes. . . .

The third item of Whitman's indictment is directed not against literature in general, but against foreign literature in particular, and especially against the dangerous influence of the great masters. America urgently needs "some two or three really original American poets." Unfortunately,

> What has fill'd, and fills to-day our intellect, our fancy, furnishing the standard therein, is yet foreign. *The great poems, Shakespeare included, are poisonous to the idea of the pride and dignity of the common people, the life blood of democracy.* The models of our literature, as we get it from other lands, ultra-marine, have had their birth in courts, and bask'd and grown in castle sunshine; all smells of princes' favors. Of workers of a certain sort, we have indeed, plenty, contributing after their kind. . . . But touched by the national test, or tried by the standards of democratic personality, they wither to ashes. I say I have not seen a single writer, artist, lecturer, or what-not, that has confronted the voiceless but ever erect and active, pervading underlying will and typic aspiration of the land, in a spirit kindred to itself.

Surely, if ever there was such a thing as valid and creative propaganda, this was it. That Whitman knew it to be propaganda is all but certain. Yet it has rarely been noticed that he himself had set forth something of the other side early in his career—in the 1855 Preface to *Leaves of Grass*.[33] There he had written that

> In the make of the great masters, the idea of political liberty is indispensable . . . Poets . . . are the voice and exposition of liberty. . . . The attitude of great poets is to cheer up slaves and horrify despots.

In criticism, however, as in everyday journalism, it is the sensational utterance that wins public notice, while the corrections, the sober second thoughts, are usually disregarded. Walt Whitman's front-page attack on Shakespeare is well remembered to this day, but hardly anyone, so far as I know, has given proper emphasis to the fact that his view underwent notable modifications. Before concluding this study, we shall have to review certain general characteristics of Shakespeare's historical plays, and, in a subsequent chapter, a remarkable suggestion of Whitman's which amounts virtually to a retraction of his earlier

33. Walt Whitman, *Representative Selections*, ed. Floyd Stovall, American Writers Series (New York, 1934), p. 326. (The last sentence of this passage is omitted in later versions of this Preface. See *Writings, Prose*, II, 175.)

charges.[34]   Meanwhile, let us observe this much: within ten years after the *Democratic Vistas* Whitman had substantially qualified the assertion that the great poems are poisonous to the lifeblood of democracy.   Of course he never ceased demanding that America produce and cherish her *own* poets, her own men and women. But he recognized, increasingly, that we cannot "afford" to do without our great heritage.   In 1881, in an essay on "Poetry To-day in America" [35] he put the case clearly.   He observes that our country, our brave new world

> proceeds on its course, on scales of area and velocity immense and absolute . . . and, like the globe itself, quite oblivious even of great poets and thinkers.   But we can by no means afford to be oblivious of them. . . .
>
> Years ago I thought Americans ought to strike out separate, and have expressions of their own in highest literature.   I think so still and more decidedly than ever.   *But those convictions are now strongly temper'd* . . . perhaps [by] the results of advancing age or . . . reflection . . . I see that this world of the West, as part of all, fuses inseparably with the East, and with all, as time does—the ever new yet old, old human race. . . . If we are not to hospitably receive and complete the inaugurations of the old civilizations, and change their small scale to the largest, broadest scale, what on earth are we for?

We must still strive, of course, to find our own native voice. But, while "democracy waits the coming of its bards," let us, says Whitman, "saturate ourselves . . . yet awhile" with the best

> of that past and those lands we spring from . . . remembering that at present and doubtless long ahead a certain humility would well become us. . . .   All serves our New World progress . . . *Shakspere has served, and serves, maybe, the best of any.*

I cannot take time to add more than one notable name to my roll call of distinguished devil's advocates for democracy and

34.  See below, pp. 35, 57 ff.
35.  *Writings, Prose,* II, 212, 229.  (My italics.)

against Shakespeare. The name of William Hazlitt, however, must not be omitted here—if only because, like Whitman, he too was a great foe of the feudal order and of its aftermath, an indomitable fighter for the liberties of the common man, and, withal, a true lover of poetry and of Shakespeare. "To see the golden sun and the azure sky, the outstretched ocean; to walk upon the green earth, to read history and witness the revolutions of empires . . . *to have read Shakespeare* and belong to the same species as Sir Isaac Newton"—this seemed to Hazlitt about the best that life has to offer. "All the people that ever lived," he wrote, are in Shakespeare's "mind," and all "the world of spirits" too.[36] As for poetry itself—he held it to be not a "branch of authorship" but "the stuff out of which our life is made. . . . It relates to whatever is most interesting in human life. Whoever therefore has a contempt for poetry has a contempt for himself and humanity." [37] Yet, like Walt Whitman he was—in certain moods—inclined to find fault with poetry because it tends to be "aristocratical"—to side against "the cause of the people."

In his discussion of *Coriolanus*, Hazlitt enters vigorously into this subject. What he has to say is important for us because this play, more than any other of Shakespeare's, seems to support the view that its author was definitely anti-democratic in spirit. Upon turning from Shakespeare's impassioned fulminations against the plebeian mob of Rome to the more calmly considered studies of his own English kings, nobles, and commoners, I think we shall find that *Coriolanus* is, after all, the exception that proves the rule—that Shakespeare, by and large, was no mere reactionary in his views on politics and the social order. Still, Hazlitt's remarks on *Coriolanus* [38] deserve careful consideration. Like Walt Whitman, he felt that

36. "On the Feeling of Immortality in Youth," "On Shakespeare and Milton," Hazlitt, *Complete Works*, ed. Waller and Glover (London, 1902-1906), XII, 153; V, 47.
37. "On Poetry in General"; *The Characters of Shakespeare's Plays*, *Complete Works*, V, 1-18, I, 271.
38. *Characters* (*Complete Works*, I, 214 ff.).

The cause of the people is indeed but little calculated as a subject for poetry: it admits of rhetoric, which goes into argument and explanation, but it represents no immediate or distinct images to the mind, 'no jutting frieze, buttress, or coigne of vantage,' for poetry 'to make its pendent bed and procreant cradle in.' The language of poetry naturally falls in with the language of power. The imagination is an exaggerating . . . exclusive . . . and aristocratical . . . faculty. The principle of poetry is a very anti-levelling principle. It aims at effect, it exists by contrast. . . . It is everything by excess. . . . It presents a dazzling appearance. It shows its head turreted, crowned and crested. Its front is gilt and blood-stained. Before it, 'it carries noise, and behind it leaves tears.' It has its altars and its victims, sacrifices, human sacrifices. Kings, priests, nobles, are its train-bearers; tyrants, and slaves its excutioners. — 'Carnage is its daughter.' — Poetry is right royal. It puts the individual for the species, the one above the infinite many, might before right.

Now Hazlitt, be it remembered, hated kings and loathed despots, oppression, and tyranny of any description. It is small wonder, therefore, that he was out of patience with Shakespeare for loading the dice against the people — as Shakespeare, the contemner of mobs, undeniably did in *Coriolanus*. "Shakespeare himself," Hazlitt observes,

seems to have had a leaning to the arbitrary side of the question, perhaps from some feeling of contempt for his own origin; and to have spared no occasion of baiting the rabble. What he says of them is very true: what he says of his betters is also very true, though he dwells less upon it. . . . A lion hunting a flock of sheep or a herd of wild asses is a more poetical object than they; and we even take part with the lordly beast, because our vanity or some other feeling makes us disposed to place ourselves in the situation of the strongest party. So we feel some concern for the poor citizens of Rome when they meet together to compare their wants and grievances, till Coriolanus comes in and with blows and big words drives this set of 'poor rats,' this rascal scum, to their homes and beggary before him.

There is nothing heroical in a multitude of miserable rogues not wishing to be starved. . . . But when a single man comes forward to brave their cries and to make them submit to the last indignities, from mere pride and self-will, our admiration of his prowess is immediately converted into contempt for their pusillanimity. The insolence of power is stronger than the plea of necessity. . . . We had rather be the oppressor than the oppressed. The love of power within ourselves and the admiration of it in others are both natural to man. . . .

But . . . the whole dramatic moral of *Coriolanus* is that those who have little shall have less, and that those who have much shall take all that others have left. The people are poor; therefore they ought to be starved. They are slaves; therefore they ought to be beaten. They work hard; therefore they ought to be treated like beasts of burden. They are ignorant; therefore they ought not to be allowed to feel that they want food, or clothing, or rest. . . . This is the logic of the imagination! . . . The history of mankind . . . is a noble or royal hunt, in which what is sport to the few is death to the many, and in which the spectators halloo and encourage the strong to set upon the weak, and cry havoc in the chase though they do not share in the spoil.

I have quoted at length because Hazlitt's account of *Coriolanus* suggests an important distinction. Perhaps this play indicates that Shakespeare could, on occasion, take his stand squarely against the popular cause — especially when he is dealing with what seems to him a mad tug of war between the insolent but established pride of power and the revolutionary mob-uprisings of "the vulture of sedition." [39] But I think we can interpret *Coriolanus* as an unqualifiedly anti-democratic document only if we disregard the fact that in the end Shakespeare allows the inexorable logic of events to bring Coriolanus, the arch-hater of the people, to absolute and dismal failure, to a futile and miserable death. (According to Walt Whitman, even the treatment of the "rabble" in *Coriolanus* is "strictly . . . the truth" as Shakespeare

39. *1 Henry VI*, IV, iii, 47.

saw it and, indeed, as it actually *was!* [40]) At all events, this play illuminates all sides and issues of its problem. It is, therefore, a document not to be ignored by anyone who is interested in the political and social travail of mankind. Hazlitt, indeed, is quick to admit this—and his verdict counts for something, since he was not merely a gifted critic but also a brilliant Parliamentary reporter and one of the shrewdest political commentators of his time. The play proves, he says, that Shakespeare was

> · well versed in history and state affairs. . . . Anyone who studies . . . *Coriolanus* . . . may save himself the trouble of reading Burke's *Reflections*, or Paine's *Rights of Man*, or the Debates in both Houses of Parliament since the French Revolution. . . . The arguments for and against aristocracy or democracy, on the privileges of the few and the claims of the many, on liberty and slavery, power and the abuse of it, peace and war, are here very ably handled with the spirit of a poet and the acuteness of a philosopher.

To recapitulate more specifically: Shakespeare weights the case unfairly against the Plebs, but this play exhibits, fairly on the whole and always significantly, many vexed strands of the complex social, economic and political fabric of its own and later times. We hear familiar complaints. "Store-houses" are "cramm'd with grain" while the poor are starving; "daily . . . more piercing" taxes are levied against them, "daily" more favorable "edicts . . . to support usurers" and rich tax-dodgers.[41] The chicanery of demagogues is given no more prominence than the insensate pride of birth and privilege. And every scene has its implied protest against the unpardonable sin in political administration—the sin of both parties in this play—the refusal to accept a reasonable compromise.[42] Many a scene, too, has its clear-eyed commentary upon the cynical folly of the war-mongers. Among them are the fine "servingmen" who want the wars for

40. See the passage quoted below, p. 50.
41. *Coriolanus*, I, 1, 80-90.    42. *Id.*, *I*, ii, 221-225; III, i, 134-137.

their money: "a stirring world again;" no more "lethargy," but "sprightly, waking, audible . . . war." [43] Then there is also the heroic Coriolanus himself, who finds one cause to welcome new wars in the hope that

> Then we shall ha' means to vent
> Our musty superfluity.[44]

This is, no doubt, a more practical method of dealing with the still unsolved problem of distribution than that suggested by Gloucester and Lear.[45] Certainly it is a significant example of the ancient escape-technique, whereby the red herring of foreign war is drawn, by desperate politicians, across the trail of domestic embarrassment. Perhaps Mussolini remembered this technique when he started upon his African adventure. Professor Charles A. Beard [46] urges that even the democracies have not altogether forgotten it. Certain it is that Shakespeare had it vividly in mind when he made King Henry IV advise his son to keep stirring abroad:

> Lest rest and lying still might make them look
> Too near unto my state. Therefore, my Harry,
> Be it thy course to *busy giddy minds*
> *With foreign quarrels*, that action, hence borne out
> May waste the memory of the former days.[47]

The causes and the vicious circle of consequences wrought by this sort of thing are too plainly operative in modern power politics. Besides illustrating them cogently, Shakespeare sums them up, time and again, in terms that might almost have been intended for this year of grace. The papal legate in the play of *King John*,[48] for example, says roundly that power

43. *Id.*, IV, v, 233-248.  44. *Id.*, I, i, 229-230.  45. See above, p. 14.
46. *Giddy Minds and Foreign Quarrels* (New York, 1939).
47. *2 Henry IV*, IV, V, 212-216.  48. III, iv, 135-138, 145.

> Snatch'd with an unruly hand
> Must be as boisterously maintain'd as gain'd;
> And he that stands upon a slippery place
> Makes nice of no vile hold to stay him up.

"How green you are and fresh in this old world," he adds. And how blind we must remain if we willfully shut our eyes to the lessons of the past thus underscored by historian and poet!

Before we leave Hazlitt and this part of our study, I should like to make another observation. Like Edwin Arlington Robinson and Walt Whitman, Hazlitt saw something of both sides of the picture. He dislikes Shakespeare's rabble-baiting and holds that "the dramatic moral" of *Coriolanus* is *immoral!* Yet he found, in Shakespeare's English history plays, delicate food to please his own taste — or rather his own disrelish — his pet abomination in the political set-up of his own time: his hatred of those "grand" conspirators "against the right of the human race to be free" [49] — tyrants, despots, Tory and Bourbon kings. Writing of King Henry VIII, Hazlitt remarks: "It has been said of him — 'no maid could live near such a man.' It might with as good reason be said of Shakespeare, 'No king could live near such a man.' " [50] If so — if Shakespeare is anti-monarchial — we had better stop to put a question, by way of turning for a moment to another side of our problem.

If Shakespeare is inimical to kings and despots, how does it happen that he is Shakespeare still, in present day Germany, in anti-democratic Germany? — There, we are informed, he remains (seconded by Bernard Shaw) the favorite attraction of the wartime theatres, even in Prussian Berlin.[51] Our question, of course, answers itself. There are indications that German scholars loyal

---

49. Preface, *Political Essays, Complete Works*, III, 31 ff.
50. *Complete Works*, I, 452, 305 (Daniel's emendation).
51. See W. L. Shirer, "Inside Wartime Germany," *Life*, February 3, 1941, p. 74.

to the present order in their country are about to proclaim
Shakespeare the true prophet of their own political faith.[52]  But
America will know a better answer.  Shakespeare was *"Unser
Shakespeare"* in Germany long before the World War.  He has
held his own there all through the vicissitudes of war and troubled
peace, and will doubtless continue to do so — for good and sufficient
non-political reasons.  Long ago, German poets, critics, and
scholars established a high and honorable claim upon Shakespeare
— and indeed upon the gratitude of Shakespeareans everywhere —
by pioneering and persevering zealously in the study of Shakespeare.  Shakespeare himself did the rest.  There is ample
*Lebensraum* in Shakespeare for all people and times.  For this
reason, among others, he belongs not only to England and America
but also to Germany and to all mankind.

Shakespeare's social and political complexion is still his own,
no matter how enthusiastically Nazi Germany may claim him.
But, by the same token, we cannot assume that he is the poet of
democracy merely because he is the national poet of embattled
Britain, nor, indeed, because he is "our" Shakespeare too —
America's Shakespeare, "the god of our idolatry."  "Washington,
Lincoln, Shakespeare," said the late Professor Thorndike [53] —
"they are the three whom Americans universally worship, and
you will not find a fourth of ours or any other nation to add to
this trinity. . . .  You can't be president of the United States
unless you have read Shakespeare!"  The writings of George
Washington and Jefferson, of the Adamses and Lincoln, of Wood-
row Wilson and the two Roosevelts, partially justify this pleasant
hyperbole.  Perhaps it does not tell the whole story, but the facts
underlying it are pertinent to our inquiry.  For nothing can be
more certain than this fact: that England's Shakespeare and
America's — like Germany's — has lived and moved vigorously,
through war and peace, in our time as of yore, in the shaping of

52. Cf. Professor Hans H. Glunz, "The State in Shakespeare's Plays," *Research and Progress* (Bi-monthly Review of German Science), V (July—August, 1939), 219-224.
53. "Shakespeare in America," *Shakespeare Association Bulletin*, III (1928), 1-8.

men and thought and events — momentous or gay, hopeful, solemn, or portentous.

John Ruskin, we know, urged that Shakespeare's histories be set down as required reading for all English schoolboys — and the Duke of Marlborough [54] got his history in just that way, except that he *elected* the course! It may be objected that Ruskin and the Duke of Marlborough were not democrats. But this objection can hardly stand in the case of the British soldiers who read Shakespeare's histories in the World War trenches; nor against H. M. Tomlinson, who drew from *Macbeth* the title of his haunting volume of recollections of that war, *All Our Yesterdays*; [55] nor yet against Ramsay Macdonald, England's prime minister — who opened the London Naval Disarmament Conference, in 1930, with a pertinent line from *Antony and Cleopatra* [56] — "Let's not confound the time with conference harsh."

"In any crisis," said *Time* on September 4, 1939 (the day after war was declared), "Englishmen crave an apt quotation from Shakespeare. The London *News Chronicle* performed great public service last week by discovering in *Hamlet*, Act IV, scene 4: 'Goes it against the main of Poland, Sir?' . . . 'Yes; it is already garrisoned.' " — *Time* was right! "Shaw Rewrites Shakespeare To Include Wallis Episode," ran the headlines in November 1937, [57] when Shaw revamped *Cymbeline* to make it foreshadow the troubles of the present Duke and Duchess of Windsor. By May 1941 German bombers had brought fiery ruin to more than six million books in British bookstores and libraries. *Bulletins*

---

54. See Coleridge's *Shakespearean Criticism*, ed. T. M. Raysor (Cambridge, 1930), I, 144.

55. New York, 1930; see pp. 341-342. — Book titles drawn from Shakespeare are always popular (see annual bibliography, *Bulletin*, Shakespeare Association of America), but they multiply in times of stress. For example — while writing these lines, in June, 1941, I find, in one day's notices of new books, two Shakespearean titles: *This Realm, This England* (editor, Samuel Chamberlain; from *Richard II*, II, i, 50), and *Come to Dust* (by Anne Fremantle; from *Cymbeline*, IV, ii, 263).

56. I, i, 45. (See London newspapers, January 22, 1930.)

57. Knoxville *News-Sentinel*, November 18, 1937.

*From Britain* [58] headline the official report on this subject by
quoting Caliban's injunction: "Burn but his books . . . for
without them He's but a sot, as I am." [59]  In this same merry
month of May Rudolf Hess landed in Scotland — whereupon the
British Press Service [60] quoted *Macbeth*,[61] "Macduff is fled to
England . . . his flight was madness."  Or — to recall another
strangely portentous international visitation by air — it will be
remembered that Mr. Chamberlain started for Munich with a
line from *Henry IV*,[62] on his lips — "Out of this nettle, danger, we
pluck this flower, safety."  (The same shallow-rooted flower,
incidentally, which Mrs. Miniver's friend, Badgecumbe the bio-
chemist, damned with faint praise not long after Munich.) [63]

Unhappily, Chamberlain did not pluck the flower he had hoped
for.  And yet, when appeasement failed, he proved himself a
true-born Englishman still, for in February 1939, he gave pointed
notice of the stiffening of British policy in another quotation from
Shakespeare, this time from the ending of *King John:* [64]

> This England never did and never shall
> Lie at the proud foot of a conqueror . . .
> Come the three corners of the World in arms
> And we shall shock them.

Statecraft, like scholarship, is not proof against the ironic
touch of time and change.  Witness the fact that this very speech,
Chamberlain's challenge to the world in arms, is cited by Professor
Tucker Brooke [65] to illustrate his point that Shakespeare's "vision
stops at the ideal of a hermit kingdom, *free from foreign entangle-
ments.*"  Shakespeare, of course, is not to be held responsible for
all the patriotic and miscellaneous uses to which his work has

58. Number 36, Supplement, May 7, 1941.   59. *The Tempest*, III, ii, 100-103.
60. As reported in the Knoxville *News-Sentinel* May 18, 1941.
61. IV, i, 142; ii, 3.   62. *1 Henry IV*, II, iii, 10.
63. Jan Struther, *Mrs. Miniver* (New York, 1940), pp. 159, 164.
64. V, viii, 112-117. Cf. *Time*, October 14, 1940.
65. *Shakespeare of Stratford*, pp. 146-148. (My italics.)

been put. It is desirable, therefore, to give due weight to Brooke's caution that Shakespeare's patriotism tended to be insular and, at times, merely rhetorical—that even so characteristic an expression of it as King Henry V's speech before Agincourt is scarcely more than "the high-water mark of football oratory." Now football is a good democratic game—as the myriad-minded Shakespeare himself intimates when he makes a great lord berate a commoner as a "base football player." [66] But it does not necessarily follow, just because Britain at war quotes Shakespeare more enthusiastically than ever, that the man from Stratford contributed anything important to the unfolding theory or practice of democracy. Yet there is often an instinctive rightness in the emotional responses of individuals and nations. So it may be that British and American devotion to Shakespeare is not merely patriotic exhibitionism but somehow consonant with the instinctive sense of the Anglo-Saxon peoples that Shakespeare does speak for our democracy. "It is a great thing" for a people, says Carlyle,[67] to possess an "articulate voice; that it produce a man *who will speak-forth* . . . what the heart of it means." Emerson in America, and some of the noblest poets of England, seem agreed that Shakespeare does speak-forth prophetically, something of what the heart of democracy means. All this in spite of the fact that he lived the better part of a century or two before England's revolution and our own brought modern democracy effectively into being.

A passage in John Milton, under-secretary of foreign affairs to the new Commonwealth of 1649, suggests as much. In that year King Charles I had been tried, found guilty, and executed for treason; and Milton had been appointed to office, with the special assignment of "preparing an answer" to foreign and domestic pamphleteers then busily attacking the government. In his

66. *King Lear*, I, iv, 95.    67. "The Hero as Poet" (*Heroes and Hero-Worship*).

official capacity—as an early but honorable minister of propaganda—he was specifically "ordered" to reply to the *Eikon Basilike*, the apologetic "Portraiture of his Sacred Majesty in his . . . Sufferings." [68] In seeking to refute the sentimental defenders of the "martyr king," who had exploited to the utmost his personal "piety and sincerity," Milton drew from Shakespeare's *Richard III* to illustrate the point that tyrants have always known how to put on, skillfully, the garment of humility. "The poets," Milton wrote in his *Eikonoklastes*,

> have been . . . so mindful of decorum as to put never more pious words in the mouth of any person than of a tyrant. I shall not instance an abstruse author . . . but one whom we well know was the closet companion of these his solitudes, William Shakespeare, who introduces the person of Richard the Third speaking in as high a strain of piety and mortification as is uttered in any passage of this [book] and sometimes to the same sense and purpose . . . Saith Richard, act II, scene 1, [69]
>
>> I do not know that Englishman alive
>> With whom my soul is any jot at odds
>> More than the infant that is born to-night.
>> I thank my God for my humility.
>
> Other stuff of this sort may be read throughout the whole tragedy, wherein the poet used not much license in departing from the truth of history, which delivers [Richard III] a deep dissembler. . . .

Though this play is melodramatic in emphasis, Milton is right in suggesting that Shakespeare meant it to be substantially in accord with the sober truth of history as he had gathered it, in this case, from Holinshed and Sir Thomas More. There is no reason to doubt that young Edward V, one of Richard's victims, expresses Shakespeare's own thought and purpose here—and elsewhere in the historical plays:

68. New Cambridge *Milton*, ed. H. F. Fletcher (Cambridge 1941), p. 32; Thaler, *Shakspere's Silences*, p. 170.          69. Lines 69-72.

> Methinks the truth should live from age to age
> As 'twere retailed to all posterity, —[70]

even if, as Edward adds, it be not actually "upon record," but only "reported successively," by tradition. Here, as Milton notes, Shakespeare did not depart from history—that is, from the chroniclers of his own time—in order to soften the odious outlines of a tyrant king. By exposing Richard's pious dissembling, he breaks a lance against all tyranny.

Across the waters long centuries after, when Walt Whitman read *Heroes and Hero-Worship*, he recognized in Carlyle "a democrat in that enlarged sense [in] which we would fain see more men democrats;—that he is quick to champion the down-trodden, and earnest in his wrath at tyranny." [71] Carlyle, of course, was not a one hundred percent democrat; and neither was Shakespeare. Tudor England under Elizabeth was not a Yorkist despotism, but democracy was still far to seek. Yet Whitman's suggestion surely points in the right direction, and neither Carlyle [72] nor Shakespeare can safely be ignored by anyone seriously interested in the past and present of democracy. As regards *Richard III* in particular, it should be noted that Milton touches upon but one of several elements of this play which emphasize the case against despotism and, to that extent, the case *for* controls or limitations which, in the long run, point toward a constitutional or democratic order. Besides dramatizing the callous hypocrisy of an unprincipled and godless tyrant, the play makes perfectly clear his calculated, resolute, and utterly ruthless use of blood and terror as a main instrument of statecraft.[73] And it exposes mercilessly the underlying chaos of selfish factional strife among the powerful nobles nearest the throne, the stupid or conniving incompetence

70. III, i, 72-77.
71. *Uncollected Poetry and Prose of Walt Whitman*, ed. Holloway, I, 129; cf. Gregory Paine, *Studies in Philology*, XXXVI (1939), 551.
72. Cf. "Democracy" (*Past and Present*), *Sartor Resartus, Latter-Day Pamphlets*, etc.
73. "Our strong arms be our conscience, swords our law" (V, iii, 311); see also, I, i, 32-40; III, iv-vi, etc.

of the city officials who are supposed to look after the interests of the commonalty, and the climbing "Protector's" deadly opportunism, his unerring skill in weaving all the elements of public weakness into the iron pattern of his rise to power. Of course Richard, like Coriolanus, by the very excess of his dubious gifts, inevitably engenders such opposition as brings about his swift destruction. But the English tyrant's downfall has another significant implication. Unlike the Roman mob, the people in this play are, on the whole, better than their leaders—less hopelessly inept politically. As always in Shakespeare, to be sure, their "hearts are full of fear"; that is, of the fear of change. But "the citizens are mum, say not a word" in response to the tyrant's blandishments which have already won over their stupid lord mayor.[74] One of these citizens, the scrivener who unwillingly draws up the fraudulently belated indictment against "the good Lord Hastings," speaks out for the commonalty:

> Who is so gross
> That cannot see this palpable device?

Perhaps he speaks to no effective purpose. Yet his condemnation of this thing—"Bad is the world and all will come to naught" [75] if these crimes are not punished—is an early sounding of that voice of public opinion which still amounts to something in democratic governments. We shall see, I think, that in his later histories Shakespeare seems to have become increasingly aware of this mighty force.


Meanwhile it is to be noted that by a curious but fitting coincidence *Richard III* was the first definitely recorded Shakespearean play to be acted in the New World. This was a performance given in New York on March 3, 1750, "by a company that

74. III, vii, 3; v, 40; II, iii, 38; cf. *Othello*, II, iii, 214.
75. *Richard III*, III, vi, 10-14.

had already acted in Philadelphia" and continued to appear "up and down the Atlantic coast until the Revolution." [76] Perhaps it is no mere coincidence that of this company's repertory of eleven plays a majority—three of the histories and three of the great tragedies [77]—were pieces seriously concerned with problems of government. In any case, *Richard III* was on the boards again during Boston's first theatrical season "in the new American post-Revolutionary world of 1792"; [78] nor was it forgotten thereafter, if we may judge from the recurring allusions to this play in the writings of such men as John Adams,[79] John Quincy Adams,[80] Walt Whitman,[81] and Abraham Lincoln.[82]

From John Milton's time in England to Abraham Lincoln's in America many another poet and statesman of the new order claimed Shakespeare for his own. Edmund Burke, for example, enriched his Speech On Conciliation with many echoes from his favorite poets—Milton and Shakespeare. A quarter of a century later, as we have seen, Wordsworth—long before he became poet-laureate and ultraconservative—hailed Shakespeare, and Milton once more, as the abiding voices of freedom. Another great poet—and a great radical—concurred heartily in this opinion. According to Percy Bysshe Shelley, "Poetry . . . is the most unfailing herald, companion, and follower of the awakening of a great people to work a beneficial change in opinion or institution. . . . Poets are the unacknowledged legislators of the world." Shakespeare ranks among the greatest of these lawmakers for mankind. For, says Shelley in the same essay,[83] "it exceeds all imagination to conceive what would have been the moral condition of the world if neither Dante . . . Chaucer, Shakespeare . . . Lord Bacon nor Milton had ever existed." In Professor D. L. Clark's

76. A. H. Thorndike, *op. cit.*, p. 2.
77. *Richard III, King John, Henry IV, Macbeth, Lear, Hamlet.*
78. E. C. Dunn, *op. cit.*, p. 39.   79. *Works*, II, 54.
80. *Diary*, ed. Allan Nevins (New York, 1929), p. 180.
81. Horace Traubel, *With Walt Whitman in Camden* (New York, 1914), II, 246.
82. See above, p. 10.   83. "A Defence of Poetry," 1821.

recent study of "Shelley and Shakespeare" [84] appears indisputable evidence to show that certain of the plays I have mentioned here— notably *Lear*, *Richard III*, and *Macbeth*—were among those which especially influenced Shelley. And Mr. Clark concludes that "Shelley found in Shakespeare what he thought was a confirmation of his own radicalism."

Now whatever be the correct definition of radicalism, it is fairly clear that Shakespeare was not a radical. In his sessions of sweet silent thought he loved to summon up remembrance of things past. "Old fashions please me best," says one of his characters; nor would Shakespeare himself have hurried "to change true rules for odd inventions." [85] He did not like "hurlyburly innovation." [86] And yet, however conservative in his everyday practice, was he not liberal in his forward-looking faith in God and man? ("What a piece of work is a man! how noble in reason! how infinite in faculty!") [87] And was he not liberal, too, in his instinctive social sympathy? Of course the answer depends upon the definition of the word—or upon the definer. "We talk about the tyranny of words," says Charles Dickens, [88] "but we like to tyrannize over them too." Mr. Stuart Chase has recently demonstrated both principles afresh! [89] Our purposes in this study, happily, do not require us to "extrapolate" nor even to *demonstrate* conclusively that Shakespeare was a liberal. Whatever he was, one essential fact has already been demonstrated here. It is the fact that Shakespeare has many significant things to say— even in the few plays we have noticed—of problems that still concern democracy to-day: of the causes of war, for example, and of the rise of tyrants; of intolerance, of poverty, of the class struggle, and of public opinion. Still, as I have already suggested, the instinctive responses of men count for something; and the responses of those among them who are endowed with livelier

84. *PMLA*, LIV (1939), 261-287.    85. *The Taming of the Shrew*, III, i, 80-81.
86. *1 Henry IV*, V, i, 78.    87. *Hamlet*, II, ii, 317.
88. *David Copperfield*, Chapter LII.    89. *The Tyranny of Words*, New York, 1938.

sensibility, with deeper vision than the rest—the intuitions of great poets—may well count for more. In the poem entitled "Why I Am A Liberal," Robert Browning states clearly the basis of his own political creed.[90] It is fair to remember this in attempting to judge the validity of his famous remonstrance against Wordsworth, written when that "lost leader" in his old age accepted the government's "handful of silver" and became the laureate of conservatism. Here Browning puts Shakespeare first among the sons of light, the poets who led the van and the freemen:

> Shakespeare was of us, Milton was for us,
> Burns, Shelley were with us,—they watch from their graves!
> He alone breaks from the van and the freemen,
> —He alone sinks to the rear and the slaves![91]

By their fruits ye shall know them! To what extent Shakespeare was and *is* truly one "of us" who believe in and hope for democracy, only a true reading of his work—especially of his sonnets, tragedies and histories—will demonstrate. I cannot hope to give an adequate indication of the challenge that awaits anyone who will reread Shakespeare for himself in the light of what is now going on in the world and of what is promised or threatened for to-morrow. But I do wish, before closing, to return briefly to Shakespeare's histories as such.[92] And I would recall, first of all, that Shakespeare's outlook upon human life in general, however wanting in "systematic" philosophy, however essentially *dramatic* in tragic solemnity or hilarious mirth, was never uncritical. Neither was his study of English history. He was a Tudor patriot, but his historical drama is a criticism of life as it

---

90. Who that is blessed with freedom, says Browning, "dares hold . . . his fellow shall continue bound?"

> Not I,
> Who live, love, labor freely, nor discuss
> A brother's right to freedom. That is 'Why.'

91. "The Lost Leader" (1845).

92. For Walt Whitman's view of these plays, see below, pp. 57-60.

is reflected in the reigns of the English Kings. Believing as he did in the gains that had been achieved under the Tudors, he dramatized without fear or favor many of the evils of ancient tyranny, oppression, or weakness in earlier English government. His work, in this sense, points toward the future and toward democracy.

There is reason to believe that something of this was at least partly recognized in his own time, and by no less a person than Queen Elizabeth herself. Certain it is that Shakespeare began his work in historical drama with a sequence of four plays—the three parts of *Henry VI* (1590-1592), and *Richard III* (1593). These attack, in one sense or another, the evil times of the Wars of the Roses, when the "viperous worm" of "civil dissension" gnawed "the bowels of the commonwealth" [93] and dynastic chaos ran riot—until Henry Tudor, Elizabeth's grandfather, conquered Richard and took the throne. It is easy to see why Shakespeare felt under no compulsion to give a flattering account of Richard Crookback, the enemy of the Tudors, nor of his immediate predecessors. Nor did Shakespeare glorify, in any sense, the uncompromising portrait of the earliest of his English kings, the worst of them all, and probably the next upon whom he wrote after *Richard III*,—the black-hearted "hero-villain" of *King John* (1594). It must be admitted incidentally, that Shakespeare does not mention Magna Charta in this play [94] though he does significantly speak of "charters and customary rights" elsewhere.[95] Perhaps he does not mention it because his source failed to do so, or possibly because the subject might not have pleased the authorities. But this play holds no brief for King John. It shows ample cause for the exactions forced upon him by his "discontented peers" [96] at Runnymede. And the failure to mention Magna Charta may be not altogether unrelated to the fact that the last of the histories in which Shakespeare had a hand—a

---

93. *I Henry VI*, III, i, 72-73.    94. Cf. Thaler, *Shakspere's Silences*, p. 15.
95. In *Richard II*, II, i, 199; see below, p. 39.    96. *King John*, IV, ii, 127.

piece which also draws a more or less realistic picture of its protagonist, King Henry VIII — was first produced in 1613, ten years after the death of his daughter Elizabeth.

Midway in his career, meanwhile, Shakespeare had written his great second sequence of historical plays, the tetralogy consisting of *Richard II* (1595), the two parts of *Henry IV* (1595-1598), and *Henry V* (1599). It is common knowledge that these are the shrewdest, the most broadly humorous, and the wisest of the histories. Upon their vast canvass Shakespeare painted in bold strokes of authentic black and white — and red — his mature vision of War and Peace, in all their checkered panoply of blood and glory and fun and tears. These plays concern us primarily because all four of them are important documents in Shakespeare's unfolding study of kingship. It is undeniable that the three plays concerning Henry IV and Henry V idealize two kings who gained power by usurpation, and sought to establish it with the aid of foreign conquest. Shakespeare, moreover, exploited to the full the popular legend of England's idol — of her Prince Hal and his unregenerate merrymakings with Falstaff, her hero-king at Agincourt. But Shakespeare also dramatizes, in effect, the main truth of sober history underlying these reigns — the fact that both these kings were immensely popular not least because they were able, magnanimous, and deeply concerned for the welfare of their country, — not to mention the fact that, as beneficiaries of Richard II's deposition, they were the first English kings who "honestly tried" to rule within the emerging framework of constitutional monarchy.[97] It is instructive, by contrast, to turn to our dramatist's sympathetic but unflinching study of their predecessor — Richard II, the most poetic, the most subtly imaginative, and the weakest of Shakespeare's kings, who was justly deposed because he himself was unjust and utterly unfit for kingship. Elizabethan England, incidentally, understood something of what Richard's deposition implied for the future of English monarchy. In 1601,

97. Benjamin Terry, *A History of England* (Chicago 1908), pp. 438-441.

on the eve of the Essex rebellion, the conspirators in his lordship's
behalf paid Shakespeare's company a special fee to revive *Richard
II*.   The conspirators hoped, of course, that the deposition scenes
would prepare the public for the drama *they* hoped to stage—
and the Queen herself had these scenes in mind when she said, a
little later, "I am Richard the Second; know ye not that?" [98]

In Shakespeare's plays, as in actual history, the leading parts
in the movement toward constitutionalism and democracy were
usually played by kings and nobles rather than by commoners.
Yet it will not do to underrate the role of Shakespeare's commoners in his scheme of things.   On general principles, he unquestionably loved a kingly king and a noble lord.   But his studies in
English history emphasize the point that each of the three
estates—king, nobles *and* commons—has its own integral rights
in the state.   While these rights are safe-guarded, each estate
contributes to the strength of the whole; if and when the rights
of one of the three are violated the whole structure tends to fall.
We hear much of Shakespeare's "traditionalism."   We should
notice, also, the fact that his demand for order and discipline is
conditioned by his sense that there must be a forward march "in
mutual, well-beseeming ranks" [99] of *all* the elements in the body
politic.   The famous speech in *Troilus and Cressida* [100] suggests
that Troy would have fallen long before it did, had not want of
discipline undermined the Greeks—the *old* Greeks, who ignored
the fact that heaven and earth themselves are strong only because they "observe degree, priority and place."   But even in
this speech mutual, coöperative strength is the desired end.   The
breach of rule and discipline lay not with the common soldiers
but with the great Achilles.   So, in *Richard II*, it lay with the
king himself—who flatly ignores his uncle's solemn warning that
ruin will fall upon the king unless he accords to his subjects the
protection of the laws which secure his own status:

98.  Cf. J. Q. Adams, *Life of William Shakespeare* (New York, 1923), pp. 316 ff.
99.  *I Henry IV*, I, i, 14.            100.  I, iii, 74-137.

> Take Hereford's rights away, and take from time
> His charters and his customary rights;
> Let not to-morrow then ensue to-day;
> Be not thyself—for how art thou a king
> But by fair sequence and succession? [101]

As for the commons themselves, the fact that Shakespeare hated the mob does not mean that he despised the common man. One recalls Lincoln's saying—that God must have loved the plain people since He made so many of them. So did Shakespeare. In this connection, I cannot do better than to quote from Professor Schelling:

> In Shakespeare poverty does not necessarily make a man vicious; nor does roguery destroy humor in a man or deprive him of his brains. The Porter in *Macbeth* is a foul-mouthed drunken lout. . . . But Adam, the old serving man of Orlando, is faithful almost to death. . . . There is no keener, droller fellow in the world than the grave-digger in *Hamlet*. If the refined modern critic . . . would learn whether Shakespeare . . . had any notions as to the mental processes and moral stability of the common man, let him read and ponder the simple incident of King Henry incognito, and the soldier Williams with their arguments pro and con as to the responsibility of princes. Williams is the type of the honest, fearless, clear-headed 'man in the street' who honors his king, not slavishly because he is a king but for the qualities that make him kingly, who respects manhood (his own included) above rank and is the more valiant that he knows the cost of valor. . . . Shakespeare . . . knew the common man and his trust was in him. . . . He depicts in his plays a feudal society, for such was the English society in his day. But there is nothing in these honest . . . pictures of English life . . . to declare Shakespeare prejudiced against any class of his fellow countrymen. . . . He found . . . in each class . . . the stupid, the ignorant, the pretentious and the absurd, but he found likewise . . . the earnest, the honorable

101. *Richard II*, II, i, 199.

and capable. . . . For their follies he ridiculed them; for their virtues, which he recognized, he loved them.[102]

It is worth noting that the remarkable exchange of views—to which Schelling alludes—between the soldier Williams and the King, occurs in *Henry V*,[103] the last of the great histories. Williams, I believe, speaks not only for himself but for all good soldiers. In a sense, indeed, he speaks for all good commoners in the later histories who, by slow but not altogether imperceptible degrees, venture increasingly to think out loud on matters of state.[104] In the voice of this common soldier King Henry hears something of the honest voice of intelligent, if not subtly articulate, public opinion. He hears it rather more plainly than others, but he was not the only royal personage in Shakespeare to be exposed to it. The scrivener's remarks in *Richard III*,[105] for example, were not altogether beside the point, even though the tyrant did not hear them. And the citizens of Angiers in the play of *King John*[106] compel the warring kings of France and England to listen—indeed to accept their plan for peace—before they agree to open their gates. "It is a common thing for Shakespeare to assume," writes Professor Tolman,[107] "that the instincts and judgments of the people as a whole are wise and right." In the *early* histories of the *Henry VI* group, to be sure, the voice of public opinion is not much more than the raucous shouting of the mob announcing its fierce determination to burn and to kill "all scholars, lawyers, courtiers, gentlemen."[108] Even this uproar, however, is not entirely unintelligible. Since the weakling King Henry VI begins by authorizing Suffolk "among the people [to] gather up a tenth" for the expenses of his marriage, it is not surprising to hear "the commons swarming like an angry hive of bees" when they are informed of the murder of their friend, Duke

102. "The Common Folk of Shakespeare," *Shakespeare and "Demi-Science,"* Philadelphia, 1927, pp. 92-97; quoted by permission of the publisher, the University of Pennsylvania Press. (See also Albert H. Tolman's "Is Shakespeare Aristocratic?" *PMLA*, XXIX (1914), 277-298.)

103. IV, i, 91-250.  104. See below, p. 41.  105. See above, p. 32.
106. II, i, 300-539.  107. *Op. cit.*, p. 294.  108. *2 Henry VI*, IV, iv, 36.

Humphrey, who "would not tax the needy commons." [109] These protests, it should be noted, gain clarity and vigor in the later play of *Richard II*. For Richard fell, as we have seen, because he violated the rights of all his subjects, nobles and commons alike: [110]

> The nobles hath he fin'd . . .
> The commons hath he pill'd with grievous taxes.[111]

These are, according to one of the King's flatterers, "the wavering commons" whose "love lies in their purses." [112] But, when nobles and commons together "shake off the slavish yoke" [113] of Richard's tyranny, the commons, like the soldier Williams once more, speak out plainly. Witness the scene, overheard by the Queen, between the gardeners. They, as she says, "talk of state, for everyone doth so against a change." Why should they in their garden, one of them asks,

> Keep law and form and due proportion . . .
> When our sea-walled garden, the whole land
> Is full of weeds . . . her wholesome herbs
> Swarming with caterpillars?

To which the other replies that the king has already had his just deserts:

> He that hath suffer'd this disorder'd spring
> Hath now himself met with the fall of leaf.[114]

Nor should it be forgotten that Henry IV, Richard's conqueror, and Henry V's father, began his career by "wooing" [115] the commons. Later, he urged upon his son the continuance of his own policy and of his honorable desire to rule his people justly — so that "Opinion, that did help" him "to the crown," might be confirmed for his son in the sincere "allegiance" of "men's hearts." [116] And so it was. For it was public opinion which, in Shakespeare's own

109. *2 Henry VI*, III, ii, 125; i, 116.
110. See above, p. 39.     111. *Richard II*, II, i, 245-246.
112. *Id.*, II, ii, 128-129.     113. *Id.*, II, i, 291.     114. *Id.*, III, iv, 40-49.
115. *Id.*, I, iv, 28.     116. *I Henry IV*, III, ii, 42-52; cf. *2 Henry IV*, IV, v, 118-138.

phrase, hailed Henry V as "the mirror of all Christian Kings." [117]

I do not mean to claim too much for Shakespeare's histories. As plays they are uneven, and much that is in them is, in one sense, water over the dam. Their troubled concern, for example, about the "right divine" of kings and of the mischief of royal favorites, their preoccupation with dynastic uncertainties, and perhaps even their "woe to that land that's governed by a child," [118] —all this belongs primarily to the past. But other recurring motives of these plays—"Uneasy lies the head that wears a crown," [119] "They that stand high have many blasts to shake them" [120]— these are not yet out-dated. Neither are their studies of the causes and consequences of despotic rule, of the dangerous potentialities of political propaganda—of loud rumor with its thousand tongues,[121] of purchased plaudits and shrewdly manipulated falsehood—[122] and of the ways and means of war, the "vengeance" of God [123]—of conscription and graft,[124] and matchless heroism,[125] and "beastly shameless" atrocities "expressly against the law of arms." [126] Of course these plays are not consciously pro-democratic in sentiment. (The *word* "democratic" incidentally, though occasionally used in Elizabethan times, does not appear in Shakespeare at all, and neither does the word "liberal," in the political sense. But then Shakespeare has but one casual mention of the word "America" [127] and none at all of the word "conservative." Hardly anyone will argue, however, that these omissions make Shakespeare a writer of no importance either for Americans or for conservatives.) Shakespeare unquestionably believed in order, discipline, and leadership—but so do we, so *must* we, if our democracy is to survive. Certainly Shakespeare in his time had no inkling of the democracy of the ballot-box, and if he had had,

117. *Henry V*, II, Chorus, 6.    118. *Richard III*, II, iii, 11.
119. *2 Henry IV*, III, i, 31.    120. *Richard III*, I, iii, 259.
121. *2 Henry IV*, Induction, 2.    122. *Richard III*, III, v, 75; vii, 34-37.
123. *Henry V*, IV, i, 178.   124. *1 Henry IV*, IV, ii, 13; *2 Henry IV*, III, ii, 235-242.
125. *Henry V*, IV, v.    126. *1 Henry IV*, I, i, 44; *Henry V*, IV, vii, 1-11.
127. *Comedy of Errors*, III, ii, 136: "Where America, the Indies?—Oh, sir, upon her nose."

undoubtedly he would have disapproved strongly. So did Thomas Carlyle almost three centuries later—and yet this same Carlyle, in writing of Oliver Cromwell, paid unstinted tribute to "that noble Struggle for constitutional Liberty" [128] which was the lasting achievement of Cromwell's time. Shakespeare's plays look prophetically toward that struggle. They refuse to gloss over the weaknesses, the wasteful exactions, the lawlessness, the tyranny of kings. Their author was no enemy of the commons, and he seems not to have been unaware of the dawning might of public opinion.

Not even Shakespeare, prophetically dreaming on things to come, could have foreseen all the hopes and fears of democracy. Certainly he would have questioned some of its methods. Yet I think he would have recognized as his own its faith and many of its objectives. In his own time, according to Professor Gayley,[129] he seems to have had "confidential" and sympathetic "relations" with certain of "the founders of American liberty" in Virginia. If he could speak to-day, I think he would find himself in substantial agreement with much that is basic to our democracy. Take, for example, the recent statement of its case in Professor Merriam's authoritative study, *The New Democracy and the New Despotism*.[130] Shakespeare would have had no quarrel with Merriam's repudiation (1) of "those who invoke . . . liberty" as a "defence of special privilege"; (2) of the enthronement of "economics alone as the lord of our social life"; and (3) of "the doctrine of despotism in government." And I think Shakespeare would have approved whole-heartedly of Merriam's basic affirmation— his faith in "the possibility of vast . . . human and . . . social

128. "The Hero as King" (*Heroes and Hero-Worship*).

129. Charles Mills Gayley, *Shakespeare and the Founders of Liberty in America* (New York, 1917), pp. VI, 4, ff.

130. C. E. Merriam (New York, 1939); see pp. 6-8. Quoted by permission of the publisher, McGraw-Hill Book Company.

. . . gains" and in the orderly control thereof; in the "advantages of rational discussion and consent . . . as against . . . brute . . . force and violence." Shakespeare would have been in substantial agreement with this position because he believed in God and man, and because he was neither a radical nor yet merely the "entrancing . . . mossback" he has been thought to be.[131] As a good Tudor, he idealized noble kingship: yet no *bad* king "could live near such a man." He was no revolutionary idealist, but he knew the value of "charters and customary rights" and "ancient freedom" [132] under the rule of law—no less than the truth that "too much" liberty "plucks justice by the nose." [133] In him was the essence of all good faith and doctrine, and of all brave dreams for the times to come. For this reason, as Dr. Johnson [134] said, "the stream of time, which is continually washing the dissoluble fabrics of other poets, passes without injury by the adamant of Shakespeare."

131. Cf. Tucker Brooke, *op. cit.*, p. 150.
132. *2 Henry VI*, IV, viii, 28; see also above, p. 41, and n. 113.
133. *Measure for Measure*, I, ii, 129; iii, 29.
134. *Preface to Shakespeare*, 1765.—For an interesting "Re-Survey" of "Anti-Democracy in Shakespeare," the reader should consult Professor Brents Stirling's article—published while this book was in press—in *Modern Language Quarterly*, II (September, 1941), 487 ff.

# II

## SHAKESPEARE AND WALT WHITMAN

IN THE Shakespeare Association *Bulletin* for January, 1939,[1] there appears, set off by itself, the passage from Walt Whitman (quoted in the preceding chapter) [2] in which we are told that Shakespeare, like all the other great poets, is out of date and unsuited for America: that he is concerned with "standards, politics . . . ranges of belief that have been quite eliminated from the Eastern Hemisphere, and never existed at all in the Western." The *Bulletin's* quotation, it should be noted, is given without a word of comment — as though the passage spoke for itself and summed up, finally, Whitman's views concerning Shakespeare. This is interesting and symptomatic. I think it expresses, fairly, the consensus of critical opinion. It apparently represents the established and accepted opinion of prominent Elizabethan scholars who have touched upon Whitman and Shakespeare, no less than the views of specialists on Walt Whitman. I believe, however, that this interpretation does not take adequate account of all the facts. Hence this Postscript to my remarks on this subject in the opening chapter.

To see for himself, first, the position of the Shakespeareans, let the reader turn to Professor F. E. Schelling's *Shakespeare and "Demi-Science"* (1927),[3] or to Professor E. C. Dunn's *Shakespeare in America* (1939).[4] Professor Schelling opens his admirable essay on Shakespeare's "Common Folk" [5] by quoting from what he de-

1. XIV, 50.    2. P. 16.
3. Pp. 85 ff. — cf. Whitman, *Complete Writings* (New York, 1902: hereafter referred to as *Writings*), *Prose*, II, 277.
4. Pp. 266-274.    5. See above, p. 40, n. 102.

scribes as Whitman's "arraignment of Shakespeare's universality and his sympathy with his fellow men,"—specifically, Whitman's charge that "there is much in" Shakespeare that is "ever offensive to democracy." Mr. Schelling, in his authoritative work on *The English Chronicle Play* (1902), had not mentioned Whitman's curious note on Shakespeare's history plays,[6] nor does he pause to notice in this essay on Shakespeare's Commoners that Whitman's views on Shakespeare were notably modified from time to time. Similarly, Professor A. H. Tolman—writing in 1914 on the question "Is Shakespeare Aristocratic" [7]—observed merely that "Walt Whitman . . . though showing a genuine appreciation of the poet's artistic greatness, has a firm belief in the anti-democratic spirit of his dramas." Finally, Professor Dunn, in her recent and thorough discussion of Shakespeare and Whitman does observe that the American poet's attitude toward Shakespeare was "not simple or consistent." She does not, however, mention Whitman's important modification of his charges against Shakespeare,[8] and she concludes that "Shakespeare was deliberately falsified in Whitman's mind that he might more sharply defend his own ideas for the relationship of poetry to life."

Whitman's biographers and critics appear to be in substantial agreement with this general position. If I read them aright, they say or imply in effect that the loftiest of the singers American democracy has yet given voice to, holds Shakespeare to "belong essentially to the buried past," [9] and consistently regards him as a foe of the democratic ideal. In the preceding study I have examined the larger issues involved in this judgment. Enough has been said, I believe, to indicate that Shakespeare's work, on the stage or in the library, still has vital significance for a democratic people. But it remains to say another word concerning Whitman's attitude toward Shakespeare—or, rather, about the critics' interpretation of that attitude.

6. See below, pp. 57-60.  
7. *PMLA*, XXIX (1914), 280.  
8. See below p. 47-53.  
9 See above, p. 16.

Critical opinion simply has not taken sufficient account of both sides, of *all* the facts. It has been content to take Whitman's attack upon Shakespeare at its face value, and to ignore his own modifications of that attack. That Whitman did significantly modify his attitude seems to me as certain as anything can well be. His own words written in 1881 state the fact so clearly, and yet they have been so little regarded and so generally overlooked, that I shall have to quote them again. If he did not altogether change his mind, he certainly modified his position. His old "convictions are now *strongly temper'd*. . . . I see that this world of the West . . . fuses inseparably with the East. . . . If we are not to hospitably receive . . . the inaugurations of the old civilizations . . . what on earth are we for? . . . All serves our New World progress. . . . Shakspere has served, and serves, maybe, the best of any." [10]

By way of confirming this matured judgment, Whitman returned to the subject the year after. On April 3, 1882, immediately after Longfellow's death, Whitman answered as follows the charge that Longfellow was wanting in "racy nativity and special originality":

> I shall only say that America and the world may well be reverently thankful — can never be thankful enough — for any such singing-bird vouchsafed out of the centuries, without asking that the notes be different from those of other songsters; adding what I have heard Longfellow himself say, that ere the New World can be worthily original, and announce herself and her heroes, she must be well saturated with the originality of others, and respectfully consider the heroes that lived before Agamemnon.[11]

I cannot believe that these utterances, *and others like them*, would have failed to impress anyone in search of all the facts. Because these utterances of Whitman's have not been noticed as they deserve to be — that is to say, cumulatively and in relation

10. See above, p. 19.          11. "Specimen Days," *Writings, Prose*, II, 32-33.

to one another—it will serve our purpose to glance at them here and now. They fall, roughly, into three categories.[12]  (1) Whitman repeatedly qualified his general charge that all the great poems "belong to the buried past," and that they are invariably "poisonous" to the ideal of liberty and democracy.  (2) He pays frequent tribute not only—as all admit—to Shakespeare's general depth and power, but also, specifically, to his timelessness; and he particularly recognizes that some characteristics of Shakespeare's are serviceable to democracy.  (3) Though ever insistent upon the principle that democracy must produce its own poets and poems, Whitman also stated—early, late, and often—that the poetry of democracy must draw deeply upon its cultural heritage, including, especially, the great poetry of times past.—To illustrate, I subjoin some passages representative of each of these categories, in the order indicated above.

I.

All the nations of this earth, diverse as they appear . . . are members of one family, and own themselves, through distant removes, and after many ages . . . fortunes and . . . developments . . . as the children of a common father ("Memoranda Preparatory to *Leaves of Grass*").[13]

When a grand and melodious thought is told to men for the first time, down within their hearts, each one says, "That music! those large and exquisite passages!  Where have I heard them before?"  ("Notes for Lectures on Literature," about 1858?) [14]

The great poet absorbs the identity of others and the experience of others . . . but he presses them all through the powerful press of himself ("Memoranda Preparatory to *Leaves of Grass*").[15]

A great poem is for all ages in common and for all degrees and complexions and all departments and sects. . . .  The greatest poet forms the consistence of what is to be from what

12. Which inevitably overlap to some extent.        13. *Writings, Prose*, VI, 139.
14. C. J. Furness, *Walt Whitman's Workshop* (Cambridge, 1928), p. 65.
15. *Writings, Prose*, VI, 120.

has been and is. He drags the dead out of their coffins and stands them again on their feet. . . . He says to the past, Rise and walk before me that I may realize you . . . he places himself where the future becomes present. . . . The prescient poet projects himself centuries ahead, and judges performer or performance after the changes of time. . . .

In the make of the great masters, the idea of political liberty is indispensable. . . . Poets are the voice and exposition of liberty. . . . The attitude of great poets is to cheer slaves and horrify despots (Preface, 1855, to *Leaves of Grass*).[16]

2.

In 1865, Walt Whitman copied into his notebooks "Ben Jonson's eulogy" of Shakespeare — "very fine and sounding:

'He was not of an age, but for all time . . .
A good poet's *made* as well as born,' "

and also Coleridge's famous phrase concerning the "Myriad-minded Shakespeare." [17] These entries are but two of many in the notebooks which testify to Whitman's general appreciation of Shakespeare's powers — witness also these lines of Whitman's written some years earlier:

Homer and Shakespeare . . . deserve all the reward that has been bestowed upon them. They did what was to be done and did the work divinely. . . . Well may Homer remain and Shakespeare remain ("Memoranda Preparatory to *Leaves of Grass*").[18]

But Whitman's praise of Shakespeare did not stop with generalities. For example, he says outright that Shakespeare was presenting the simple truth — as he saw it, and perhaps as it still *is* — even in his unsympathetic accounts of the rabble:

16. *Id.*, II, 182, 169, 181, 175; see above, p. 18, n. 33.
17. *Id.*, VI, 74, 189 (Whitman's italics).
18. *Id.*, VI, 123, 124 (about 1856).

> His renderings of . . . the rabble . . . the . . . stupid
> canaille that Coriolanus cannot stomach . . . in so rendering
> humanity, Shakespeare strictly rendered what was to him the
> truth—and what was the truth. The class of mechanics,
> tailors . . . attendants, etc. in Europe then, perhaps even now,
> are they or are they not properly reflected by such reflections as
> Shakespeare gives of them? ("Memoranda Preparatory to
> *Leaves of Grass*") [19]

And Whitman adds specifically that Shakespeare's inspired and
luminous study of human character—his exaltation of *personality*
—is invaluable for democratic America, because it too, like the
other nations, must grow by cultivating the "personal character"
of its manhood and leadership.

> It almost seems [Whitman writes] as if only . . . feudalism
> in Europe, like slavery in our own South, could outcrop types
> of tallest, noblest character . . . invincible courage, generosity,
> aspiration, the spines of all. Here is where Shakespeare and
> the others I have named perform a service incalculably precious
> to our America. Politics, literature, and everything else, centers
> at last in perfect *personnel* (as democracy is to find the same as
> the rest). Hence the great value of the foreign . . . lessons
> . . . which we are to work over, and popularize and enlarge and
> present again in our own growths ("Poetry To-Day in Amer-
> ica," 1881).[20]

For the same reason Whitman prefers the "lessons" of Shakespeare to those of Burns, the democrat. Though Whitman
"blessed . . . the memory of the warm-hearted Scotchman" who
was "essentially a Republican" and "would have been at home"
in America, he held that

> the splendid personalizations of Shakespeare, formulated
> on the largest, freest, most heroic, most artistic mould, are to

19. *Id.*, VI, 75.—This question perhaps answers, in part, Whitman's complaint to
Traubel: "Everything possible is done in the Shakespeare plays to make the common
people seem common indeed"; Shakespeare "looks upon the people with something like
despair" (Horace Traubel, *With Walt Whitman in Camden*, New York, 1914, I, 240; III,
444).

20. *Id.*, II, 207-208.

me far dearer as lessons, and more precious even as models for Democracy, than the humdrum samples Burns presents ("Robert Burns," *November Boughs*, 1888).[21]

### 3.

With reference to Whitman's roundest attack upon the great old poems—the 1888 pronouncement that the "underlying basis" of all of them is "a denial and insult to democracy" [22]—it has not usually been remembered that in this very essay Whitman also described himself as "the grateful and reverent legatee of the past."

> If I were ask'd [he says] to name the most precious bequest to current American civilization from all the hitherto ages, I am not sure but I would name those old . . . songs ferried hither from east and west. . . .[23]

Again and again we may observe in Whitman this tendency to balance insistent attack upon the old, or urgent demand for original American productivity, with due recognition of the fact that the old poems, the old culture, have their indubitable claims upon those who would sing nobly for the New World. For this reason, as we have seen, Whitman wrote in 1881 that America could not afford to do without the great poets and thinkers of old, and that Shakespeare "has served" and *still* serves. By the same token, Whitman, in certain of his manuscript "notes for lectures," returned to his favorite theme—and to the familiar reservation. America's poets have been feebly imitative:

> Ye have feebly followed and feebly multiplied the models of other lands. Its own literature, to a nation, is the first of all things. Aping but others, ye are but intelligent apes ("Addresses on Literature").[24]

21. *Id.*, III, 128, 137.   22. Preface, *November Boughs*, quoted above, p. 16.
23. *Writings, Prose*, III, 50, 52.   24. Furness, *op. cit.*, p. 67.

And yet, side by side with this denunciation appears another note for an "address on literature" which makes reasonable concession to the old poets, of all lands:

> The very greatest writers can never be understood or appreciated forthwith—any more than the very greatest discoverers. It takes some ages to unfold the scope of the invention of steampower or printing, or the discovery of America, or the commencement of the greatest breed of poets.[25]

Let us observe, finally, that his balancing of values was as thoroughly characteristic of Whitman early in his career as at the very end. For example—into one of his notebooks, probably of the eighteen-fifties, Whitman wrote the following

> *Caution*—Not to blaart constantly for *Native American* models, literature, etc. and bluster out 'nothing foreign.' The best way to promulge native American models and literature is to supply such . . . superb specimens of the same that they will . . . put foreign models in the second class. . . . Best *not at all* to bother with arguments against the foreign models . . . but *just go on supplying American models*.[26]

He returned to the subject many years later in *Good-bye My Fancy* (1891), one of his last utterances. "My own opinion has long been," he recalls,

> that for New World service our ideas of beauty (inherited from the Greeks, and so on to Shakespeare) . . . need to be radically changed [27] and made anew for to-day's purposes. . . . But, if so, it will all come in due time. . . . What could humanity and literature do without the mellow . . . averaging, bringing-up of many years . . . ? Every really first-class production has likely to pass through the crucial tests of . . . several generations. . . .

25. *Id.*, p. 67.        26. *Writings, Prose*, VI, 30 (Whitman's italics).
27. Later in this paper Whitman says that "ideal Americanism would take the Greek spirit and law and democratize and scientize and Christianize them for . . . all history, all ranks and lands."

> The most important principle of all [is] that *Art is one*, is not partial; but includes all times and forms and sorts — is not exclusively aristocratic or democratic or oriental or occidental. My favorite symbol would be . . . the old Dutch flour miller, who said, 'I never bother myself what road the folks come — I only want good wheat and rye.' . . . Democratic art results of democratic development. . . . [28]

It is strange, I think, that utterances such as these seem to have gone virtually unnoticed by students of Whitman and Shakespeare. Perhaps they have left their mark [29] somewhere in the pages of books on Whitman not accessible to me; or perhaps the critics were busy with more important matters. In venturing these remarks concerning Whitman, I write as an amateur troubled by omissions in the testimony of experts. But I think that this matter is not unimportant, and I can find little to indicate that its implications have been given the notice they deserve. The fact seems to be that distinguished students of Whitman, like the Shakespeareans, have not given us both sides of this picture. A brief — but, I hope, representative — summary of some half-dozen of their findings, old and new, will serve to illustrate my point, and also to prepare the way for a final glance at Whitman himself.

(1) I begin with Bliss Perry's *Walt Whitman* (1906, 1908).[30] This relatively early critical interpretation is still a wise, a gracious and a generous book — but it does not enlarge upon Whitman's Shakespearean views. I find but two allusions to the subject. Both are quotations from Whitman and both characterize Shakespeare as "feudal" and "lacking" in "democratic" spirit.

(2) Mr. Basil de Selincourt's *Walt Whitman, A Critical Study* (1914),[31] especially notable for its challenging closing chapters on

28. *Writings, Prose*, III, 287-288, 293.

29. Brief incidental mention of Whitman's admission of the desirability of continuity in literary tradition — but without reference to Shakespeare — is made in William Clarke's *Walt Whitman* (London, 1892), p. 40, in John Addington Symonds' work of the same title (London, 1896), p. 122, and in Floyd Stovall, *Walt Whitman, Selections* (New York, 1934), p. LI.

30. Pp. 197, 260.                    31. See p. 247.

"Democracy and the Individual" and "Whitman and America," touches upon our problem only in very general terms. Once more the conclusions drawn show but one side of the picture. Whitman "saw that there was no American tradition in poetry and that the English tradition, if only because of its consanguinity, must be worse than useless to him. He was prepared to dispense with what he could not have." (Yet Walt Whitman wrote, virtually in so many words, that "we cannot afford to be oblivious of" [32] that tradition. — This admission of Whitman's supplies the logical answer also to the converse of Mr. de Selincourt's proposition — Mr. John Bailey's statement of the case in the English Men of Letters *Whitman*.[33] Here it is written that Whitman "was wrong in supposing that American poetry could cut itself off from the parent stock of Europe.")

(3) Professor Emory Holloway's collections and editorial labors have given him a just claim to the unqualified gratitude of all students of Whitman. But his valuable "Interpretation in Narrative," *Whitman* (1926), in its treatment of the Whitman-Shakespeare relationship resembles the works already noticed in the preceding paragraphs. In his discussion Mr. Holloway speaks of Shakespeare a dozen times over. At least thrice-repeated is the familiar emphasis upon Whitman's view of Shakespeare as the poet of kings and feudalism: [34] but I find no mention of Whitman's recognition that Shakespeare "has served" and may still serve America.[35]

(4) By all odds the most important study of our subject — the most comprehensive survey of the varied and extensive correlations between *Walt Whitman and Shakespeare* — is the late Professor R. C. Harrison's posthumous article by that title (1929).[36] Unhappily Professor Harrison did not live to write his proposed —

32. See above, p. 19.          33. 1926, p. 70.
34. *Whitman*, pp. 13, 119-120, 250.
35. Nor is there any such recognition in John Burroughs (*Whitman*, Boston, 1896) who also writes of Shakespeare as the dramatist of feudalism (p. 233).
36. *PMLA*, XLIV, 1201-1238.

and much-needed—book on the subject. At least one sentence in his article suggests that this book might have helped to correct the excessive emphasis given, in all the other works I have mentioned, to Whitman's attack upon Shakespeare as a foe of democracy. Mr. Harrison writes that Whitman's "*preponderant* insistence . . . upon a democratic genius in literature as opposed to an aristocratic one, and his identification of Shakespeare with the latter, and of himself or his ideal with the former, has led me, by its cumulative force, to discern an actuating motive, which became . . . one of the springs of Whitman's poetry." [37] The word "preponderant" here indicates that a fuller discussion in the proposed book might have struck a juster balance between Whitman's varying pronouncements upon Shakespeare and democracy than the article suggests. For, with this one exception, Mr. Harrison reduces the issue almost to a simple affirmation of faith—to the thesis that Whitman's single-minded conception of Shakespeare as the poet of the old order became a main spring, a "dominant motive" [38] of Whitman's "own literary activity." Mr. Harrison points out that "Whitman always came back to what he most opposed in Shakespeare . . . the Shakespeare who was a reflector of ideals not consonant with American Democracy," [39] who "catered to the nobility" and was "inimical to democratic institutions and democratic art." [40] The article illustrates by many pertinent quotations "Whitman's life-long obsession with the idea that a democratic American literature, rather than a literature distilled from an older, aristocratic one, should be the chief concern of American poets." [41] But it does not mention Walt Whitman's own early qualification of his general attack upon the old poets—in the 1855 Preface to *Leaves of Grass*—his observation that all "great poets . . . are the voice and exposition of liberty," that their "attitude . . . is to cheer up slaves and horrify despots." [42] Nor does the article mention Whitman's "temper'd conviction" of 1881, that

---

37. *Id.*, p. 1203 (my italics).  38. P. 1219.  39. P. 1210.
40. Pp. 1220, 1218-1219, 1211.  41. P. 1218.  42. See above, p. 49.

our new world must "hospitably receive the inaugurations of the old civilizations," and Shakespeare in particular. Incidentally, Professor Harrison names, but does not discuss in any way Whitman's final qualification of his views, his significant note of 1888 on Shakespeare's historical plays. The import of that note we shall have to consider in closing.

(5) Edgar Lee Masters' *Whitman* (1937),[43] while it does not specifically mention this note of Whitman's, does allude to his speaking enthusiastically of the historical plays. For the rest, this book devotes several pages to the familiar summing-up of Whitman's exceptions against Shakespeare (the anti-democrat), but it does not touch upon the other side.

(6) Neither did Professor Newton Arvin, a year after Masters, in his illuminating study,[44] chiefly of the socio-political background and meaning of Whitman's work and personality. The plan of this volume virtually excludes close consideration of Whitman's literary relationships, except as regards his contacts with the work of certain of the romanticists and their successors, such as Burns and Scott, the German philosophic idealists, and Emerson and Carlyle.[45] Shakespeare receives little more than casual mention here, and that but in two or three places in the book. Even so, this work underscores a principle of first importance for all future interpreters of Whitman and not least for our inquiry. It urges home the truth that criticism which over-simplifies, which fails to take account of the "vital contradictions" of Whitman's thought, is likely to remain "green and raw."[46] It demonstrates that there was "nothing easefully simple about Walt Whitman" as man, thinker, doer, and artist; that beneath his radicalism ran strongly conservative undercurrents; that there were unpredictable manifestations of "practical conformity in this non-conformist"; and that by no means all his convictions were — or remained — "clear-cut."[47] In view of what I have written in the

43. Pp. 233, 237-240.    44. *Whitman*, New York, 1938.    45. *Id.*, pp. 176 ff.
46. *Id.*, p. 5. Quotations by permission of The Macmillan Company, Publishers.
47. *Id.*, pp. 6, 30-31.

preceding pages it seems reasonable to conclude that the "magnificent inconsistency" [48] of Whitman's thought and action — traced in this book through the complex of his social-political and scientific-religious interests — is characteristic also of his varying reactions to Shakespeare.

Mr. Arvin, of course, does not say this; but neither does he deny it. He sticks to his own subject, admirably — except possibly at one point. This is his allusion to Whitman's note on Shakespeare's historical plays,[49] which note he mentions only to dismiss it as an example of Whitman's increasing fondness, as he grew old, for the obscure or the enigmatic: in Whitman's own words, for "that inexplicable element of every highest poetic nature which causes it to cover up . . . its real purpose and meanings."

Now it is true that Whitman may have enjoyed his little mystification, or the mild delight of helping to *solve* a "mystery," when he wrote this sentence into his note, "What Lurks Behind Shakespeare's Historical Plays?" published in *November Boughs*,[50] 1888. But more important, surely, is the fact that in writing this note — or query — Whitman sought, rationally and fairly on the whole, to explain the new light he had come to see in these plays. His new view of the histories is distinctly interesting in itself. And it is important for our purposes because it contains another notable qualification — not to say an outspoken retractation, almost at the end of Whitman's career — of his charges against Shakespeare. These observations of Whitman's have been so little noticed that they deserve full review, the more so because some of their implications are directly at variance with the conclusions of the critics. Professor Dunn,[51] for example, writes that *"Whitman did not know what staunch elements of independence and what adaptations to an English public already headed for democracy, Shakespeare exemplified in his plays."* This, in my judgment is admirably

48. *Id.*, p. 37.     49. *Id.*, pp. 222-223.
50. *Complete Prose*, pp. 390-392; *Complete Writings, Prose*, III, 120-123.
51. *Shakespeare in America*, p. 273. (My italics.) Quoted by permission of The Macmillan Company, Publishers.

and exactly right—that is, all but the first four words quoted. The fact is that Whitman did know, or at least that he found out in time if he did not know at first. This is shown by his "speculations" in the note on the histories.

These speculations may be summed up as follows. (1) He had come to look upon them as Shakespeare's most notable work. To quote his own words:

> The English historical plays are to me . . . the most eminent as dramatic performances (my maturest judgment confirming the impressions of my early years, that the distinctiveness and glory of the poet reside not in his vaunted dramas of the passions, but in those founded on the contests of English dynasties and the French Wars). . . . Conceiv'd out of the fullest heat and pulse of European feudalism—personifying in unparallel'd ways the mediaeval aristocracy, its towering spirit of ruthless and gigantic caste, [it would seem as though only] some born descendant . . . of the 'wolfish earls' so plenteous in the plays themselves . . . might seem to be the true author of those amazing works—works in some respects greater than anything else in recorded literature.

(2) Whitman had come to believe that Shakespeare's study of English history, beginning casually with the *Henry VI* trilogy, *developed systematically;* that the unfolding sweep of the histories, and even of certain of the great tragedies vitally concerned with kings and government, was the result of an *essentially controlling plan.* "It is plain to me," he writes,

> that as profound and forecasting a brain . . . as ever appear'd in literature, after floundering somewhat in [*Henry VI*, Part One,] afterwards developed and defined his plan in the Second and Third parts, and, from time to time, thenceforward, systematically enlarged it to majestic and mature proportions in "Richard II," "Richard III," "King John," "Henry IV," "Henry V," and even in "Macbeth," "Coriolanus," and "Lear." For it is impossible to grasp the whole cluster of those plays

without thinking of them as, in a free sense, the result of an *essentially controlling plan*.

(3) The "real purpose and meaning" of this "controlling plan" was purposely "veil'd," but Whitman had come to believe that its import is inescapable. Briefly, by virtue of the very power of their "barbarous and tumultuous gloom," the histories *intentionally undermine* the theory and practice of government they portray. This suggestion Whitman owed to his friend William O'Connor, whom he quotes approvingly as follows:

> The atmosphere of the histories is one of barbarous and tumultuous gloom, — they do not make us love the times they limn. . . . It is impossible to believe that the greatest of the Elizabethan men could have sought to indoctrinate the age with the love of feudalism which his own drama in its entirety, if the view taken of it herein be true, certainly and subtly saps and mines.

(4) To this Whitman adds flatly: "I defy any one" who will read the histories "in the light" of this suggestion, "to escape such new and deep . . . meanings." And he intimates that in the future Shakespeare may be remembered in America primarily because he exposes most powerfully the evils of the old order, the "necessity" for the new order, which is still the American way:

> Will it not indeed be strange if the author of "Othello" and "Hamlet" is destin'd to live in America, in a generation or two, less as the cunning draughtsman of the passions, and more as putting on record the first full exposé — and by far the most vivid one, immeasurably ahead of doctrinaires and economists — of the political theory and results . . . which America has come on earth to abnegate and replace?

This question, incidentally, answers Whitman's complaint written seven years earlier, that "Scott and Tennyson, like Shakespeare, exhale that principle of caste which we Americans have come on earth to destroy." [52]

A half century of Shakespearean criticism stretches between Whitman's final pronouncements and the renewed outbreak of the world struggle now confronting democracy. At this distance it cannot be said that Whitman's views have won, or are likely to win, unqualified acceptance. It is unlikely, for example, that Shakespeare's "glory" will ever reside pre-eminently in any one portion of his work. Time and change will naturally make more precious now one and then another part of the mighty treasure-trove he bequeathed to mankind. But Shakespeare is destined to live because he wrote the tragedies *and* the comedies *and* the sonnets *and* the histories. As regards the histories in particular, nothing has come to light to substantiate adequately the conjecture that they are the product of a systematically conceived or essentially controlled *plan*, and that they were *consciously intended* to sap or undermine the old order. Shakespeare was not primarily a political philosopher. He was a practical dramatist busily engaged in writing plays to please the public. Yet there is a residuum of compelling common sense behind the general trend of Whitman's argument. As I have pointed out above,[53] Shakespeare's histories dramatize times past for what they are worth. They do not disguise or prettify the ancient evil of weak or ruthless absolutism, of civil disunion, and tyranny. To this extent at least they point the way toward, or, as Whitman suggests, they demonstrate the "necessity" for the new order—for "the inauguration of modern democracy."

One could hardly hope to find a more beautiful illustration of Whitman's "contradictoriness" than in his utterances concerning the democratic foreshadowings in Shakespeare's historical plays—

52. "Poetry To-Day in America" (1881), *Complete Writings, Prose*, II, 209.
53. Pp. 35 ff.

for his note on the subject was first printed in the very same volume of *November Boughs* (1888), which, in its Preface, charges that all the great poems are an insult to democracy and of no concern to the Western Hemisphere.[54] Whitman was in his old age when he published this book, but he had always had the creative inconsistency of life itself. And he knew this — better than did some of his critics. "Do I contradict myself?" he queries, in the "Song of Myself" —

> Very well then I contradict myself,
> (I am large, I contain multitudes.) [55]

As a democratic propagandist, he did not hesitate to stress *one* side of Shakespeare, or of anybody else, to suit his own immediate purpose. But he was no mere propagandist. The man and the poet in him also speak out, to set things right and to strike a balance.

54. See above, pp. 15-16.
55. Lines 1325-1327; cf. Arvin, *op. cit.*, p. 219.

# III

## SHAKESPEARE ON STYLE, IMAGINATION, AND POETRY [1]

THE IRRESISTIBLE whirl of change moves faster as the world grows older, but the student of history and letters may still take uneasy comfort in the reflection that old legend dies hard. It lives long and, grown old, may be born anew if it be good legend — a challenging fable, a pointed parable, a tale which holds old men from the chimney corner because it has poignancy, beauty, truth, even if it be not the whole truth. And as with legend so with certain legendary literary judgments which have captured the imagination of men. So it is, for instance, with Wordsworth's famous dictum concerning Milton: Milton's soul was like a star, but he did not dwell far apart from the world of affairs nor from warm and kindly human relationships. Yet Wordsworth's Milton lives, not only because the conception has in it an element of real, though partial truth, but more especially because it is dramatically effective — because it characterizes a complex figure in sharp, clean-cut, easily understandable lines. So it is also, I believe, with a fascinating old half-truth of critical legend which has had a curiously varied revival in our own time: the legend — one of Milton's own sponsorship though neither of his only begetting nor yet of Ben Jonson's — concerning the divine "easiness," [2] the gloriously unstudied artlessness of "sweetest Shakespeare, Fancy's child," warbling "his native woodnotes wild."

Fancy's child in modern critical costume seems more mature,

1. Reprinted, with additions, from *PMLA*, LIII (1938), 1019 ff.
2. Hemings and Condell, "To the . . . Readers," First Folio.

but he still smiles, "out-topping knowledge" and all but scorning conscious art. Distinguished scholars find that he was "a little shy of talking shop": [3] disinclined even to mention poets and poetry. "One of the most curious things about Shakespeare," we read, is "his ridicule of poetry and poets."

> He does not handle genuine poetry and poets; he may have thought that unprofessional. He doesn't 'talk shop' in his plays. In the two plays in which he introduces professional poets, *Julius Caesar* and *Timon of Athens*, they are treated with utter contempt. [In] Bartlett's *Concordance* . . . the words 'Poem,' 'Poetical,' 'Poet,' and 'Poetry,' combined, do not make a half a column. . . . He has more references to worms than to poets! The first if not the only passage that occurs to anyone as Shakespeare's tribute to his art is that in *A Midsummer Night's Dream* beginning 'The poet's eye in a fine frenzy rolling'; and all it says is that it is 'airy nothing'. . . . The word 'feign' occurs six times out of the thirty-two that the words 'poet,' 'poetry,' and 'poetical,' occur. . . . It is interesting to hear poetry thus condemned. [4]

Other critics agree that Shakespeare was unconcerned about the problems of the theory and technique of Poetry. "Poetry, or the poet," they say, "Shakespeare barely mentions."

> If the well-known passage in *Midsummer Night's Dream* and phrases in the *Sonnets* may be said to be praise, other passages are in sardonic vein; and Shakespeare 'shows singularly little desire to magnify his office as artist,' as Sir Edmund K. Chambers says. . . . In Shakespeare no conscious art is apparent. Shakespeare holds no theory about himself as artist, about the ideas which may be said to pervade his work, or about the form which embodied them. [5]

3. "The passages which indicate that Shakespeare was . . . keenly interested in the actor's art . . . as compared with the allusions to sport . . . are few in number, as if the author were a little shy of 'talking shop' " (J. M. Manly, "Shakespeare Himself," *Memorial Volume to Shakespeare and Harvey, University of Texas Bulletin* No. 1701 (1917), p. 20).

4. Henry David Gray, "Shakespeare: A Person," *Shakespeare Association Bulletin*, VII (1932), 159.

5. Arthur H. R. Fairchild, *Shakespeare and the Arts of Design, University of Missouri Studies*, XII (1937), i, 173.

In the face of the evidence, does the new costume fit much better than the old? Questions of taste and critical emphasis permit of no dogmatic answer; but perhaps it will be granted that, roughly speaking, the new view appears to be akin to the old. For example, Ben Jonson's tart observation that Shakespeare (sometimes) "wanted art" can hardly have failed to contribute something to the still widely prevalent belief that Shakespeare was not a "conscious" artist. Again, Dryden's emphasis upon that "comprehensive soul" of inspired genius in Shakespeare which drew all things "not laboriously but luckily," would not seem to have been forgotten by modern critics who, by way of exalting the native genius of the man, hold that he stood, in Olympian aloofness, above art, as it were—perhaps positively disinclined to take his own art seriously, or at least reluctant to talk about it. Curiously enough, Shakespeare's contemporaries had not made these discoveries. Ben Jonson's eulogy effectively disposes of Matthew Arnold's idea that Shakespeare walked on earth "unguessed at," and, so far as I know, neither his contemporaries nor the critics of the next century and a half, though there was then almost universal agreement as to his wanting art, found him guilty of wanting shop talk. I mean to examine the evidence. Does it exhibit conscious art in Shakespeare? Have not certain critics erred by failing to take account of Hazlitt's [6] observation— that much of what is greatest in Shakespeare is "blended together with the greatest art *and without any appearance of it*"? And, conversely, does Shakespeare, or does he not, discuss his art frequently and significantly? From the plays and poems I shall seek to show that current generalizations concerning Shakespeare's artlessness require qualification. To this end I shall examine, first, what he himself says concerning "style" in prose and verse; next, his comments upon the place of imagination in poetry; and, finally, his utterances upon poetics in general—such matters as

6. *Characters of Shakespeare's Plays, Complete Works*, ed. Waller and Glover, I, 238. (My italics.)

metrics, rhyme, diction, and the "kinds" of poetry—and upon dramatic poetry and the theatre in particular.

With regard to style in Shakespeare, I think it may safely be said that his works early and late, his poems as well as his plays, exhibit clearly: (1) his perfect and delighted awareness of it; (2) his instinctive and yet studied—i.e., consciously wrought—use of all its shades and levels in the building of character, situation, or background; (3) his ready and unmistakable pleasure in talking about it. My illustrations indicate that his comment upon style is not deeply concerned with its merely formal aspects; that it touches, not infrequently, upon its most subtle implications. Again, it will appear that many of these comments are virtually written in the first person—not in the sonnets only but also in the plays, being made without dramatic compulsion or necessity by personages who, in these matters, speak with the recognizable accents of their creator. "Pat he comes," says Edmund in *King Lear* [7]—when Edgar conveniently arrives at just the right moment for the initial move in his brother's plot against him—"Pat he comes, *like the catastrophe in the old comedy*." Hector quotes Aristotle, but this is not a case of Edmund, in the ancient days of Lear, alluding to Plautus or Menander! It is not Polonius pontificating. Illegitimate Edmund's goddess was nature, not art, and he was not afflicted by the curiosity of nations or of critics concerning details of dramatic technique. He is merely the mouthpiece of Shakespeare—pleasantly talking shop. By way of avoiding the bother of motivating Edgar's pat appearance, Shakespeare genially likens his management of the scene to the free and easy disregard of motivation in the "lamentable" old "comedy" of Tudor times—*King Cambyses*, *The Old Wives Tale*, and their predecessors.

Deprecating but certainly not unconscious reference to style in the formal sense appears over and over again in the *Sonnets*, not

7. I, ii, 146.

only with regard to the stylistic achievements of the rival poet, but in somewhat voluble protest against the admitted artificialities of the *genre*.  For himself, Shakespeare, like Sidney, will look in his heart and "true in love, but truly write"; [8] unlike those "stirred by a painted beauty" to their verse, he rejects for himself their "laboring for invention," [9] their "proud" — and "false" — "compare"; [10] yet he hopes that his sincerity, his lack of sophisticated artifice — the "barren rhyme" of his "pupil pen" [11] — will win him the tribute of loving memory over "better" craftsmen.  Of their work, and of his, he hopes his friend will say, "Theirs for their style I'll read, his for his love." [12]  And yet, here as in the plays, none of the Elizabethans, not even Sidney or Spenser, for all their learning, paid higher tribute to that essential quality of style, that conscious, painstaking removal of surplusage which Shakespeare acclaims in Sonnet 85.  For here, though once more modestly asserting his own "unlettered" simplicity (which merely "think[s] good thoughts whilst other[s] write good words"), he writes in eloquent praise of the elemental but studied power of the poet's word, the "precious phrase by all the muses filed."  Something of the same consciousness of the power of words as an essential element of style, "Words sweetly placed and modestly directed," appears in a casual remark by the Earl of Suffolk, in one of the earliest of the plays, the first part of *King Henry VI*.[13]

These passages in themselves should almost suffice to refute the view that no conscious art is apparent in Shakespeare.  Jonson rightly observed that Shakespeare sometimes wanted art.  But Jonson, no less justly, gave high praise where that is due:

> Yet must I not give Nature all: Thy Art,
> My gentle Shakespeare, must enjoy a part.
>
>                    . . . He
> Who casts to write a living line, must sweat
> (Such as thine are) and strike the second heat

8. Sonnet 21.      9. *Id.*, 59.      10. *Id.*, 21, 130.      11. *Id.*, 16.
12. *Id.*, 32.          13. V, iii, 179.

Upon the Muses' anvil: turn the same
(And himself with it) that he thinks to frame;
Or for the laurel he may gaine a scorne,
For a good poet's made as well as borne.
And such wert thou.

And so he was.   Benedick, in *Much Ado*, testifies to this purpose.
Benedick himself was no poet born, though he did manage to grind
out a sonnet or two to his mistress' eyebrow.   But he knows and
fills in (with quizzical protective coloring) the great names of
romantic poetry: "Leander the good swimmer, Troilus, the first
employer of panders, and a whole book full of" others.   Better
still, he knows how the true poets have *worked* to make these
"names yet *run smoothly in the even road of a blank verse.*"   Benedick was simply not "born under a rhyming planet"; turn and file
as he will, he, like Hamlet the Dane, is but "ill at these numbers."
The great names which still run smoothly in the masters' verse
were "never so *truly turned over and over*" as his "poor self in love."
Even so, he can achieve nothing better than a "hard" or a "bab-
bling" rhyme, probably set—even if "the . . . lame . . . feet
might bear the verses"—to something not much better than Orlando's jog-trot: "the very false gallop of verses," "the right butter-
woman's rank to market." [14]

It cannot be that Shakespeare was artlessly unconscious of all
this.   For, as though to anticipate the critics, he smilingly denies
the allegation.   Says Rosalind to Touchstone, "Thou speakest
wiser than thou knowest."   To which, be it remembered, Touchstone replies, "Nay, I shall never be ware of mine own wit till I
break my shins against it." [15]—"One can imagine Shakespeare
smiling" at Matthew Arnold in the Elysian Fields (so Matthew
Arnold himself suggests) [16] upon being reproached by that distinguished critic for certain "false . . . lines," certain "strains
quite . . . unworthy" of his art.   His smiling reply, of course,

14. *Much Ado*, V, ii, 30-41; iv, 86-88; *As You Like It*, III, ii, 174-180, 119, 104.
15. *As You Like It*, II, iv, 57-60.
16. "Wordsworth," *Essays in Criticism*, Second Series.

would have been "that he knew it perfectly well himself, and what did it matter?" Yet Shakespeare was not altogether content to smile and smile (like King Claudius in *Hamlet*) and be a—slipshod craftsman! Witness the notable but frequently misinterpreted remark by the time-serving poet in *Timon of Athens*, one of the lying knaves come to sell Timon his shoddy wares above their worth. Here Shakespeare speaks directly if somewhat less genially to the point. This huckster poet describes his work, deprecatingly and disingenuously, to his fellow-peddler, the painter, as

> A thing slipped idly from me:
> Our poesy is as a gum, which oozes
> From whence 'tis nourished.[17]

This is not Shakespeare's confession of faith. True poetry, "beauty making beautiful old rhyme," does not "ooze." It is turned over and over on the muses' anvil till it becomes the precious phrase by all the muses filed. Lack of painstaking workmanship, lack of art, mere spontaneity as the definition of the sum-total of the poetic process—this, the passage ironically implies, is shallow pretense, quackery worthy of a peddler poet.

Of the *word* "style" in the narrower sense, Shakespeare makes sufficiently pointed use, especially in the earlier plays. But what really matters is not so much the word as the lively consciousness of the thing itself which remains in his work to the end, in *Lear* and *Timon*, for instance. Therefore I shall not dwell upon his use of the mere word, "familiar style," [18] "high . . . style," [19] "large style," [20] "the style of gods," [21] "harsh . . . style," [22] "tedious . . . style," [23] "a silly stately style," [24] and the like. More important and very much in evidence, especially in certain of the great romantic comedies (*As You Like It, Twelfth Night, Much Ado*), but also in *Love's Labour's Lost, Romeo and Juliet*,

---

17. *Timon*, I, i, 180, 20-22.
19. *Much Ado*, V, ii, 6.
21. *Much Ado*, V, i, 37.
23. *1 Henry VI*, IV, vii, 72.

18. *Merry Wives*, I, iii, 51.
20. *2 Henry VI*, I, i, 111.
22. *Richard III*, IV, iv, 360.
24. *Id.*, IV, vii, 70.

*Hamlet*, and elsewhere, are certain observations on style in the larger sense — and certain applications thereof.

It is late in the day to labor further the obvious fact of Shakespeare's exquisite and delighted consciousness of words — from Berowne's "taffeta phrases, silken terms precise" to the same gentleman's "russett yeas and honest kersey noes," [25] or the gracious Duncan's recognition of the fitness of martial words on the lips of martial men,[26] or Osric's summer-flies of ostentation and Hamlet's forswearing of the triple emptiness of words such as poets like Timon's write.[27] But, even at the risk of underscoring the obvious, I cannot yet dismiss this subject. Berowne's taffeta phrases suggest at least one word more concerning the lively "civil war of wits" and words which is *Love's Labour's Lost*. Not even in Shakespeare are the "epithets" elsewhere so "sweetly varied"; nowhere else is there so consciously wrought and yet so fantastically and uproariously high-spirited an uprearing of words, such a mint of euphuisms and malapropisms and figures pedantical, of puns and quibbles and sweet smoke of rhetoric, of "high-born" words and "fire-new" words and "magnificent" words — or, as Costard might say, such "guerdon," such "remuneration" for the lover of words and poetry as Shakespeare achieved in this, the best dramatic essay ever written on words and their ways.

*As You Like It*, too, has its full share of "brave words" and "Ethiop words" [28] and what not; but also much of larger significance in the matter of style. Sufficiently obvious, besides the remarks already noticed concerning such matters as lame feet, conventional versifying, and the like,[29] is the wide-awake comment by Jaques upon Orlando's entrance with his "Good day and happiness, dear Rosalind." Jaques misses no points; he recognizes among other things, something of the natural affinity between

25. *Love's Labour's Lost*, V, ii, 406-413.
26. "So well thy words become thee as thy wounds; They smack of honour both" — *Macbeth*, I, ii, 43-44.
27. Cf. above, n. 17 and text; *Hamlet*, II, ii, 193-195; V, ii, 84-202.
28. III, iv, 44; IV, iii, 35.
29. See above, p. 67, n. 14.

English prose—in certain moods—and blank verse: "Nay then, God b'wi' you, and you talk in blank verse!" [30]  And no less wide-awake, no less unconscious, surely, on Shakespeare's part, if less obvious to the critics, is Rosalind's dictum, in the same scene, concerning the creative contribution of the "foolish chroniclers"—and the wise poets—toward the upbuilding of romantic legend. Troilus, Hero and Leander, and all the fabled patterns of love—what would have become of them but for the chroniclers and the poets?  In mere prose—"men have died . . . and worms have eaten them, but not for love." [31]  (With this utterance on the romances compare the equally notable remark, in *Richard III*, on the provenience of the chronicle play materials—the leading question of the young Prince concerning the Tower of London, and historic truth and the effect of *recorded* legend in the shaping and interpretation of tradition.) [32]

*As You Like It* contains much additional evidence which proves that Shakespeare the stylist consistently knew what he was about.  Witness, for example, his unchanging habit of calling a spade a spade when telling the audience about it.  Thus, the letter of Phebe, the cruel shepherdess, is written in

> a boisterous and cruel style,[33]
> A style for challengers.  Why, she defies me
> Like Turk to Christian! Women's gentle brain
> Could not drop forth such giant-rude invention!

"Did you ever hear such railing?" queries Rosalind.  The answer might be "No"—unless one happened to recall also, for example, the "railing" of Falconbridge in *King John*,[34] when the Citizen of Angiers has said his say to the embattled kings:

30. IV, i, 31.                              31. IV, i, 107-108.
32. "Did Julius Caesar build that place . . . ?"  "He did, my lord, begin that place . . ."  "Is it upon record, or else reported Successively from age to age, he built it?"  "Upon record . . ."  "But say . . . it were not registered, Methinks the truth should live from age to age, As 'twere retailed to all posterity, Even to the general all-ending day?" (III, i, 69-78).
33. I.e., "Art thou god to shepherd turned" etc.; IV, iii, 30-46.
34. II, i, 423-467.

> Here's a stay
> That shakes the rotten carcass of old Death
> Out of his rags!  Here's a large mouth indeed
> That spits forth death and mountains, rocks and seas,
> Talks as familiarly of roaring lions
> As maids of thirteen do of puppy dogs . . .
> Zounds!  I was never so bethumped with words
> Since I first called my brother's father dad.

Or, to return to Rosalind, let us recall her delicious comment on what might be termed the wolverine style—the *word* "style," once more, is not there—in pastoral love-making.  It is toward the end of the play.  The quartet—Phebe and Silvius, Rosalind and Orlando—chant to one another in flowing dithyrambs "what 'tis to love," until Rosalind ends the scene with a winged word quizzically recognizing the near approach of the sublime to the ridiculous: "Pray you, no more of this; 'tis like the howling of Irish wolves against the moon." [35]  Nor can it be said that this is merely Rosalind speaking.  Professor Manly [36] pays just tribute to Shakespeare's "unequalled capacity for self-criticism," and *As You Like It* proves this, if proof be needed.  After the good Duke's great speech on the uses of adversity comes the superb—because utterly calm and true—self-appraisal in the words of the courtier whose voice is that of Shakespeare delighting nobly in a piece of work well done:

> Happy is your Grace
> That can translate the stubbornness of fortune
> Into so quiet and so sweet a style. [37]

Like Chaucer, Molière, Dryden, Carlyle, and other skillful craftsmen in verse and prose, Shakespeare dared to look upon his work and at once see and *say* that it was good.  This is the true tenor of Orsino's comment on the old plain chant sung by the spinsters and the knitters in the sun, which so movingly "dallies with the inno-

35.  V, ii, 89-119.          36.  *Op. cit.*, p. 10.          37.  II, i, 18-20.

cence of love/Like the old age, . . ." and this also is the implication of his response to the charming words Viola had spoken in praise of the music:

> It gives a very echo to the seat
> Where love is throned.

> *Orsino.* Thou dost speak masterly.[38]

Yet Carlyle and Ruskin and Hazlitt and Emerson and many another romantic worshipper of "the doctrine of the unconscious" solemnly insist, in Carlyle's phrase,[39] that " 'genius is ever a secret to itself' . . . The sign of health is unconsciousness . . . Shakespeare" was "everyway an unconscious man." He "takes no airs for writing *Hamlet* and *The Tempest;* understands not that it is anything surprising. . . . On the other hand what cackling and strutting must we not often hear and see when . . . this or the other well-fledged goose has produced its goose-egg!" Shakespeare delights in the sweet and quiet style of *As You Like It,* but Ruskin [40] assures us that "the moment a man can really do his work, he becomes speechless about it. . . . Art must not be talked about." Hazlitt [41] agrees, at least in part. Shakespeare, he says, had "the unconsciousness of nature . . . imagination to be perfect must be unconscious, for nature is so." And Emerson [42] adds that "the works of genius cost nothing. There is no painful effort, but it is the spontaneous flowing of the thought. Shakespeare made his *Hamlet* as a bird weaves its nest." —What is the answer? I believe it may be read in the second thoughts of these very critics, and in the fact that their practice was better than their theory. Ruskin, for example, talked about art, to good effect, during most of his long lifetime. Carlyle was right, of course, in

38. *Twelfth Night,* II, iv, 44-49, 21-23.
39. See "Characteristics," and "The Hero as Poet" (*Heroes and Hero-Worship*).
40. "The Mystery of Life and Its Arts" (*Sesame and Lilies*).
41. *Characters of Shakespeare's Plays, Works,* I, 294.
42. "Works and Days," *Works* (Centenary edition), VII, 182; cf. R. P. Falk, *PMLA,* LVI (1941) 536.

insisting that "Shakespeare's Art is not Artifice"—as Ben Jonson, indeed, had testified long before, even while praising Shakespeare for sweating at the muses' anvil. But Carlyle was right also in branding as "a heedless notion . . . our common one, that" Shakespeare "sat like a bird on the bough and sang forth, free and offhand." [43] And, as regards Carlyle's strictures against "cackling and strutting"—let the reader of *Sartor Resartus* turn again to Carlyle's own luminous self-appraisal; i.e., to his remarks about the "rapt earnestness," the "inequality," the "rather beautiful apostrophe[s]," and the "true inspiration" of Professor Teufels-droeckh's "style"! [44] Hazlitt's faith in unconsciousness did not keep him from recognizing Shakespeare's power to achieve great art—partly because "he was not above" giving "attention to the smallest . . . things" [45]—without leaving behind the visible signs of endeavor. Nor did Emerson [46] fail to realize that "a multitude of trials . . . a thousand rejections" must have played their part in the making of Shakespeare's greatest work.

All this, to quote Professor Bradley in another connection,[47]

[does] not imply that Shakespeare always deliberately aimed at the effects which he produced. But no artist always does this, and I see no reason to doubt that Shakespeare often did it or to suppose that his method of constructing and composing differed, except in degree, from that of the most conscious artists. . . . Inspiration is surely not incompatible with considerate work-manship.

Another great English stylist lends the weight of his authority to this view of the matter. In "that lavish richness of style" which Cardinal Newman had "noticed in Shakespeare," he saw "no mark of trick or artifice." It is sound art:

43. "The Hero as Poet."
44. Cf. *Sartor Resartus*, ed. Archibald MacMechan (New York, 1896), pp. 25-26, 97.
45. *Characters*, *Works*, I, 185; see above, p. 64.
46. *Journals*, III, 478. (See above, p. 72, n. 42.
47. On Shakespeare's architectonics in tragedy; see *Shakespearean Tragedy*, p. 68; quotations by permission of The Macmillan Company, Publishers.

> I cannot grant that genius need never take pains, that genius
> may not improve . . . never finishes off at leisure what it has
> thrown off in outline at a stroke. . . . Is it wonderful that
> . . . our greatest poet . . . should sometimes . . . pause,
> write, erase, re-write, amend, complete, before he satisfies him-
> self that his language has done justice to the conceptions which
> his mind's eye contemplated? [48]

If Shakespeare took conscious and pleasing pains in the matters
I have thus far discussed, what, roughly, was the result? We
have seen that he was marvelously attuned to words, deliberately
and delightedly word-conscious, style-conscious, and self-critical,
though never [49] self-conscious. I will not presume to estimate the
total effect of these qualities upon his work; but, before turning to
other matters, I should like to indicate two or three fairly specific
and perhaps not insignificant results.

One appears to be that Shakespeare's style-consciousness
helped to shape and tighten his own style from the very first. My
quotations from *1 Henry VI* [50] would seem to point in that direction. So, I think, does *Titus Andronicus*, though Professor Bradley [51] holds that "if Shakespeare wrote the whole" of this play,
"he did so before he had either a style of his own or any characteristic tragic conception." One might argue, for example, that its
language, at least in part, is unmistakably, though perhaps not
demonstrably, in Shakespeare's style:

> What fool hath added water to the sea
> Or brought a faggot to bright-burning Troy? [52]

48. "Literature," *Idea of A University, Works*, ed. 1923, pp. 283 ff. — Mr. Granville-
Barker, in the most recent of his *Prefaces to Shakespeare*, Third Series (1937), pp. 1-2,
genially pretends to defer to the popular cry. "Let us cheerfully admit," he writes, "that
[Shakespeare] 'wanted art'; he was the genius of the workshop." But the art he "wanted"
is merely "a *scheme* of consistent principles and a *studied method* of expressing them. . . .
There is an aspect of him which turns towards pure beauty of form, and the discipline and
the limitations involved" (Italics mine).
49. Unless it be, here and there, in the *Sonnets*.
50. See above, p. 66, n. 13; p. 68, nn. 23-24
51. *Op. cit.*, p. 4; see above, n. 47.          52. III, i, 69-70.

More demonstrably in Shakespeare's style — or, at least, an interesting early manifestation of a stylistic sense which, if it partook of artifice at first, became art before the end — is an earlier speech of Titus, his farewell to his sons:

> *In peace and honour rest you here, my sons:*
> Rome's readiest champions, repose you here in rest,
> Secure from worldly chances and mishaps!
> Here lurks no treason, here no envy swells . . .
> No noise, but silence and eternal sleep.
> *In peace and honour rest you here, my sons!* [53]

The effectiveness of the choric repetition speaks for itself, and Lavinia's words, immediately after, drive it further home: "In peace and honour live Lord Titus long!" Certainly Shakespeare did not miss it — witness his skillfully studied use of similar choric effects later on. Take, for example, the incremental repetition which links Orlando's challenge, upon his entrance into the forest of Arden, and the good Duke's reply:

> *Orlando*   If ever you have looked on better days,
> If ever been where bells have knolled to church,
> If ever sat at any good man's feast,
> If ever from your eyelids wiped a tear,
> And know what 'tis to pity and be pitied,
> Let gentleness my strong enforcement be;
> In the which hope I blush, and hide my sword.

> *Duke*   True is it that we have seen better days,
> And have with holy bell been knoll'd to church
> And sat at good men's feasts, and wiped our eyes
> Of drops that sacred pity has engendered;
> And therefore sit you down in gentleness
> And take upon command what help we have . . . [54]

53. I, i, 150-156.
54. *As You Like It*, II, vii, 114-125.

So, again, in the farewells between Brutus and Cassius:

*Brutus*    For ever and for ever farewell, Cassius!
         If we do meet again, why, we shall smile;
         If not, why then this parting was well made.

*Cassius*   Forever and for ever farewell, Brutus!
         If we do meet again, we'll smile indeed;
         If not, 'tis true this parting was well made.[55]

A larger effect of Shakespeare's self-critical style-consciousness grows out of the utterly unreserved clarity and frankness with which he sees what he is about and makes others see it. Matthew Arnold's signpost method of organizing and presenting his doctrine was not invented in the nineteenth century. Every writer—like every age—has his own whimsies, his own Philistines, and his own favorite technical devices; but Shakespeare knew the essentials of this method, and never tired of using it. His superb and unquestioned skill in exposition, the matchless clearness of his character drawing, the certainty and finality of his tone-color ("Fair is foul, and foul is fair") grew to no small extent out of his consistent habit of calling a spade a spade for himself and for his audience. Smilingly but skillfully he all but labels his characters, tags his themes, and provides bold markers to designate the channels and cross current of his plots. Many of his titles, of course—*A Midsummer Night's Dream, Measure for Measure, Twelfth Night, The Winter's Tale, As You Like It*—point the way; but obviously this is not all. In *As You Like It* pastoral fantasy plus unclouded good humor blossom into poetry by virtue of a sweet and gracious style—and Shakespeare says so in so many words. The "weak and idle theme" of *A Midsummer Night's Dream* (Shakespeare himself to the contrary notwithstanding) yields *more* than a dream, more than the course of true love not running smooth, the sadness of bright things coming, too soon, to confusion—for in the crowd of mortals and fairies there is also Puck, deftly defining his

55. *Julius Caesar*, V, i, 117-122.

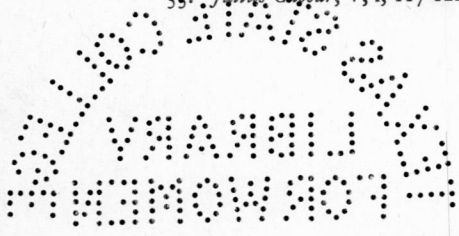

pleasantries, "(Those things do best please me / That befall pre-posterously)," and Bottom the Weaver, mellifluously roaring forth his varied virtues, expounding *his* dream.  So in *Love's Labour's Lost*.  The "odoriferous flowers of fancy," the "jerks of invention," the pedants and curates carousing at the feast of languages and stealing the scraps—these do not, after all, monop-olize the feast.  Youth and poetry also sit at the table, and promise to turn it before the end, since "young blood doth not obey an old decree."  And so it is once more—though by no means once more only—in the flood-tide of *Lear*, when the audi-ence is unequivocally informed that the Fool's function is to "outjest" his master's "heart-struck injuries," and that Lear's daughters are drawn to scale with Gloucester's sons in the shaping and crossing of the two stories: "He childed as I fathered."

As I see it, finally, Shakespeare's style-consciousness left its recognizable mark upon his work through his instinctive awareness and studied use of what may be termed the *levels* of style, deftly "lackeying the varying tide" of his dramatic purpose.  Shake-speare, of course—like Edmund—was not another Polonius.  He smiles at academic-pedantical differentiation merely for the sake of differentiation: "pastoral, pastoral-comical, historical-pastoral, tragical-historical," and all the rest.  And yet, being a true crafts-man, he delighted in pertinent distinctions, for he knew from the first that there is excellent music to be drawn from the stops and frets of style.  Early and late, he played upon this pipe, and he must have enjoyed the sense of growing mastery.  One does not forget, for example, Falstaff's merry parody of the Euphuists, and his mock-heroics "in King Cambyses' vein" for the benefit of the fluttering hostess ("Weep not, sweet queen, for trickling tears are vain"); nor Bottom the Weaver in "Ercles' vein"; [56] nor Romeo's opening essay in the artificial amatory-romantic style:

> Why then, O brawling love! O loving hate!
> O anything, of nothing first create!

56. *1 Henry IV*, II, iv, 425-461; *A Midsummer Night's Dream*, I, ii, 42.

O heavy lightness! serious vanity! . . .
Feather of lead, bright smoke, cold fire, sick health!

On the heel of this comes Romeo's revealing question to Benvolio
—a delightful anticipation of Rosalind's afterthought concerning
the Irish wolves—"Dost thou not laugh?" There is no such
leading question to set off the wailing chorus-quartet of pseudo-
elegiacs later in the play, after Juliet's supposed death—

| | |
|---|---|
| *Lady Capulet* | Accursed, unhappy, wretched, hateful day! |
| | Most miserable hour that e'er time saw . . . |
| *Nurse* | O woe! O woeful, woeful, woeful day! |
| | Most lamentable day, most woeful day . . . |
| | O woeful day! O woeful day! |
| *Paris* | Beguiled, divorced, wronged, spited, slain! |
| | Most detestable Death . . . |
| | By cruel cruel thee quite overthrown . . . |
| *Capulet* | Despised, distressed, hated, martyred, killed! |
| | Uncomfortable time why cam'st thou now . . .[57] |

Nobody says "Dost thou not laugh" here, but it seems reasonable
to suppose that Shakespeare wrote these falsetto ejaculations with
an eye and ear to the audience, which knows that real mourning,
so far, is not in order, since Juliet is still very much alive. Who
can doubt, moreover, that Shakespeare "paused, amended"—
in short, achieved consciously, discerningly, even while sweeping
aloft on mighty wings, the impassioned rapture of sense and style
which transfigures Juliet's epithalamion—"Gallop apace, you
fiery-footed steeds"—and Romeo's farewell—"Shall I believe
That unsubstantial Death is amorous . . . ?" Shakespeare himself virtually marks his most famous essay in the fanciful lyric-
descriptive style as a somewhat undramatic intermezzo—witness
Romeo's impatient comment after the Queen Mab speech, "Peace,
Mercutio . . . Thou talkst of nothing." Not all the notable
lyric-descriptive pieces (Oberon's, for example, concerning Cupid's

57. IV, v, 49-60. (Cf. the equally artificial choric wailing in *Richard III*, II, ii, 77-79;
IV, iv, 26-45, etc.)

fiery shaft and the imperial votaress, and Queen Gertrude's on Ophelia's watery grave) are set off by this sort of author's notation. Yet it is clear enough that Shakespeare was aware of his objectives in these and other variations. The bloody gules style ("roasted in wrath . . . o'ersized with coagulate gore") of the Dido passages in *Hamlet*, and the protesting declamatoriness of the Mousetrap speeches, are not casual or accidental. Their rant sets off, sharply, and no doubt purposely,[58] the contemplative style of the main play. And the pastoralism of *As You Like It*, *Cymbeline*, and *The Winter's Tale*, is not less lovely in its own right even though in achieving it Shakespeare worked in the studied literary tradition of Sidney and Spenser.[59] Polonius, when all is said and done, had a substratum of heavy-handed sense. And Polonius, reading Shakespeare, might catch good fish for his net. Pastoral, pastoral-comical, lyrical-descriptive, histrionic-declamatory-elegiacal-tragic: all are there, and more to boot. Shakespeare, of course, touches deftly upon these things. He does not overburden his plays with talk about nice distinctions in style. But he used them with an open eye.

Again, Shakespeare's utterances upon poetry in general do not suffer from an overplus of uncritical praise or stiff solemnity. "Truth," writes Mark Van Doren, "contains many mockeries" — and Hotspur was not the only one whose teeth were set on edge by "mincing poetry." "One can imagine that . . . the seventeenth-century poets . . . agreed to be men first and poets afterwards . . . The habit of Shakespeare's best poets—Hotspur, Mercutio, Hamlet—is to berate poetry. But for what? For pretending, as it so often does, that it is an end in itself . . . They agree to keep poetry in its place."[60] Yet true poetry has its place and its

58. As Professor Kittredge has observed (see his edition of *Hamlet*, New York, 1939, pp. 197-198).

59. Cf. Greenlaw, "Shakespeare's Pastorals," *Studies in Philology*, XIII (1916), 154 ff.

60. Professor Van Doren has kindly allowed me to quote from his essay on Metaphysical Poetry read at the 1937 meeting of the Modern Language Association.

power. "Much is the force of heaven-bred poesy." So says the Duke in *Two Gentlemen* [61] — but by what power can poets make its music most charming to mortal ears? Shakespeare leaves us in no possible doubt as to the answer. Consciously, luminously, consistently, almost insistently, he replies: by the supreme poetic gift of all, the creative imagination. Nor does he stop here. Criticism has rightly observed that Shakespeare, as a rule, was not disposed to dwell upon theoretical concepts concerning general principles or processes of art; but critical generalization not infrequently slights the exception which proves the rule. Certainly Shakespeare's interest in "strong imagination" was not casual but pervasive and open-eyed. His statement of the theory of the subject, however, is also a declaration of faith. Hence those memorable utterances which acclaim in solemn and moving iteration the power and the splendor of the creative imagination as the prime and essential gift of poet and player, artist and audience, and those others in which if he does not absolutely define the thing itself, the nature of the creative imagination, he does explore its limits and lament its limitations.

The Duke's speech in *A Midsummer Night's Dream*, though it happens to be the most familiar utterance on the subject, does not tell the whole story, and it is too often read out of its context. "Cool reason" leads Theseus, so he tells Hippolyta, to misdoubt the very glory he extols, the "tricks" of "strong imagination" of which the poet is all compact. But Theseus, the doubter, puts aside his unbelief. For the moment, at least, he speaks with conviction and finality:

> The poet's eye, in a fine frenzy rolling,
> *Doth* glance from heaven to earth, from earth to heaven,
> And as imagination bodies forth
> The forms of things unknown, the poet's pen
> Turns them to shapes, and gives to airy nothing
> A local habitation and a name.

61. III, ii, 72.

But the other mood, the other truth, reasserts itself. It is the ever-present threat, the inescapable fact: the utter ineffectiveness of these airy nothings — these "visions" and "shadows," this "weak and idle theme, / No more yielding but a dream," whether it be Puck's dream, or Mercutio's or Prospero's or Shakespeare's — unless the audience contribute its quota of imaginative response. Pyramus and Thisbe do talk the silliest stuff ever heard, yet the best in this kind are but shadows. That the worst need be no worse if the audience's imagination amend them, is a round statement of principle which Shakespeare forcefully reasserts elsewhere, though with a notable — if merely implied — qualification. In the chorus-prologues heading the successive acts of *King Henry V* he emphasizes this principle again and again. "Let us," he urges —

> Let us, ciphers to this great accompt,
> On your imaginary forces work . . .
>
> Piece out our imperfections with your thoughts:
> Into a thousand parts divide one man
> And make imaginary puissance . . .
>
> Behold
> In the quick forge and working house of thought . . .
> Play with your fancies, and in them behold
> Upon the hempen tackle ship-boys climbing . . .
>
> Our scene must to the battle fly,
> Where — O for pity — we shall much disgrace
> With four or five most vile and ragged foils . . .
> The name of Agincourt . . .
>
> Thus with imagined wing our swift scene flies . . .
> Work, work your thoughts, and therein . . . still be kind,
> And eke out our performance with your mind.[62]

But the audience does not have to do it all. The poet is no cipher to this great accompt. To eke out the audience's part, there is the

---

62. Prologue, Acts I, V, III, IV, III. (Cf. *The Winter's Tale*, IV, i, 19-21; *Pericles*, III, Gower 58-61.)

full-winged splendor of the poet's imaginative challenge. His "muse of fire" kindles and burns. The king's "brave fleet, / With silken streamers the young Phoebus fanning," tugs at no shadowy moorings. Poet and audience, by virtue of their combined forces, make room enough in their little wooden *O* for the vasty fields of France, give local habitation and a name unfaded by time to warlike Harry and to Agincourt.

It is natural that Shakespeare should have given clear and oft-repeated recognition to this transcending power of the creative imagination, this soaring above space and time, this bodying forth, by the poetic-imaginative will to believe what from the realistic-skeptical point of view is nowadays termed unreal or "feigned." It is strange, therefore, that this conception has latterly been interpreted as a quasi-condemnation of poetry on Shakespeare's part, or perhaps an implied questioning of its worth.[63] This interpretation, surely, cannot be right, even though the word *feigning* does repeatedly appear in Shakespeare's remarks concerning poetry. Touchstone's dictum, "Truest poetry is the most feigning," is not, in spite of its intentional puzzlement of poor Audrey,[64] a reaffirmation of the ancient libel—newly debated by Stephen Gosson and Sir Philip Sidney, and freshly documented by Francis Bacon[65]—that poetry is the mother of lies. Shakespeare knew this libel,[66] but Touchstone says only what Duke Theseus had already said. "Truest poetry is the most feigning" means that the most genuinely inspired poetry is the most imaginative. So say Viola and Olivia in *Twelfth Night*: if a thing is truly "poetical," "it is the more like to be feigned."[67] In these and in many other passages Shakespeare of course plays upon the secondary meaning of *feign*, in the sense of pretend or sham (e.g.,

63. See above, p. 63.

64. Nor yet in spite of Apemantus's cynical exchange with Timon's poet: "Art not a poet? . . . Then thou liest . . . In thy last work thou hast feigned him a worthy fellow. . . . That's not feigned" (*Timon*, I, i, 226-230; *As You Like It*, III, iii, 17-27).

65. "Of Truth": "Poesy filleth the imagination, and yet it is but with the shadow of a lie"; cf. Gosson's *School of Abuse* and Sidney's *Apology*.

66. Cf. above, n. 64.          67. I, V, 207-208.

"most friendship is feigning").[68] But there can be no doubt that, beneath the jest, he knew and in his remarks on poetry meant to press seriously the primary sense of *feigning*—i.e., bodying forth, imagining (as in "all that poets feign of bliss and joy"),[69] which Sir Philip Sidney in his *Apology* had authoritatively set down as the very essence of poesy: "It is not rhyming and versing that maketh a poet, but . . . *feigning* of notable images of virtues . . . or . . . vices . . . with . . . delightful teaching."[70]

In short, and in spite of Sir Francis Bacon, it is not the lie that vitiates the poet's feigning. Yet there is in Shakespeare's analysis of the grip and ultimate range of the poet's imagination a solemn sense almost of frustration, or at least of a beating against bounds not to be outsoared. Nor was Sidney, for all his joy in poetry, unaware of this. "The poet's persons and doings," he writes, "are but pictures." The best in this kind are but shadows—dreams [71] unsubstantial and impermanent: "too flattering-sweet to be substantial," "swift as a shadow, short as any dream." How soon—Shakespeare says it again and again—these dreams, poetry itself, like all "bright things" of creation, "come to confusion." [72] For in one sense, as Mercutio observes after the Queen Mab speech, they are *merely* dreams,

> Begot of nothing but vain fantasy,
> Which is as thin of substance as the air,
> And more inconstant than the wind, who wooes
> Even now the frozen bosom of the North
> And, being angered, puffs away from thence,
> Turning his face to the dew-dropping South.

68. *As You Like It*, II, vii, 181; cf. "flatter, face, or feign," *I Henry VI*, V, iii, 142.

69. *3 Henry VI*, I, ii, 31; cf. *Merchant*, V, i, 79: "The poet Did feign that Orpheus drew trees, stones, and floods," and *Timon*, I, i, 64: "I have upon a high and pleasant hill Feigned fortune to be throned." (On "feigning" and "feign," cf. *N. E. D.*, which does not, however, cite these passages, nor those from Sidney quoted immediately below.)

70. Later in the *Apology* Sidney adds: "a feigned [imaginary] example hath as much force to teach as a true example."—Gregory Smith, *Elizabethan Critical Essays*, I, 160, 169.

71. "A dream . . . is but a shadow" . . . *Hamlet*, II, ii, 266.

72. *Romeo and Juliet*, II, ii, 141; *A Midsummer Night's Dream*, I, i, 144, 148.

Ultimately, however, this is no shortcoming properly chargeable to the nature of poetry or to the imperfections of the creative imagination. It grows out of the artist's longing for permanence and perfection in a finite, imperfect world. The poet's creation, when all is said and done, is scarcely less insubstantial than humanity itself, than the great globe itself, and all which it inherit — the physical creation of the "Heavenly Maker":

> We are such stuff
> As dreams are made on, and our little life
> Is rounded with a sleep.

The preceding review of Shakespeare's observations upon style and imagination indicates incidentally that he often touches upon poetics in general — unobtrusively but with keen relish. The ways and means of "a staff, a stanze, a verse," [73] of rhyme and "numbers," the flavor and the cadence of verse, the differences between Orlando's drasty rhyming and the truly turned phrases, so well remembered by Benedick, which yet run smoothly in the even road of a blank verse; all that concerns what Holofernes terms "the elegancy, facility, and golden cadence of poesy"; [74] in short, the mechanism and devices, the kinds and species, the moods and the limitations of poetry, and of the theatre and the drama to boot: Shakespeare talks about them all. Or, at least, Hamlet does and Benedick, Touchstone and Edmund, Macbeth and Cleopatra, [75] Ulysses and Benvolio, [76] Hotspur [77] and Holofernes, Jaques and Coriolanus, [78] Bottom the Weaver and Sly the Tinker (to mention no others) — each in his own voice, all with the accent of Shakespeare, who happened to know, as Ben Jonson did, and Molière, and Bernard Shaw, that audiences like nothing better than shop talk from behind the scenes. Shakespeare's people talk

73. *Love's Labour's Lost*, IV, ii, 107.    74. *Id.*, IV, ii, 125.
75. *Macbeth*, I, iii, 127-129; *Antony and Cleopatra*, V, ii, 217.
76. *Troilus and Cressida*, II, iii, 230; *Romeo and Juliet*, I, iv, 7-8.
77. *I Henry IV*, III, i, 134.
78. *Coriolanus*, V, iii, 40. — Other references, *passim*.

of songs and sonnets (from Petrarch to Tottel's Miscellany),[79] of epitaphs and blank verse, of ballads and tragedy, of the catastrophe in the old comedy and the happy ending in the new, of properties and prologues and rehearsals, epilogues, choruses and dumb-show, of revels and theatrical "shares," child actors and strolling players—and of what not else? If Shakespeare "barely mentions"[80] poetry, what then, to echo Audrey, *is* poetical? And even though the mere number of Shakespeare's allusions to poetry and drama is smaller than the number of allusions to various other subjects, it does not follow that these technical allusions are qualitatively insignificant. The qualitative test suggests that even if Shakespeare had written nothing more than the sonnet which lauds the "precious phrase by all the muses filed," or Benedick's remark on blank verse, or Hamlet's advice to the players, he would still have demonstrated adequately his workmanly interest in his own art, his readiness to talk about it, and his obvious awareness of his audience's interest in what he had to say. But any reasonable accounting shows that these passages make but a small fraction of the whole. Nor is the sum total merely a product of Shakespeare's natural fondness for the imagery of his profession. The oft-repeated and varied "All the world's a stage" may be important,[81] but the thing is not merely a matter of imagery. It goes further and deeper. Everywhere in Shakespeare there are manifestations of innate stage sense and stage consciousness,[82] but also of a growing sense of poetic and dramatic values. Sometimes, to be sure, these are strangely compounded. Even at the risk of obviousness, let us recall that *Hamlet*, for example, contains not only the advice to the players and its definition of the purpose of all drama, but also, among

79. "Now is he for the numbers that Petrarch flowed in."—*Romeo and Juliet*, II, iv, 41; "I had rather than forty shillings I had my Book of Songs and Sonnets here"— *Merry Wives*, I, i, 206.

80. See above, p. 63.

81. Though Miss Spurgeon in *Shakespeare's Imagery*, p. 45, finds but "a small number" of images "from the theatre."

82. See, for example, *Twelfth Night*, III, iv, 140.

other things, Polonius's theatrical reminiscences and critical divagations, the remarks on the dumb-show, the allusion to the children's companies, and, in the very whirlwind of passion, Hamlet's exchange with Horatio on the subject (of all things!) of actors' shares —

> A fellowship in a cry of players! . . . Half a share!—
> A whole one, I —

an allusion which must have been relished by the audience, if one may judge by the crowning exhibit in this kind, Ulysses' comment, in *Troilus and Cressida*,[83] upon the strutting Ajax: " 'A would have ten shares!" I need not review all the evidence here, but I cannot resist quoting the best definition yet written of what comedy is *not*. "Is not," quoth Christophero Sly, "Is not a comonty a Christmas gambold or a tumbling trick?"[84]

In conclusion, Shakespeare has much more to say on poetry and upon his art in general than the sum total listed in Bartlett under *poem, poet*, and their derivatives.[85] How much more, Bartlett will readily indicate if one starts, as I have suggested above, by turning to the *word* itself. This runs through Bartlett for many solid columns, approximately a thousand entries. Most of these, of course, have no immediate bearing upon poetry, but a good many have. "Words sweetly placed and modestly directed," "Ethiop words," "bitter words," "brave words," "true plain words," "old words new," "dedicated words," "sportive words," "idle words," "the wind of words," "the helpless smoke of words," "heart-easing words," "words, words, words"—many of these are of the very stuff of poetry. To take a true account of Shakespeare's utterances upon his chosen art one must count them in, and others like them which deal with related terms. I cannot stop to enumerate many of them—these "singular and choice *epithets*" so "sweetly varied," these "taffeta *phrases*, silken *terms* precise," this mint of "soldier-like" phrase, of "grand-

---

83. II, iii, 230; *Hamlet*, III, ii, 289-291.  84. *Taming*, Induction, 139-141.
85. See above, p. 63.

sire" phrase and "stewed" phrase and "swinish" phrase, the "phrase of war" and "the soft phrase of peace": all "good phrases" which "are surely, and ever were, very commendable," all jolly "holiday and lady terms" — "alligant," "high," and "precise." Happily, all this "sweet smoke of *rhetoric*," this paraphernalia of "a thousand *similes*," of "three-piled *hyperbole*" and "gay *comparisons*" — this "world of *figures*" is neatly compacted in Bartlett, where the entries under these headings run into many scores. To these must be added at least as many others already noticed here but not usually counted by the critics — under *imagination*, for example, and its near relations, including (in part) *fancy* and *conceit*. Further, there are the entries under rhyme and verse, numbers and cadence, sonnet and blank verse, epitaph and ballad, comedy and tragedy, masque and revels, prologue and epilogue, chorus and catastrophe, dumb-show and extempore, pastoral and history, theatre and playhouse, plays and players, comedians and tragedians, theme and action, scene and act, and (lest the line stretch out to the crack of doom!) actors and spectators. All in all these entries approximate another thousand, but in the last analysis it is not their number which proves that Shakespeare was a conscious artist. Their quality does. It proves also his generous readiness to give the audience a taste of *his* quality from behind the scenes.

Of course there is an element of truth, even so, in Ruskin's pronouncement. If art *must* be talked about, the talking should be done by great artists, or at least by great critics. Samuel Taylor Coleridge,[86] therefore, may well have the last word here. "What then shall we say? even this; that Shakespeare, no mere child of nature; no automaton of genius; no passive vehicle of inspiration possessed by the spirit . . . first studied patiently, meditated deeply, understood minutely, till knowledge, become habitual and intuitive, wedded itself to his habitual feelings, and at length gave birth to that stupendous power, by which he stands alone."

86. *Biographia Literaria* (London, 1817), II, 19.

# IV

## THE "LOST SCENES" OF *MACBETH* [1]

SOME years ago one of the most distinguished of the recent editors of *Macbeth* contended unequivocally that "several . . . portions of Shakespeare's play are lost or intentionally omitted" [2] in the Folio, the original text of the play. Specifically, Professor J. Q. Adams argues that three scenes—one each in the first, second, and last acts—have been lost. For various reasons this contention challenges reconsideration. It is an integral though not necessarily a vital part of the commentary in this edition, and it revives—though with a decided difference—an old and much-debated hypothesis concerning textual losses from this play. Furthermore, it requires, if certain aspects of the reasoning underlying it are to be accepted, a not inconsiderable readjustment of current views as to the swift and compelling structural efficacy of the play as it stands—not to mention a fresh appraisal of no less a personage than Lady Macbeth. Yet Professor Adams's edition adheres scrupulously—except possibly in the three instances to be noted—to the principle which prompts the present inquiry. "We ought," says Bradley [3] in a similar connection, "to do our best to interpret the text"—i.e., the text *as it stands*—"before we have recourse to this kind of suggestion." Granting that an able exposition of textual difficulties is a boon in itself, do these difficulties

1. Revised from *PMLA*, XLIX (1934), 835 ff.
2. *Macbeth*, ed. J. Q. Adams (1931), p. 253. Quotations from this edition, in the pages immediately following, by permission of Houghton Mifflin Company, Publishers.
3. *Shakespearean Tragedy*, p. 483, n. Quoted by permission of The Macmillan Company, Publishers.

justify the conclusions just mentioned as to losses or purposive omissions from the text at the several points definitely marked by Mr. Adams?

He himself silently rejects the most noteworthy of the older claims for a scene supposedly omitted at one vital point in the play. But the relationship between certain of his contentions and some of the older ones in this kind is close enough to compel me to begin fairly near the beginning.

Koester [4] and other late nineteenth-century critics urged that Lady Macbeth's allusion to Macbeth's "breaking" the enterprise of Duncan's murder to her previously — when, though neither time nor place "adhered," he swore to "make both" [5] — must point to a "former scene . . . omitted, lost, or cut out by some stage manager." [6] This because no such scene between them is actually *staged* in the extant text, and because:

> such a scene is too important to have been overlooked by Shakespeare, who is always so exact in such matters. Without it Duncan's murder takes place too early, and it is needed to counterbalance artistically the long-drawn-out, almost epic scenes between Malcolm and Macduff towards the close. . . .

Mr. Adams, like most sound critics, rightly refused to be alarmed by this reasoning; but it remains to be seen whether some of it is altogether remote from the considerations he urges in behalf of his own list of scenes lost or omitted from the text. With an eye to this list, therefore, and with particular reference to Bradley's [7] discussion of the earlier claim, it will be useful to recall the reasons which make Koester's hypothesis untenable. These I may summarize as follows.

    1. It is unnecessary to suppose an early scene (lost, cut, or set

4. *Shakespeare Jahrbuch* (1865), I, 146 ff.

5. *Macbeth*, I, vii, 47-52.

6. This quotation and the next are from Furness' (substantially fair though not altogether accurate) summary translation of Koester in the Variorum *Macbeth*, p. 79.

7. *Op. cit.*, pp. 480-484. See above, p. 88, n. 3.

before the opening of the play [8]) in which Macbeth "broke" the enterprise to his wife and the two predetermined the murder of Duncan.   Macbeth's *letter*,[9] written when neither place nor time yet "adhered," is sufficient to explain Lady Macbeth's nervous and not necessarily accurate allusion to earlier passages between them on this subject.   This is especially so because both must long since have been aware—without necessarily cherishing a guilty ambition—of Macbeth's closeness to the throne, by birth and by military prowess in difficult times and under a quasi-elective succession.   If a scene must be sought in which Macbeth definitely yielded to his wife's urgings, this scene—*unwritten*,[10] i.e., compressed to a mere suggestion, for reasons of artistic economy in an opening action consciously keyed to a swiftly tense crescendo [11]—would logically have come *between scenes*, after I, v, which closes with Macbeth's promise, "We will speak further."

2. A predetermination upon the murder in a lost scene at or before the beginning of the play would make at least the whole of the first act a long-drawn-out anticlimax.   It is all but precluded by Macbeth's "violent agitation" upon first hearing the witches' prophecy, and by his palpable and long-continued indecision, which is not resolved until, at the very last of Act I, he yields to Lady Macbeth: "Bring forth men-children only."

3. As Bradley observes, "practically all" readers and audiences "continue to imagine"—even after meeting Lady Macbeth's "When you durst do it, then you were a man"—the situation as it looks on the face of it; i.e., contrary to Koester's hypothesis, they think of the murder as not "planned and sworn to beforehand." If it be granted that Shakespeare knew something of his audiences and wrought no intentional ambiguities to confuse them, then it would seem to follow that their natural and obvious interpretation

8.   The latter alternative wins more or less support from numerous editors, including Sir E. K. Chambers (Heath's Arden *Macbeth*, p. xviii, n.) and, perhaps, Professor Adams (see below, p. 91, nn. 12-13).

9.   I, v.

10.   See below, p. 105.

11.   See below, p. 92, n. 15, p. 94, n. 17.

rather than a devious subtlety imagined after almost 300 years of critical meditation is the more likely to represent his own conception.

Mr. Adams, as already stated, rejects Koester's hypothesis, but he also rejects some of the fundamental objections (just noted) thereto. He believes, for example, that at the time of the witches' first "soliciting" "the plan of attaining the crown has . . . long been . . . in" Macbeth's "mind . . . clearly formulated," [12] that "of course . . . they spoke to a man who was . . . already . . . deliberately contemplating murder." [13] Still other points of contact between this interpretation and that underlying Koester's hypothesis will appear in the following excerpts, which present, *seriatim*, the main portions of Adams's argument for the three scenes he believes to have been lost.

I. The first of these he locates in I, iv of the present text, marking it in his edition by the dash in the third line of Duncan's speech of thanks to Banquo, just before the announcement of the proposed elevation of Malcolm and of Duncan's visit to Macbeth at Inverness:

> My plenteous joys
> Wanton in fulness, seek to hide themselves
> In drops of sorrow.—Sons, kinsmen, thanes,
> And you whose places are the nearest, know
> We will establish our estate upon
> Our eldest, Malcolm, whom we name hereafter
> The Prince of Cumberland; which honour must
> Not unaccompanied invest him only
> But signs of nobleness, like stars, shall shine
> On all deservers. From hence to Inverness,
> And bind us further to you.

Mr. Adams writes: [14]

> The sudden transitions of thought here, and the inadequacy in expression, suggest that the text is corrupt . . . Something

12. Adams, p. 134.　　13. *Id.*, p. 128.　　14. Pp. 21, n. 1; 139.

seems to have gone wrong . . . [1] We lose a day . . . during
which Macbeth is supposed to have made inquiry about the
Weird Sisters, and to have dispatched a letter to his wife re-
garding them . . . [2] The weak Duncan, from shedding tears,
suddenly . . . on this inappropriate occasion, and without
adequate explanation, attempts to arrange for his son to succeed
him on the throne . . . an important proclamation, almost
revolutionary in its nature . . . [3] He announces, in a clause,
unexpected, and so brief as to be almost unintelligible, that he
proposes to visit Macbeth at Inverness.   We may therefore suspect that portions of the original Shakespearean text have been
lost, possibly even that two scenes, separated in time, have been
awkwardly run together.

The fact that Duncan's proclamation does come with startling
abruptness at what certainly seems to be an inappropriate moment is, of course, altogether undeniable, nor have other critics
failed to observe the difficulty.[15]  And yet, by way of attempting
to meet Adams's outright challenge to the adequacy of the existing
text, one might ask whether the ineptitude of the announcement
is not, after all, quite in keeping with the character of the weak
king who makes it?   Because or in spite of his weakness, even
Duncan might have seen substantial reasons for quick action and
few explanations at this point.   Specifically, as regards (1) the
"loss" of a day, there is, surely, but small support for a hypothetical lost scene on this ground.   No day is really lost, any more,
for example, than while Hamlet, off-stage, is adventuring with the
pirates.   There is merely an interval, during which Macbeth inquires about the witches and writes to his wife.

(2) It is perfectly true that Duncan offers no "adequate explanation" for his sudden attempt to preëmpt the succession for
his son.   But is it not equally true that no adequate explanation
for this attempt would have been possible or feasible under the

15. Bradley, for instance, admits that "it is difficult not to suspect some omission or
curtailment here," but adds that "Shakespeare may have determined" to secure "rapidity
in the First Act" at almost any reasonable cost.   "That any *extensive* omissions have been
made seems not likely" (*op. cit.*, p. 468).

circumstances? Tyrants—even weak or would-be tyrants—about to proceed with an almost revolutionary act usually do so by proclaiming a *fait accompli* rather than by starting a public debate. Lear similarly proclaims, without allowing debate, his "darker purpose" of dividing his kingdom in three; and King Claudius, in a similar speech from Hamlet's throne, briefly announces that he has taken Gertrude to wife and started action against young Fortinbras. In Lear's case, to be sure, Kent and Gloucester have had preliminary information of what may have been previously discussed in council. But Duncan, too, may have had time for councils while Macbeth, on the battlefield, was proclaiming himself the foremost man in the kingdom. And Duncan's sudden announcement, Duncan being what he is, may possibly be a not altogether unpremeditated nor unkind attempt to time an act of self-defense for his house at the very moment when the chief sufferer from this act would have been propitiated by the bestowing of great honors well-deserved, sincerely offered,[16] and, for the moment, gratefully accepted. If it be objected that this is too Machiavellian an explanation of Duncan's ineptitude, the answer is that Duncan, at best or worst, is a secondary figure at this point. The audience is primarily interested in Macbeth. It has little time or inclination, at the very moment when Macbeth is about to "fall down, or else o'erleap," to want more information as to the whys and wherefores of Duncan's announcement. And Shakespeare has already prepared it to expect ineptitude from Duncan, the stay-at-home king who wantons in drops of sorrow and whose former *speeches* (". . . There's no art To find the mind's construction in the face," at the very moment of his first greeting to Macbeth) are informed by the same tragic irony as this his first real *act* in the play. In short, it may well be that preliminary explanations of Duncan's proclamation are missing because Shakespeare wanted none. Macbeth holds the centre of the stage. The very

16. Though some commentators emphasize the point that he sounds "noticeably less cordial" toward Macbeth than to Banquo in thanking them.—See Brooke, Cunliffe and MacCracken, *Shakespeare's Principal Plays* (New York, 1935), p. 702.

suddenness of Duncan's announcement is the spur here needed to prick him on to evil against his better nature. The whole tempo of the play, moreover, or at least the consciously wrought speed of the first act, [17] makes against the assumption that a further scene enlarging upon or explaining Duncan's motives is needed or desirable.

(3) The extant text's sudden announcement of Duncan's proposed visit to Inverness is perhaps less readily defensible than the rest, and possibly another line or two here might have been useful —especially to moderns less familiar than the Elizabethans with the sometimes sudden and costly honors bestowed upon the nobility by royalty on its progresses. But anything more than a brief phrase or two from the king to emphasize the compliment of the intended visit would have been, for the reasons just outlined, undesirable at this juncture. And possibly *any* elaboration would have made against the abrupt challenge of the announcement as it stands. In any case, though a king might pause to consider the import of a crowning favor he is about to bestow upon a victorious subject, he need not stop to explain it in public. And the "From hence to Inverness" is surely not altogether unintelligible as it stands, if read in its context. Honors, "signs of nobleness," shall shine on all deservers: the greatest honor at once—a royal visit in immediate reward for a royal victory—upon Macbeth.

II. Professor Adams argues that another scene may have been lost from the text, as it now stands, of II, i, 29-30; that is to say, immediately after Banquo and Macbeth have bidden each other good night ("Good repose the while . . . The like to you") and just before the dagger soliloquy, two lines below. The commentary here is extraordinarily far removed from the traditional view. To discuss it fairly I must quote in full: [18]

> At this point—it will be noted that there is a break in the metre—we may suspect that the play has again lost some of its

17. *Macbeth*, I, ii; v, 37; II, iii, 51.
18. Adams, pp. 164 f.

original Shakespearean text.     Up to the present moment the scene is clearly timed as shortly after midnight; Duncan has just shut himself up "in measureless content," and Banquo and young Fleance, leaving the King's bedroom, are retiring to rest. Yet Macbeth at once proceeds to the murder.   As we learn from the sleep-walking remarks of Lady Macbeth, the murder took place after two o'clock; the Porter declares that the servants were "carousing till the second cock" (i.e., three o'clock); and even before the deed is entirely completed, Macduff comes to arouse Duncan for the next day's journey.   It would seem, therefore, that two scenes, separated in time, have here been run together; and, possibly, that an intervening scene has been omitted.

If so, we may guess that the omitted scene represented Lady Macbeth in her attempt to kill Duncan without assistance from her husband.   She had, we know, resolved to do the deed her-self — there is much emphasis on this point; and she had more than once definitely promised Macbeth to relieve him of the actual murder.  We know, too, from a passage in a later scene, that she made the effort.   She entered the death-chamber, stood with knife poised, and then suddenly lost her nerve.   Finding herself unable to strike, she was forced to abandon her original care-fully-laid plan, and to call upon her husband, unwilling and shrinking, to take the dagger, enter the chamber, and perform the deed.   A scene representing this important episode seems called for.    It would help us to understand much better Lady Macbeth's subsequent breakdown, and would make Macbeth's conduct throughout more consistent.   As the text now stands, however, Lady Macbeth's failure to do the deed, as first planned, is unexplained; and Macbeth proceeds to the murder immediately after Duncan has retired to his room, and before Banquo and Fleance have had adequate time to get to bed.   We are wholly unprepared for the situation thus thrust upon us.

To sum up, the case for the lost scene appears to be based pri-marily upon the following considerations: (1) the break in the metre; (2) the present text's failure to allow sufficient time for the murder; (3) its failure to stage the consummation of Lady Mac-beth's "resolution," "definite promise," and "carefully-laid plan . . . to relieve" Macbeth "of the actual murder" and "do the deed herself"; (4) a scene staging Lady Macbeth's attempt at murder seems needed to make more comprehensible than does the present text Lady Macbeth's subsequent breakdown.  I shall outline, in the order indicated, the chief objections, as I see them, to this interpretation.

(1) As regards the break in the metre: Before examining details here it is to be observed once more that the text of *Macbeth* is, unquestionably, troublesome.  The "badly printed" Folio cannot be checked by any other early text, for none exists; and there is no doubt that additions — Middleton's Hecate scenes — were made to Shakespeare's original.  At the other end, Professor Adams is by no means the only critic who believes something may have been lost.  Thus, Sir E. K. Chambers [19] thinks it "not unlikely" that "the unusual shortness of the play," together with certain apparent "discrepancies in the incidents" may be due "to the excision of speeches or parts of speeches." [20]  In this connection, however, Chambers makes a significant reservation.  "I cannot believe," he writes, "that it is possible to disentangle [minor] alterations from the original stuff of the piece."  Are the chances much better for the detection, and for the exact placing and description, of possible omissions?  As for the unusual shortness of *Macbeth*, one recalls also that Bradley [21] is not alone in the belief that the play does not seem short in the reading or acting and is in all probability substantially as long as Shakespeare felt it ought to be.  Nor is it by any means clear that the "discrepancies" as to small details of incident or character are any greater in *Macbeth* than in other plays, for some of which the Folio text may be checked by early quartos,[22] and in which no one suspects the loss of entire scenes.  In short, though each difficulty deserves consid-

19. Arden *Macbeth*, p. vi.
20. By "cutting" for stage purposes, or, as Adams (p. 258) suggests, by damage, badly "restored" subsequently, through such an accident as the Globe fire of 1613.
21. P. 469.
22. E.g., *Hamlet* (the difficulty concerning Hamlet's age) and *Romeo* (Juliet's forty-two hour sleep); or, to mention another Folio play, the Fair Maudlin episode in *All's Well* (cf. the writer's *Shakspere's Silences*, pp. 57-59).

eration on its merits, it is hard to escape the familiar conclusion that Shakespeare was frequently inexact about details because he was preoccupied with major issues and did not expect his audience to be too exacting as regards non-essentials.

Specifically, it seems to me that the broken line at II, i, 30 (Macbeth's "Thanks, sir; the like to you!"),[23] leaves but little room, and that hazardous, for the conjecture that a scene has been omitted at this point. There are more than a score of such broken lines in the play.[24] Not a few of these are excellent lines, in excellent sequence—witness my italics in the following passages:

> O, never
> *Shall sun that morrow see!*
> Your face, my thane, is as a book where men
> May read strange matters . . . (I, v, 61).

> Macb.                 . . . No, this my hand will rather
> The multitudinous seas incarnadine,
> *Making the green one red.*

> Lady M.   My hands are of your colour; but I shame
> To wear a heart so white . . . (II, ii, 61).

(Compare also *Julius Caesar*, II, i, 61:

> Since Cassius first did whet me against Caesar,
> *I have not slept.*
> Between the acting of a dreadful thing
> And the first motion . . .

where the broken line, once more, does not signalize an omission.) Certainly no such broken line in itself can safely be adjudged to

23. Immediately followed by his directions to the servant—

> Go bid thy mistress, when my drink is ready
> She strike upon the bell. Get thee to bed.

24. The banquet scene (III, iv) in and by itself has half a dozen such broken lines, but no omissions are suspected. (For other broken lines cf. I, ii, iii; II, iii; III, i, ii, iii; IV, iii, 139, etc. In my reckoning of a score or more I have purposely left out the witch scenes.)

signalize an omission, any more than the vast majority of such lines in the play which no one would take to indicate anything of the sort.

(2) I have already pointed out that the supposed inadequacy of time, upon analysis, yields little support to the argument for the "lost" scene of Act I, any more than to Koester's hypothesis. Nor can I believe that it is necessary, on this ground, to seek out a lost scene just before the murder of Duncan. Professor Adams states that up to the moment of Macbeth's soliloquy "the scene is *clearly* [25] timed as shortly after midnight. . . . Yet Macbeth at once proceeds to the murder." In the sleep-walking scene, of course, Lady Macbeth says it was "time to do it" when the clock struck two — but it might be recalled that the sleep-walking reminiscence comes long after the event, and long after slight inaccuracies concerning its timing — if there are any — would trouble an audience. It is also true, however, that Macduff is first heard knocking at the gate while Duncan's blood is still fresh upon Macbeth's hand — at a time which the drunken Porter puts after the "second cock"; i.e., roughly the same as Lady Macbeth's two o'clock.[26] Macduff, it must be remembered, had orders to call Duncan "timely," for an early start. But, if this juxtaposition puts the murder at a seemingly late time, it may also be noted (1) that long and terrible pauses (in the course of the breathless conference between Macbeth and Lady Macbeth) have fallen between the actual murder and the first sound of the knocking; and (2) that in the Porter's scene, as in the sleep-walking scene, the audience, tense with expectancy as to the discovery or the consequence of the murder, has other things to do than to calculate the exact number of minutes between events. Indeed, even if it were in a calculating mood, it could scarcely find any loss or confusion sufficient to justify the suggestion that "two scenes separated in time have been run together." For I am not sure that Professor Adams puts the case altogether as it stands in the play. Is it

25. My italics.        26. Or between then and three.

certain, for instance, that even before Macbeth joins Banquo and Fleance, the scene is "*clearly* timed as shortly after midnight"? It is after the going down of the moon, which disappeared at twelve; and Fleance emphatically suggests that the scene starts "later" than twelve.[27]  And is it altogether accurate to say that Macbeth proceeds "at once" to the murder?  First comes the bestowal of Duncan's diamond; then Banquo's uneasy recollection of his dream of the witches, followed by Macbeth's hint of future "words upon that business" between him and his friend; and then Banquo's significant rejoinder.  Finally Macbeth sends his servant to Lady Macbeth to request her to sound the bell — when all is ready. He does not do the murder at once, for all is *not* ready.  He has yet to pull himself together once more: to attempt, vainly, to make the dagger of the mind yield to the bad virtue of the blade he draws from his side.  In short, the murder has to wait upon Macbeth's soliloquy; that is to say, for a space of time which the clock may tick off in not many minutes, but which in his own consciousness and in that of the audience might well seem to stretch over an agonizing eternity of suspense.  The soliloquy epitomizes the long inward struggle that has gone before, and *expands* the last lingering moments before the murder into intolerable stretches of time.  (There is a strikingly similar use of the soliloquy in *Cymbeline*,[28] where *four* hours are supposed to pass between Imogen's falling asleep and her re-awakening after Iachimo's invasion of her chamber.  Imogen's query, "What hour is it?" is answered by the Lady: "Almost midnight"; whereupon Imogen begs that she be called by "four o' the clock."  After praying for protection against the tempters of the night, she sleeps. Then follows a long pause — like that after the murder of Duncan — here broken by Iachimo's emergence from the trunk:

> The crickets sing, and man's o'erlabour'd sense
> Repairs itself by rest . . . 'Tis her breathing that
> Perfumes the chamber thus . . . But my design

27.  "I take't, 'tis later, sir" (II, i, 3).          28.  II, ii, 2-7, 49-51.

> To note the chamber: I will write all down,
> Such and such pictures . . .

He notes them, screws them into his memory, takes her bracelet, observes her book—the tale of Tereus—and then concludes his long soliloquy by hastening back into the trunk *before the clock strikes four*.   During the long opening pause and the forty lines of the soliloquy, the dragons of the night have flown far and fast:

> . . . I lodge in fear;
> Though this a heavenly angel, hell is here. [*Clock strikes.*]
> One, two, three: time, time! [Goes into the trunk.])

Macbeth's soliloquy forwards the essential action in relentless and unerring sequence—from Banquo's earlier midnight gloom to the impending horror which suits the later time of deep sleep unsuspecting of the violator: when "o'er the one-half world nature seems dead" and only the wolf's howl and the owl's scream strike the dark hour of Duncan's taking-off.   In short, the present text allows ample time for the murder, for the soliloquy provides a more than sufficient interim—the terrible interim, at once timeless and unending, between the acting of a dreadful thing and its first motion or its last, before the event.   This interim, Shakespeare reminds us, far from being too brief, may be as endless as "a phantasma or a hideous dream." [29]

   (3) I find it difficult to subscribe to the view that Lady Macbeth had (a) emphatically "resolved to do the deed herself"; (b) "definitely promised Macbeth to relieve him of the actual murder," and (c) made a "carefully-laid" plan to that end.   The text, I think, does not justify this interpretation.   She had resolved to do one thing only: to help—indeed to force—her husband to "catch the nearest way," by ruthlessly and relentlessly putting down his scruples.   To keep his better instincts under control she must not only chastise with the valor of her tongue but dominate

---

29. *Julius Caesar*, II, i, 63.

his spirit with her own iron purpose. It is true that in the mounting excitement of her first murderous vision, when she calls upon the spirits of evil to unsex her, she identifies herself imaginatively not only with the crime but with its perpetration —

> Come, thick night,
> That *my* keen knife see not the wound it makes —

and true also that upon first sight of her husband, to put the essential point beyond dispute, she proposes, in general terms, that he shall put

> This night's great business into *my* dispatch . . .
> Leave all the rest to *me*.

Let it also be remembered, however, that this sort of language comes natural to Lady Macbeth. She is mistress of her household:

> The raven is hoarse
> That croaks the fatal entrance of Duncan
> Under *my* battlements.

Not only is she her husband's dearest partner of greatness, but, as hostess to boot, it is her place to take charge —

> He that's coming
> Must be provided for.

Macbeth, however, has left matters open: "We will speak further." He does. Nor must we forget that he had already spoken long before, that is to say immediately after the witches' first suggestion,

> Whose horrid image does unfix my hair,

and again, upon hearing of the Prince of Cumberland —

> Let not light see my black and deep desires;
> The eye wink at the hand; yet let that be
> Which the eye fears, when it is done, to see.

When next we hear Macbeth, he and his wife *have* spoken further, and his soliloquy and their next speeches make all but certain that valour's minion, the warrior Macbeth, was not so craven a scoundrel as to require his wife's promise to relieve him of the actual *deed* of butchery. He, not she, is "to bear the knife myself." [30] Throughout the play it is clear that he fears no deed in itself [31] but only the "horrible imaginings" that run before, and the untrammeled consequence that follows in inexorable judgment. Lady Macbeth's task, first and last, is to keep her husband keyed up to their mutual purpose, even though she has to taunt him with cowardice and to protest that she would have slain the baby at her breast had she so sworn as he. Specifically, the text assigns her no other part in any carefully-laid plan for the actual perpetration of the murder that I can discover, other than to drug the grooms. The rest is a question—which Macbeth answers. While the grooms sleep

> What cannot *you and I* perform upon
> The unguarded Duncan?

As regards the crime itself, as distinguished from the actual butchery, they are, of course, full and equal partners. As always—and perhaps with especial warmth here because Macbeth needs his wife's support in shouldering the terrible responsibility immediately before him—he gladly recognizes the partnership:

> Will it not be receiv'd
> When *we* have mark'd with blood these sleepy two . . .

Immediately afterwards Macbeth answers *our* question as to who was actually to do the deed:

30. I, vii, 16.

31. His refusal to return to smear the grooms with blood is merely a momentary nervous-hysterical revulsion *after* the act.

> *I* am settled, and bend up
> Each corporal agent to this terrible feat . . .

Lady Macbeth proceeds to carry out her only definitely planned part in the actual perpetration of the crime — to drug the grooms. At the critical moment Macbeth all but ruins their hopes by his untimely and terrible outcry, "Who's there? What, ho!" Thereupon, wracked with uncertainty and almost breaking under the strain, Lady Macbeth frantically tries to see the situation: a frustrated attempt will spell ruin, but how could Macbeth have failed? She herself had laid the daggers ready. She herself — *so she now thinks*, and *perhaps* she actually thought so at the time — "*had* done't" (as she formerly *would* have slain her babe, surely without any carefully laid plan!) had not Duncan resembled her father as he slept. But meanwhile her husband's resolution to achieve the terrible feat has borne fruit: "I have done the deed." — I shall not stop to urge that the actual staging of two attempts to murder the gracious Duncan might have been too much even for the Elizabethans. Lear, of course, has *two* Pelican daughters, but he was a king of another stamp; and even in that terrible play the atrocity of Gloucester's blinding is achieved once only.

(4) As I have just indicated, the proposition that Macbeth required his wife's promise to relieve him of the actual butchery, is to stamp him a craven and a coward — which he is not, according to the play at large, nor, in spite of Lady Macbeth's taunt, according to his wife, who knows him best. Similarly, the suggestion that a scene representing Lady Macbeth as actually attempting to perpetrate the crime would make her subsequent breakdown more comprehensible, seems to me to degrade the character unnecessarily and unreasonably. Is not the crime enough without the butchery? Could the smell of the blood upon her little hand have been much stronger if she had drawn it instead of merely smearing the grooms withal? And, if actual perpetration of murder be necessary to help us to understand her breakdown, how account for the compunctious visitings of nature which lead her, in

the sleep-walking scene, to recall the fate of another woman whom she had certainly not planned to butcher: "The Thane of Fife had a wife; where is she now?"

III. Traces of the last of the lost scenes, according to Professor Adams,[32] are to be seen in another remark of Lady Macbeth's in the sleep-walking scene — "I tell you yet again Banquo's buried; he cannot come out on's grave." This passage, we are told, "is significant in that possibly it brings before us a scene — omitted when the text was revamped — in which Macbeth, trying to find sleep, was tortured by the image of Banquo's ghost. She then was called upon to make another supreme effort to save him from the painting of his fear." Again, I cannot see the necessity of supposing that Shakespeare ever wrote such a scene; and even the possibility that he did seems slight. Lady Macbeth's remark need not be anything more than a somewhat distorted recollection of her original effort to save the situation immediately after the murder of Banquo. Of that impending event she had had a shrewd hint. She knew "nature's copy" to be "not eterne" in Banquo and Fleance: "they are assailable." Consequently she must have been able to guess whose ghost she would have to try to lay when Macbeth, after challenging the fates ("Were the grac'd person of our Banquo present!") saw Banquo's spectre in his own place at the table. "O proper stuff!" she cries (i.e., There is no ghost! Even if Banquo *is* dead!) —

> This is the very painting of your fear;
> This is the air-drawn dagger which, you said,
> Led you to Duncan. O, these flaws and starts! . . .
>             When all's done
> You look but on a stool.

Or, even though it be granted that this spectre reappeared in Macbeth's subsequent dreams, and that Lady Macbeth might have endeavored to repeat the effort to calm her husband, it by

32. P. 219.

no means follows that Shakespeare would have written an anti-climactic scene to *stage* these much-belated flaws and starts. He does stage Macbeth's "initiate fear"; thereafter he is too busy depicting the onward rush of events—at the witches' cauldron, at Macduff's castle, in England and in Scotland—to give room to redundancies. What's done is done, so far as the stage is concerned. Yet it is not the least effective part of Shakespeare's artistic economy to *suggest* many things which he does not actually stage.[33] Thus, Lady Macbeth's allusion to the air-drawn dagger which "you *said*, Led you to Duncan," clearly suggests an *unwritten* scene between the two in which they discussed further the dagger of the mind. As already indicated above, with reference to Macbeth's "We will speak further," [34] there are in this play numerous instances of scenes deftly suggested—to sound deep overtones of meaning in characterization and action—but purposely left unwritten,[35] to keep tense the movement of the play. If any further scene between Lady Macbeth and Macbeth is to be predicated on the sleep-walking passage, it was in all probability not a scene written and then lost or omitted, but one of these unwritten scenes.

33. I have discussed this subject more fully in *Shakspere's Silences*, pp. 48-54.

34. See above, p. 90.

35. Among other unwritten scenes in *Macbeth* I may mention: (1) Macbeth's inquiries concerning the witches (I, v); (2) two scenes between him and the murderers of Banquo ("This I made good to you in our last conference" and "I'll come to you anon"—III, i, 79, 139); (3) a scene between him and the murderers of Lady Macduff (IV, i, 155); (4) Duncan's sending forth largess; (5) the doctor's double watch before the Sleep-walking.

# V

## SPENSER AND *MUCH ADO ABOUT NOTHING* [1]

IN THIS study I propose to re-examine pertinent documents and critical opinion concerning the sources of the Hero-Claudio story in *Much Ado About Nothing*. I mean to call attention, especially, to certain materials which suggest that Spenser may have exerted more influence upon the shaping of the play than has generally been supposed. For I hope to show that in at least three fairly substantial details of motive, incident, and characterization, *Much Ado* is close to the story of Phedon and Claribell in *The Faerie Queene* (II, iv, 16-46), and relatively remote from the versions of the more commonly accepted sources, Bandello's novel of Timbreo and Fenicia, and Ariosto's *Orlando Furioso*.

Elsewhere I have recently presented a considerable body of evidence which, in sum, indicates that Shakespeare frequently remembered Spenser.[2] The specific suggestion, therefore, that he may have remembered something of him in *Much Ado*, may now be examined with reasonably close reference to the general probabilities of the case. This suggestion, we shall see, has occasionally had some favorable notice from earlier students,[3] but it deserves more systematic analysis, in the light of all the facts and probabilities, than it has hitherto had. In attempting this analysis, I ask the reader to bear in mind Shakespeare's general tendency to remember Spenser, and to judge Spenser's specific claims upon

1. Reprinted, with additions, from *Studies in Philology*, XXXVII (1940), 225 ff.
2. "Shakespeare and Spenser," *Shakespeare Association Bulletin*, X (1935), 192-211; XI (1936), 33-40; "Mercutio and Spenser's Phantastes," *Philological Quarterly*, XVI (1937), 405-407. — See also Thomas P. Harrison Jr.'s "Primitivism in Shakespeare and Spenser," University of Texas *Studies in English*, 1940, pp. 39 ff.
3. See below, p. 113.

*Much Ado* by noting the cumulative resemblances between that play and some portions of the Phedon-Claribell story which differentiate it from Bandello and Ariosto and may indicate that it served Shakespeare as an intermediate source. I shall review Bandello's contribution to *Much Ado* and then Ariosto's [4] before turning to Spenser. But I must first underscore certain basic principles of definition and procedure.

(1) As regards "sources," I do not suggest that all are equally important. There are sources *and* sources, though some critics hold otherwise. They insist, for example, that even Ariosto's claims upon *Much Ado* are negligible—that "one exceptional reminiscence"—the "likeness" between him and Shakespeare in the use of the maid disguised as the mistress in the slander plot—"by no means requires us to regard the *Orlando* as one of the sources of *Much Ado*." [5] For our purposes, however, even *one* really significant "reminiscence" might justify consideration of its point of origin as a contributory "source," even though it be less important

4. I exclude three other items sometimes listed among the sources of *Much Ado*.

(1) The Greek romance of Chaereas and Callirhoe (ca. 400 A. D.). It is generally agreed that some portions of Bandello's story may be traced to this romance, but the romance is "prehistoric so far as Shakespeare is concerned"—G. L. Kittredge, *Shakespeare* (Boston, 1936), p. 159; Shakespeare *Jahrbuch*, XXXIV (1898), 339.

(2) A hypothetical lost play (English, "feeble," and "modelled" on Bandello) for which Furness (Variorum *Much Ado*, p. xxvi) argues valiantly but unconvincingly. Nothing beyond the names of one or two English plays from the late 1570's and 80's—which may or may not have been connected with Bandello or Ariosto—is actually known. One or two German and Dutch plays, notably Ayrer's *Die Schöne Phönicia*, are directly or indirectly indebted to Bandello, but not otherwise connected with Shakespeare. Cf. Kittredge, *op. cit.*; J. C. Smith, American Arden *Much Ado* (Boston, Heath, n.d.), p. xi; Neilson, Cambridge Poets *Shakespeare* (Boston, 1910), p. 180; etc.

(3) Belleforest's French adaptation of Bandello's story in *Les Histoires Tragiques*. Some editors still believe that "Shakespeare may have derived his story from Belleforest"—Gollancz, Temple *Much Ado* (London, 1894-1900), p. 6; cf. Porter and Clarke, First Folio *Much Ado* (New York, 1907), pp. 98 ff., Parrott (see p. 113, n. 28, below), etc.; but the majority dismiss this source, for the reason that "Shakespeare shows no acquaintance with Belleforest's rather numerous deviations from his original"—Tucker Brooke, Yale *Much Ado* (New Haven, 1917), p. 124; cf. Neilson, Kittredge, J. C. Smith, etc.

5. F. Holleck-Weithmann—*Zur Quellenfrage von . . . Much Ado* (Heidelberg, 1902), pp. 3-4—who quotes A. W. Ward, *English Dramatic Literature* (London, 1899), II, 133: "There is no necessity for supposing Ariosto's version to have been used by Shakespeare." Cf. pp. 110-111, below.

than others. It is as legitimate, surely, to recognize likenesses in kind as differences in degree. Plautus is the main source of *The Comedy of Errors*, and Florio's Montaigne is not the main source of *The Tempest*. Even so, Florio's work is part of the source material, as surely as Holinshed, Sidney, Spenser, and the old *Leir*, respectively, are among the more or less substantial sources of *King Lear*. *King Lear* demonstrates the point that Shakespeare made his sources — like his actors — play many parts, large or small, formative or casual; that certain sources served him again and again from play to play; and that usually he drew together in one play many suggestions of varying importance from many sources. So, in the case of *Much Ado*, I shall indicate that he seems to have drawn from Spenser, *among others*.[6]

(2) It is important to recognize the implication of the basic fact to which I have just referred — Shakespeare's conscious,[7] open-eyed, consistently eclectic use of his sources. The happy efficacy of his workmanship is, from this point of view, especially notable in *Much Ado*. I shall illustrate it later [8] in comparing Shakespeare's Margaret with her predecessors in Ariosto and Spenser; but I wish to supply at once another illustration which, so far as I know, has not found its way into the commentaries. Hero's father, Shakespeare's Leonato — certainly based on Bandello's Lionato [9] — differs from his prototype and from the King of Scotland, the corresponding figure in Ariosto.[10] Each of the earlier fathers stands by his daughter, never for a moment doubting her innocence. Shakespeare's Leonato, on the other hand, blows hot and cold. He indulges in long-winded, self-pitying speeches enlarging upon his child's guilt, and, in all but the same breath, threatening dire vengeance upon her false accusers.[11] His sentimental weakness throws into sharp relief — doubtless intentionally — the common

6. Certainly not that Spenser was his "particular source," as Professor C. T. Prouty would have me say ("The Sources of *Much Ado*," *Studies in Philology*, XXXVIII (1941), 215).

7. See above, Chapter III.                        8. See pp. 112-118.
9. See below, p. 109, and n. 16.                  10. See below, summary, pp. 110-111.
11. *Much Ado*, IV, i, 121-193.

sense and the sturdy loyalty, in a critical moment, of Benedick and Beatrice.  Here as elsewhere in *Much Ado*, Shakespeare leaves his sources far behind.  "No other play," to quote one of its ablest editors, "better reveals his skill in selection and rejection . . . in the transmuting of diverse elements." [12]  Let us review these diverse elements.

Almost all investigators [13] are agreed that the Hero story is primarily indebted to Bandello's novel.  Editors have properly emphasized the fact that therein only, as in Shakespeare, "the scene is laid in Messina at the close of a successful war," [14] and that the story "includes a King Pedro [15] and a Messer Lionato.  The concurrence of" names and scene "and the personation plot would seem to amount to proof." [16]  To summarize Bandello's plot:

> Timbreo—a very wealthy gentleman, distinguished soldier, and favorite of the king—falls in love with the fair Fenicia, daughter of an honorable family of relatively modest means. She accepts, eventually, his offer of marriage.  Nothing of all this is made known to Timbreo's bosom friend, Girondo, who had also fallen secretly in love with the lady.  When the match is publicly announced, Girondo, finding his hopes forestalled, "bethought himself to sow discord between Don Timbreo and his mistress, that the match should be broken off, *in which case, demanding her of her father to wife, he hoped to have her.*" [17]  To "the service of his *blind and unbridled appetite*" Girondo wins "*a young courtier*" who quickly succeeds in making Timbreo believe that he has seen a "*perfumed gentleman*" ascending Fenicia's chamber window.  Timbreo thereupon sends to the family an "ambassador," to make known—privately, and with comparative mildness—Fenicia's guilt and the withdrawal of his suit.  They dismiss the charge as a belated subterfuge of Timbreo's— to enable him to avoid an undistinguished marriage, into a family

12. G. R. Trenery, English Arden *Much Ado* (London, 1924), pp. xi ff.
13. With the exception of Furness (see above, p. 107, n. 4) and Holleck-Weithmann (see above, p. 107, n. 5).
14. Neilson, *op. cit.*, p. 180.          15. "Piero d'Aragona" in Bandello.
16. Quiller-Couch and Dover Wilson, *Much Ado* (Cambridge, 1923), pp. ix-xi.
17. Quotations from John Payne's translation; Furness, Variorum *Much Ado*, pp. 311 ff.

of small means — but announce that Fenicia has died of the shock.
In fact, she quickly recovers, and is secretly sent to stay with
friends in the country. Timbreo and Girondo, however, are
deeply moved. Girondo confesses his villainy and is quickly for-
given by Timbreo. The facts being made known to the family,
both men are soon restored to favor, and, after a year, they are
allowed to marry, respectively, the restored Fenicia and her
sister.

Over and above the identity of scene and name, the likenesses
between this story and Don John's villainous plot against Hero
are sufficiently evident. The differences,[18] however, are also significant. It should be observed (1) that the villain's *motive* and
general character differ sharply from Don John's, who is a mali-
cious and revengeful evildoer, and not a disappointed and intri-
guing lover. (2) The deceit of the "hero" — on the whole a less
reprehensible fellow than Claudio — is less skillfully motivated
than in Shakespeare. Specifically, he is not led to believe — as is
Claudio — that he has been shamed by the lady's favors to a base
"ruffian." (3) No waiting woman or maid corresponding to Shakespeare's Margaret appears in Bandello's story. The prototypes of
Margaret, however, do appear in Ariosto and Spenser.

Ariosto's tale of Ginevra and Ariodante [19] is actually told by
Ginevra's maid, Dalinda,[20] who bears a heavy share of responsibility for the troubles of her lady, the Princess of Scotland.

> Dalinda had been seduced by Polynesso, Duke of Albany,
> who had been for many months her private visitant in Ginevra's

18. Partly marked by my italics in the summary above.
19. Book V of the *Orlando*, Harington's translation, stanzas 7-74; Furness, pp. 295-
307.—Harington mentions an earlier (lost) version of this story by George Turberville,
and Furness (*op. cit.*, p. xxiii) conjectures that another early version (1565) by Peter
Beverley may have been the foundation of the (lost) play of Ariodante and Ginevra acted
by Mulcaster's children in 1582. Professor Prouty (see above, p. 108, n. 6) promises "a
synthesis of all the now-known sources and analogues" of *Much Ado*, including Beverley's
version and a similar tale by George Whetstone.
20. In the manner of Daniel's *Rosamond* and the tragic raconteurs of *The Mirror for
Magistrates*.

chambers. At length, his "love" for Dalinda cooling, he informs the maid that he is "enflamed . . . on faire Ginevra" (partly for ambition's sake), but that he will continue "to love" Dalinda "best" if she will help him win the Princess. The maid "straight consented," but her efforts to plead her duke's cause with the lady proved vain because Ginevra's affections were fixed upon the noble Ariodante. Thereupon Polynesso, "Greeved with repulse and vexed therewithal, to see this stranger thus to be preferred," plots vengeance:

> The love that late his heart so sore had burned
> Was cooled all and into hatred turned,
> Intending by some vile and subtile train
> To part Ginevra from her faithful lover,
> Yet with so cunning show . . .
> That her good name he will so foul distaine
> Alive nor dead she never shall recover.

This he manages to do by having Ariodante, accompanied by his brother Lurcanio, watch the Duke ascending the Princess's room, where—though they do not realize the deceit—Dalinda meets him. She wears Ginevra's clothes—persuaded thereto, without "perceiving" his "shameful drift," by his plea that she please his "fond conceit" that in meeting the maid, so dressed, he is conquering the mistress! Ariodante, heartbroken at what he thinks he has seen, twice tries suicide. His brother publicly accuses Ginevra of unchastity, and, under the strict Scottish law, compels the king, who believes his daughter innocent, to submit her cause to trial by combat. From this she emerges vindicated, thanks to the intervention of Ariodante, who returns to serve as her unknown champion.

"That Shakespeare had his eye upon Ariosto," writes Professor Kittredge, "seems certain. His Claudio is challenged to mortal combat by Leonato and Antonio and again by Benedick. There is nothing of the kind in either Bandello or Spenser." [21] Kittredge and others,[22] however, have also noted that Spenser, too, almost

---

21. *Op. cit.*, p. 160.
22. See below, pp. 113-117, and F. W. Clarke and W. G. Boswell-Stone, The Old Spelling Shakespeare *Much Ado* (New York, 1908), pp. viii-ix.

certainly followed—and improved upon—Ariosto in making the intrigue turn upon the maid's participation. With regard to Ariosto and *Much Ado*, though the challenge in the play is allowed to go by default and though Claudio is far from harboring thoughts of suicide, most commentators [23] agree that Margaret's relatively important part in the action owes something to Ariosto's story. My reason for thinking that it may owe something also to Spenser's intermediate version thereof is that besides the resemblances between Ariosto and Shakespeare, there are also notable differences. Thus, in Ariosto as in Bandello—but not in Spenser or Shakespeare—the villain's motive is bitter jealousy aroused by his rival's successful wooing. Again, Ariosto employs the duke himself in the supposed shaming of the heroine—not a base "ruffian," as do Spenser and Shakespeare. Finally, I think the following comparison of Spenser's version with Shakespeare's will show that the maid in Ariosto is made to bear much more guilty responsibility than in *The Faerie Queene* and in *Much Ado*, in both of which she is comparatively blameless and less awkwardly conspicuous in the action.

In judging the evidence for himself, the reader will find it useful to have at hand a summary of the astonishingly wide and persistent divergence of critical opinion concerning Spenser's possible influence upon *Much Ado*. One-fifth of some thirty editors and commentators I have consulted dismiss Spenser absolutely, either by failing so much as to mention him among possible sources of *Much Ado*, or else by tacitly accepting Furness's view that Spenser's story exerted not "the remotest degree of influence . . . on *Much Ado*," [24] or W. A. Wright's, that it "is of no value" in this connection "except as an illustration of a literary commonplace." [25] Indeed, it is not unlikely that this view, perhaps with with some modification, is held by the majority. At any rate, all

23. Among many others, early and late: Langbaine (see n. 26, below), Trenery, Neilson, Tucker Brooke (see above, nn. 12, 4), et al. (But see also above, p. 107.)

24. *Op. cit.*, p. 307.    25. *Much Ado* (Oxford, 1905), p. vii.

but some half-dozen are non-committal as to Spenser's claims. Generally speaking, the majority mention Spenser's story merely as an analogue, somewhat as Langbaine did long ago: "The contrivance of Borachio is borrowed from Ariosto . . . the like story is in Spenser." [26] Yet some among this majority, I think, are non-committal with a difference. "Doubtless Shakespeare knew Spenser's version," writes Professor Kittredge,[27] and such scholars as Parrott,[28] Neilson,[29] Quiller-Couch and Dover Wilson, among others, agree outspokenly or by implication. It is not surprising, therefore, that some have gone a step further—far enough, that is to say, to suggest that in some one particular or other Shakespeare "may have borrowed either from . . . *Orlando* or from *The Faerie Queene*." [30] Finally, at least three editors, English and American, have expressed the definite conviction that in some respects Shakespeare "preferred" Spenser's version to Ariosto's and therefore "adopted" it. On looking into the books to check my conclusions, I find that MacCracken [31] and Smith,[32] the two scholars just quoted, agree with the English Arden editor,[33]—and with my own first impressions—in giving special emphasis to the fact that the only recognizable prototype of the "ruffian" Borachio is the "base groom" in Spenser.[34] The evidence should be worth looking at closely. Taken together with the preceding comparisons of *Much Ado* with Bandello and Ariosto, it

26. *English Dramatick Poets* (Oxford, 1691), p. 461; cf. Grant White, *Works* (Boston, 1859), III, 223.

27. See above, p. 111.

28. *Shakespeare* (New York, 1938), p. 480. (He and Quiller-Couch and Dover Wilson substitute "certainly" and "of course," respectively, for Mr. Kittredge's "doubtless.")

29. *Op. cit.*, p. 180.

30. Quiller-Couch and Dover Wilson, *op. cit.*, pp. ix-x. The same suggestion is implicit in Parrott's discussion (see n. 28 above) and in F. E. Budd's—New Eversley *Much Ado* (London, 1936), pp. xxxiii-xxxiv; and possibly also in Neilson's (see n. 29), and Tucker Brooke's (see p. 107, n. 4), to mention no others.

31. Brooke, Cunliffe, and MacCracken, *Shakespeare's Principal Plays* (New York, 1935), p. 373.

32. American Arden *Much Ado*, p. xiii.

33. *Op. cit.*, pp. xi ff. (See above, p. 109, n. 12.)

34. See summary below.

should supply an adequate basis for judgment. With regard to
Spenser in particular, I think it indicates some formative influence
beyond that connected with the base Borachio—in the shaping of
the characters and motives of Claudio and Don John and Margaret.

Spenser's tale of the tragic loves of Phedon and Claribell, like
Ariosto's, is told by one of the principals, Phedon himself. He
recounts the successful wooing of his "lady fayre of great degree," [35] and the fatal consequences of the treachery of a "faithless
squire," his friend, Philemon. This "friend" is fully apprised of
Phedon's "love and all [his] privicie." Actuated—like Shakespeare's Don John, but unlike Bandello's Girondo or Ariosto's
Polynesso—not by any desire to win the lady for himself but by
sheer malice [36] ("envy" or "treason"), he charges Claribell with
unchastity:

> He, *either envying my toward good,*
> *Or of himself to treason ill disposed,*
> One day unto me came in friendly mood
> And told for secret how he understood
> That . . . [Claribell] . . .
> Had both distained her honorable blood
> And eke the faith which she to me did bind
> And therefore wished me stay till I more
>           truth should find.

Don John the bastard in *Much Ado*, is also a born malcontent
and mischief-maker, though a clumsy one withal.[37] He has not the
remotest inclination for Hero or any woman.[38] In his own words,
he is simply a "plain-dealing villain" who "would bite" if he had
his "mouth." [39] Embittered by his defeat in his futile rebellion

35. *The Faerie Queene*, II, iv, 19, and (for the long quotation below) 22.
36. As Phedon himself, in this allegory, is moved by and symbolizes wrath (see stanzas
34-35).
37. "Will it serve for any model to build mischief on?" (*Much Ado*, I, iii, 48.)
38. "What is he for a fool that betroths himself to unquietness?" (*Id.*, l. 50.)
39. *Id.*, ll. 33-37.

against his brother, his rancorous malice fixes upon Claudio, "the young start-up" who had "all the glory" of his "overthrow." He therefore jumps at the chance to "cross him any way,"—i.e., to "be the death of this marriage," by Borachio's plot against Hero.[40]

Next, to make his "craftie engin" [41] the more deadly, Spenser's "treachour" Philemon envenoms the point of his charge by the twice-repeated [42] assertion that

> It was *a groome of base degree*
> Which of my love was partener paramoure:
> Who used in a *darkesome* inner bowre
> Her *oft to meete:* which better to approve
> He promised to bring me at that howre
> When I should see that would me nearer move
> And drive me to withdraw my blind abused
>     love (Stanza 24).

So Borachio and Don John in *Much Ado*, and they only—for this devilish refinement of the hero's torture is not in Bandello nor in Ariosto—stage-manage their trick. Deceived "partly by the dark night," [43] but chiefly by the villainy of Don John's slanders and his henchman's impersonation, Claudio and Don Pedro, "planted and placed" by Don John "afar off in the orchard," watch Hero's supposed encounter with the base ruffian. In Don Pedro's words, they

---

40. *Id.*, ll. 68 ff.; II, ii, 19-20.        41. *The Faerie Queene*, II, iv, 27.
42. In the line next quoted in the text, and in stanza 27, where Phedon, led by Philemon, becomes "the sad spectator" of his "tragedy," while the other, "his owne false part played,"

> Disguised like that *groome of base degree*
> Whom he had feigned th' abuser of my love to bee.

43. *Much Ado*, III, iii, 159-169. (Cf. *The Faerie Queene*, II, iv, 28:

> Her proper face
> I not discerned in that darksome shade
> But weened it was my love with whom he played.)

> See her, hear her, at that hour last night
> Talk with *a ruffian* at her chamber window,
> Who hath, indeed, like a most liberal villain,
> Confessed the vile encounters they have had
> A thousand times in secret.[44]

It seems to me that the maid's part in all this is progressively strengthened as it develops from Ariosto through Spenser to Shakespeare. Critics have not observed, apparently, that Spenser's Pryene is less obtuse than Ariosto's Dalinda, less blameworthy for her part in the deceit, and less disproportionately obtrusive in the action. In all this she anticipates Shakespeare's Margaret. Pryene, like Margaret, remains the maid and not the mistress of the plot. Dalinda tells the story and remains in the foreground to the last; the other two, if not altogether "below stairs" (as Margaret suggests),[45] stay in the background. Dalinda's affair with her duke antedates and dominates her story; Pryene and Margaret do not appear until after the respective villains have laid their plots and all but achieved their deviltry.[46] Shakespeare, indeed, withholds for seemingly casual but really skillfully unemphatic notice in the fifth act,[47] the fact that Borachio courted Margaret "in Hero's garments." Thereby he conceals effectively the chief weakness of the plot—the difficulty of accounting for Margaret's allowing herself—sensible and loyal as she is—to be used, however innocently, in this scoundrelly masquerade, and then maintaining silence when it turns into near-tragedy for her mistress.

This difficulty amounts to less in *The Faerie Queene*, chiefly because Pryene is a story-book maid involved in an intrigue, rather than an authentic human being. Even so, Spenser improves upon Ariosto at least to the extent of rationalizing Pryene's part in the masquerade. Dalinda agrees to wear her lady's clothes to please her duke's equivocal "conceit";[48] Pryene does it to please

---

44. *Much Ado*, IV, i, 91-95.  
45. *Id.*, V, ii, 10.  
46. Cf. *The Faerie Queene*, stanzas 22-25.  
47. *Much Ado*, V, i, 245.  
48. See above, summary of Ariosto's story, pp. 110-111.

her own—a relatively good feminine reason!  Philemon suggests to her that if her beauty were but "adorned" like her mistress, it would "deface" that lady's "blazing pride": if fortune had not spited her, "thus lowly to abase" her beauty,

> If she had her least helpe to thee lent,
> T' adorne thy forme according thy desart,
> *Their blazing pride thou wouldest soone have blent.*[49]

Pryene acts upon this suggestion.  Hero's "good Meg" is no mere story-book maid, but this is a motive which she could have understood.  Shakespeare, too, would scarcely have missed its point.  One does not forget the lively scene in which Hero's maids rhapsodize upon her wedding garments and Margaret expresses her particular delight in the "fine, quaint, graceful, and excellent fashion" of her lady's gown.[50]  Ariosto's Dalinda, the villain's conscious and willing agent in his efforts to win the mistress after seducing the maid, is, to all intents and purposes, his guilty accomplice in crime.[51]  Pryene and Margaret, comparatively speaking, are innocent transgressors.[52]  In closely similar language, Spenser and Shakespeare signify that their maids were not criminals, though both were imprudently at fault.  Claribell's

> *faultie* handmayd . . .
> Confest how Philemon her wrought to chaunge her weede;[53]

and

> Margaret was in some *fault* for this,
> Although against her will, as it appears
> In the true course of all the question.[54]

---

49. *The Faerie Queene*, II, iv, 25-26.
50. *Much Ado*, III, iv; especially lines 22-23.
51. Remorseful in the end, she enters a nunnery.
52. Pryene accepts Philemon's "vile affections" for herself without suspecting his designs upon her lady. On Margaret, see text below.
53. *The Faerie Queene*, II, iv 29.    54. *Much Ado*, V, iv, 4-6.

Margaret's faults and virtues illustrate perfectly Shakespeare's mastery of his sources, his unerring selective instinct in giving essential human life to such shadows as Spenser's Pryene. The great virtue of "sweet Mistress Margaret," with all her curious tricks, is that she is thoroughly alive. Her "fault," as we have seen, is carefully kept under cover; and in the end we are assured by Leonato that, at worst, she erred "against her will," or, as Borachio puts it, she "knew not what she did. . . . But always hath been just and virtuous."[55] Her own straightforward and spirited utterances are all in her favor. There is no harm in her, for all her love of mischief and all her spicy talk.[56] And perhaps even her part in Borachio's masquerade is not so utterly incomprehensible as has been thought.[57] For one might guess, judging by Margaret's emphatic dislike of the prospect of remaining permanently "below stairs" and husbandless,[58] that, like Maria in *Twelfth Night*, she might not have been altogether averse to the idea of achieving marriage with a none too sober "gentleman," even at the cost of a more or less innocent trick at someone else's expense!

Of course the most telling strokes in the character of Margaret are of Shakespeare's own devising. But, as we have seen, her responsibilities and limitations in the spinning of the plot are, in some respects, closer to Spenser than to Ariosto. So too is the malice of the villain, and the invention of the "base groom" who serves as his tool.

55. *Id.*, V, i, 310-311.          56. To Benedick, for example, in V, ii, 1-25.
57. Cf. Trenery, *op. cit.*, p. xviii.          58. *Much Ado*, V, ii, 9-10.

# VI

## THE ORIGINAL MALVOLIO?[1]

IN HIS most recent pronouncement upon *Twelfth Night* Sir E. K. Chambers[2] states that "there is no clear source for the Malvolio episodes." Gollancz, he adds, "has suggested an analogue . . . in a quarrel at court"; and Chambers himself had suggested another of a similar nature.[3] Neither suggestion, however, ultimately satisfied him — possibly because the two together, tempting as each may have seemed in itself, are mutually destructive? The reader may judge for himself, for I shall presently review the case for these, and one or two still earlier, attempts to explore Malvolio's "sources" and origins. All this (to screw my courage to the sticking-place!) because I think I have found the original Malvolio myself — or at least a personage who looks more like the living model from whom Shakespeare might have drawn than any yet suggested. I believe that this model — for the *man* Malvolio, not necessarily for nice details of the episodes in which he is concerned — was William Ffarington, Esquire (1537-1610), of Worden, Lancashire, steward (until 1594) to Lord Ferdinando Strange, Earl of Derby and patron of Shakespeare's company.

The concluding years of Ffarington's stewardship marked the period of Shakespeare's *Lehrjahre*. I think it is altogether likely that Shakespeare, as a young actor and budding dramatist, might have noticed, for future reference, the arrogant pomposity of this important functionary of the Derby household. For Ffarington wielded great power in his official domain. He had under him

---

1. Revised from The Shakespeare Association *Bulletin*, VII (1932), 57 ff.
2. *William Shakespeare* (Oxford, 1930), I, 407.
3. *Shakespeare: A Survey* (London, 1935), pp. 177-179.

some 150 servants and retainers, and he appears to have been un-
friendly to the players, particularly, if I am not mistaken, to
Shakespeare's company,[4] when they came to act at Knowsley,
Lathom, and New Parke, the Lancashire residences of the Stanleys, Earls of Derby.   Let me say at once that Ffarington sketched
the essential lines of his own portrait in the records of his stewardship, that is to say, in the *Derby Household Books*,[5] a document
unaccountably neglected by Elizabethan students.   And Canon
Raines, the able editor of this document, has filled in most of the
outlines of Ffarington's sketch.   I mean to confront Mr. Ffarington with self-comparisons by putting him side by side with Malvolio.   I shall also have to consider more definitely the probabilities as to the contacts between Shakespeare's company and
Lord Strange's steward, but first I shall venture still another
claim in his behalf.   Malvolio may not have been his only off-
spring.   Malvolio and Oswald, Goneril's steward in *Lear*, are, in a
sense, two lodged together.   They differ from one another, of
course, as comic figures inevitably differ from more serious ones;
but both are negative studies informed with, and perhaps inspired
by, a sort of lingering distaste for the type of solidly faithful but
exasperatingly stupid and self-important officialdom they represent.   I hope to show that Lord Strange's important Mr. Ffarington gives us so satisfactory a composite portrait of these two —
with possibly a touch or two of Polonius thrown in to boot!— that
he ought to be the great original even if he is not.   Let us see
whether, in any case, he is not much more likely to be the man

4.  See below, pp. 126, 134, 153, and notes.
5.  Chetham Society *Remains*, 1853, XXXI, ed. F. R. Raines (hereafter referred to as
*D. H. B.*).—Some time after the completion of this study, Professor Abel Lefranc informed
me that in 1919, subsequent to the publication of his *Sous le Masque de William Shakespeare*, he reread *D. H. B.*   Thereupon, "struck by the many resemblances between Ffarington and Malvolio," he took copious notes (still in MS.) for future publication.   "Quelle
curieuse concordance de résultats!" adds M. Lefranc; "la chose vaut vraiment la peine
d'être notée."   Professor Lefranc's Shakespearean studies had not come to my attention
until this essay was completed.   As regards the question, therefore, concerning the original
Malvolio, independent inquiry by two investigators representing entirely different points
of view, has brought the same answer: Ffarington.

than any of those hitherto thought to be Malvolio's forebears.

Two of these I shall dismiss rapidly, for neither of them, at best, could have supplied more than a name. Thus, Hunter suggested long ago that Shakespeare might have *named* Malvolio from Messer Agnol Maleuolti, an obscure participator in the induction to *Gl'Ingannati*, one of the not impossible sources or analogues of *Twelfth Night*. Furness, however, observed that "there is nothing whatsoever in Malevolti . . . which corresponds to the character which Shakespeare gives to Malvolio," and doubts that Shakespeare even "took the trouble" to borrow the name.[6] Even if he did not invent it, as he surely might have done, the Italian comedy does not supply even the shadow of a model for Malvolio. Neither does Fleay, who, because he was able to concoct the anagram I O [H N] M A [R S T O N] out of the fustian riddle (the "M O A I doth sway my life") in Maria's letter,[7] decided that "Malvolio was a representative of Marston's vanity." [8] For, as Small [9] has noted, Fleay's insistence upon the "singular likeness between the names" of Malvolio and Malevole (in Marston's *Malcontent*) is of small account—in the first place because there is no resemblance between the two characters except in name, and, secondly, because, if it be granted that there was any borrowing, Marston must have been the borrower, since *The Malcontent* is almost certainly at least a year or two later than *Twelfth Night*.

The suggestions of Gollancz and Chambers are much more useful and plausible than this one. Accordingly, I shall excerpt enough of their materials to supply a fair basis for comparison with my claims for Ffarington. Gollancz,[10] to begin with, thought he recognized the original Malvolio in the person of "Sir Ambrose Willoughby, Queen Elizabeth's Chief Sewer and Squire of the Presence," whose quarrel with the Earl of Southampton is thus

6. Furness, Variorum *Twelfth Night*, pp. xix-xx; 2, n. 12.
7. *Twelfth Night*, II, v, 118.
8. *Shakespeariana*, I (1884), 136; Furness, p. 168.
9. *The Stage Quarrel* (Breslau, 1899), p. 139; cf. Chambers, *Elizabethan Stage*, III, 431.
10. *A Book of Homage to Shakespeare*, (Oxford 1916), pp. 177-178.

described in a letter by Rowland Whyte, dated January 12, 1597/8:

> Southampton [and] Willoughby . . . with Sir Walter Raw-
> ley and Mr. Parker being at Primero in the Presence Chamber,
> the Queen was gon to bed, and he being there as Squier for the
> Body, desired them to giue over.  Soon after he spoke to them
> againe, that if they would not leaue he wold call in the Gard to
> pull down the Bord, which Sir Walter Rawley seeing, put vp his
> Money and went his Wayes.  But my Lord Southampton took
> Exceptions at hym and told him he wold remember yt.  [Where-
> upon ensued a hairpulling match, in which Southampton was
> worsted.]  The Queen gave Willoughby Thanckes for what he
> did in the Presence, and told hym he had donne better yf he had
> sent hym to the Porters Lodge, to see who durst haue fetcht
> hym out.[11]

Such a quarrel, Gollancz goes on to say, would have caused
much gossip, and "what more likely" than that Southampton's
"devotee, Shakespeare, should cleverly utilize the incident?"  The
question has its point; but other questions, of which I shall mention only one or two, suggest themselves.  If Willoughby was
Malvolio, was Raleigh Sir Andrew, and Southampton Sir Toby?
If so, would not the thing have been a rather left-handed compliment to Southampton?  If, moreover, the allusion was recognizable, it might well have been dangerous, since the Queen had
publicly supported Willoughby and might have had the last word
if this quarrel had really been translated to the stage.  At all
events, this Willoughby, who spoils a belated cardgame for the
Queen's favorites, supplies few definitely recognizable lines for the
model of Malvolio the steward — for his dour surliness to servants
and jesters, or his suppressed passion for fine feathers and high
station.

Possibly Chambers meets the requirements more nearly.
"The sort of criticism," he writes,[12] "which endeavors to trace and

11.  *Sidney Papers* (*Letters and Memorials of State*, ed. A. Collins, London, 1746), II, 83.
12.  *Shakespeare: A Survey*, pp. 177-179.

interpret topical allusions in Shakespeare's plays can easily be overdone." Yet he could not resist the temptation to illustrate the scene wherein Malvolio rebukes the "uncivil rule" by night of Maria and her disreputable consorts (only to be invited by Sir Toby, in turn, to go rub his chain with crumbs), by "an amusing incident" in which, according to a seventeenth-century anecdotist, Sir William Knollys, the Comptroller of the Royal Household, played the leading rôle:

> Knollys . . . had his lodging at court, where some of the . . . Maydes of Honour used to friske . . . about in the next room, to his extreame disquiet a nights. . . . At last he getts one to bolt their own backe doore when they were all in one night at their revells, stripps off his shirt, and so with a payre of spectacles on his nose and Aretine in his hand, comes marching in at a posterne doore . . . reading very gravely, full upon the faces of them. Now let the reader judge what a sadd spectacle and pitiful fright these poor creatures endured, for he faced them and often traversed the roome in this posture above an hour."

Now Knollys, though elderly and married, "had amorous relations with one of the Maids of Honour, the audacious and frail Mary Fitton," who, after his wife's death, failed to keep a promise to marry him. And so, Chambers concludes, "I like to think that the pompous and besotted old Comptroller gave Shakespeare his hint for Malvolio, and that Mary Fitton," though not the lady of the sonnets, "does . . . make her appearance in the plays as . . . the pert and ingenious hussy, Maria."

With due respect to a great scholar, I am bound to add that to my ear this anecdote sounds apocryphal. Even if it is not, one recalls, with reference to the maids of honor, that the "uncivil rule" of *Twelfth Night* is not that of the monstrous regiment of women but of Sir Andrew and Sir Toby, whom Maria, indeed — with certain anticipatory wifely-proprietary stirrings — admonishes *against* too many late drinky hours and too much caterwauling,[13] though it is perfectly true that she dislikes Malvolio's airs far more than Sir Toby's excessive libations. For the rest, I cannot see that Chambers' anecdote, except for Knollys' pomposity (which he, unlike Malvolio, strips off, of his own volition, with his shirt!) furnishes us, any more than does the Willoughby story, a clearly recognizable model for Malvolio, the sour steward and petty Jack-in-office. "Art any more than a steward?" Sir William Knollys [14] was, decidedly. To wit: of high family connection (his mother was a first cousin of Queen Elizabeth), he was, like his father before him, a tried soldier and diplomat. Moreover, he stood in high personal favor with the Queen, who made him treasurer of the royal household, gave him many important and delicate tasks, and took pleasure in describing him as "one that appertaineth to us in blood." The danger involved in staging a recognizable caricature of one so close to the Queen makes strongly against the likelihood of any such intention in *Twelfth Night*. In any case, I do not think Knollys *fits*, any more than Willoughby. He did not, like Sir John Oldcastle, die a martyr, but this is not the man.

Yet there is virtue in these suggestions in so far as they look toward a living model within Shakespeare's range of observation. I think, however, that Gollancz and Chambers looked too high. Shakespeare certainly kept his eyes open at court as well as elsewhere, and used, directly or indirectly, much of what he saw there. Yet it does not follow that he put into his plays nearly so many full-length allegorical portraits of great personages as some enthusiasts would have us believe. Certainly some of the most interesting discoveries of recent scholarship—Manly's, for example, and Hotson's— [15] support the belief that Shakespeare, for many good reasons, is less likely to have modeled his characters upon princes, potentates and powers, than, like Mark Twain or Dickens, upon his uncles, his cousins, and his aunts—or, like Chaucer, upon his personal and professional associates, neighbors,

13. *Twelfth Night*, I, iii, 14; II, iii, 76.          14. See *D. N. B.*
15. *New Light on Chaucer, Shakespeare vs. Shallow,* etc.

or acquaintances. I am confident, therefore, that in seeking the original Malvolio among Shakespeare's quasi-associates I am at least pointing in the right direction, though Ffarington's claims must rest finally not upon certainties but upon comparative probabilities. As steward to Lord Strange and occasional host to Shakespeare's company, he was, at all events, a person of sufficient consequence, though not too dangerously near the throne nor to the London players. And, as a candidate for the honor I would thrust upon him, he was blessed with a personality which, I think it will appear, could not easily have been forgotten by anyone who had had anything to do with him.

Ffarington, as Raines has shown, was born in 1537, and inherited from his father, Sir Henry Ffarington, a large property, an official connection with the Stanley family,[16] an inordinate "appetite for law," [17] and, in his conduct as a public official, an authoritative and unyielding manner which his inferiors and even "the surrounding gentry . . . felt . . . sometimes to be inconvenient . . . and at other times oppressive." [18] Ffarington cultivated his heritage assiduously. He increased his property by a prudent marriage [19] to a wealthy young daughter of the house of Stanley and by shrewd legal management, but his unpleasantly habitual litigiousness (for, like his father, and like Oswald, he was preëminently an "action-taking" gentleman) [20] involved him in an unending "series of disputations with his neighbors as well as with members of his own family." [21] Meanwhile, he had become Justice of the Peace in his home county and comptroller of the household to Edward, Earl of Derby; and he

16. The elder Ffarington had been secretary to Edward, Earl of Derby.

17. *D. H. B.*, p. xxii.                18. *Id.*, p. xxi.

19. Later, he objected strenuously to his son's *imprudent* marriage (see below, pp. 128-129, n. 42.)

20. Cf. *Lear*, II, ii, 18, and, below, p. 131. (Possibly the mild Oswald is described as an "action-taking" rogue because Shakespeare was thinking of some functionary like him who exemplified this trait.)

21. *D. H. B.*, pp. xxi ff., etc. He studied law at the Middle Temple and is said to have attended Oxford, though he is not listed among its graduates, as is his son, William (*Alumni Oxoniensis*, Oxford, 1891, II, 483).

remained "an influential magistrate . . . throughout his life."
In 1572 "he received a patent as Steward of the household" to
the next Earl, and took up his new duties with vigor and enthusiasm, if one may judge by the sharpened household regulations,
extant in his handwriting, with which he celebrated his inauguration. According to these rules it appears that he would have
exterminated altogether, if he could have had his way, such
nuisances as "Doggs," "boyes," "slaves," and "vagrants." [22]
Doubtless, however, this was merely his conception of his duty,
which, as his editor has it, was "to censure delinquents, to check
extravagance, to overlook the accounts . . . and to pay wages."
Raines adds that Ffarington's record of his many years of service
to the Stanleys "clearly proves that he had a just estimate of
what was due to the rank and station" of this great family. Unquestionably, he had also a just estimate of the exalted respect
due to the family's connection by marriage, its steward, Mr.
Ffarington, who, meanwhile, by frugal [23] and dextrous management of his own affairs and in spite of his numerous and expensive
law-suits, was thriving apace and steadily accumulating wealth,
dignity, and importance. For during these years — between 1572
and 1594 — he acquired lands, rebuilt his ancestral seat, "sought
confirmation of the heraldic honours" of his family, lent money to
his neighbors, settled disputes, and (like Malvolio) busied himself
with "arguments of state" ranging all the way from the putting
down of May games [24] to the raising of local funds to support the
wars. [25] As steward of the Derby household he seems literally to
have worn his "cheane" of office — which is reverently mentioned
in a letter from one of his sycophants — [26] with an air that might

22. See below, p. 136, n. 71.        23. See below, p. 137, n. 71, p. 128, n. 41.
    24. In 1580 a fellow magistrate expressed his confidence that Ffarington would sup-
press — quickly and on his own responsibility — "Robyn hoode and the May games" and
such-like "lewde sportes tendings to . . . wantones" (*Ffarington Papers*, Chetham Soc.
*Remains*, xxxix, pp. 128-130).        25. *D. H. B.*, pp. xlv, xl, ff.
    26. One Richard Kellet, who wrote his "Right welbeloved Maister, my dutie remem-
bered," that Ffarington was "greatlie missed" in 1584 when he did not accompany Derby,
who "saied he wolde have geven ffortie powndes to have youe w^th him," on an embassage to
France. Kellet adds: "I see that M^r Warren doeth weare your Cheane" (*D. H. B.*, p. li).

well have roused a Sir Toby or a cry of visiting players to bid him go rub it with crumbs. But perhaps this is humanly understandable. He was not of their element. At home he had a "great golde Chaine" of his own,[27] and there, like Count Malvolio in his contemplation of future greatness,[28] he could sit in his state and call his officers about him to his heart's content, for his personal establishment was "large and well organized, his servants amounting to upwards of twenty, including his gentleman, steward, clerks, and others." [29] His records show that he was not incapable of doing good deeds — in 1580, for example, he paid a boy's expenses at Christ Church, Oxford; and he willed a year's wages to his servants — [30] but he appears to have been an intolerably magisterial, opinionated, and self-righteous person for all that.[31] There can be no question, however, in his case any more than in that of Malvolio or of Oswald, that he discharged his duties to the entire satisfaction of his principals, and that they, whatever the visiting players may have thought, held him in high regard and reposed the utmost trust in him.[32] Lord Ferdinando Strange, in particular, relied upon him in all business matters, and, when he became Earl, confirmed Ffarington in all his offices.[33] The *Derby Household Books*, unfortunately, close with the year 1590, so that to trace the later years of Ffarington's career we have to turn to other sources of information. Canon Raines was unable to find any evidence to show that Ffarington continued to serve the house of Derby after the sudden and mysterious death of Lord Ferdinando in April, 1594.[34] It may be pertinent to add, however, that Ffarington was, at least for a time, on most friendly terms with William Stanley, the next Earl,[35] who, as will appear

27. Valued at £100 (*D. H. B.*, p. xcii). 28. *Twelfth Night*, II, v, 35-55.
29. *D. H. B.*, p. xxxv. 30. *D. H. B.*, pp. xli, lxxii ff.
31. See below, p. 128, nn. 39-42.
32. "They confided in him . . . entirely" (*D. H. B.*, pp. xciv ff.; Cf. *Lear*, IV, ii, 18; *Twelfth Night*, III, iv, 69.
33. *Id.*, p. lxiii.
34. This sensational event, incidentally, was the talk of all London, including, undoubtedly, the players.
35. He was Ffarington's guest in May, 1594 (*D. H. B.*, p. lxiv).

below,[36] continued in noteworthy fashion his family's traditional interest in plays and players. Ffarington died in 1610. Of his later years it is enough to say that he was frequently in London — in 1594, for instance, and 1597— [37] where he might have been seen or heard of by old acquaintances, and that during this decade or earlier there must occasionally have been high gossip about him below stairs in Lancashire, which might likewise have come to the ears of the players. For Ffarington had notorious trouble the while. He was constantly in the courts,[38] and his stiff-necked integrity did not compensate for the lack of humor and human sympathy he exhibited in his own home. He was "disappointed in all his children" and he absolutely disinherited Thomas Ffarington, his eldest son. This young man, described by Raines as "a gentleman of some accomplishments and learning," with "a taste for music . . . painting, and poetry," [39] was not a young Malvolio. Sometime between 1590 and 1598 [40] he refused point-blank to achieve greatness by a prudential marriage such as might have established him in a nearer relationship to a noble house. According to William Ffarington's will, written just before his death in 1610, his son twice married "w^{th}out my co[n]sent & w^{th}out any preferm^t to himselfe obtayned or yet to the obtaining of any frends thereby," his second wife being so "base and beggar[l]ye" [41] and so "undvtifulle, vnqwiet & disobedient" withal that she had the effrontery to beard her father-in-law in his own house at Worden in order "to take possessyon in the same." The husband and wife offered abject "submission," apparently soon after this event, but Ffarington's will proves that he nursed his grudge until the end.[42]

36. See p. 132.                           37. D. H. B., pp. lxiii, lxvi, etc.
38. Id., pp. lxvi, lxxvi, xlix, etc.       39. Id., p. lxxxvii.
40. See below, n. 42.

41. "It is just possible," says Raines, that to the fist-hardened elder Ffarington "to want money" may have been tantamount to wanting "everything" (Id., p. lxxxi).

42. The passage from the will reads as follows:
  "Forasmvche as Thomas ffarington . . . my eldest sone . . . hath not onlye bestowed himselfe at two severall tymes, since the beryall of his first wieffe, in marryadge w^{th}out my pryvitie & co[n]sente & greatlye to my . . . discontentm^t & w^{th}out

Now this side of Ffarington — his unimaginative self-righteousness as a man, his "superserviceable" [43] devotion to his principals, his surliness toward servants,[44] and his instinctive distaste (still to be shown) for players — is that of which Shakespeare may well have seen and heard something. To let the reader see something more of it, I shall quote here a passage from the concluding character sketch of Ffarington by Raines, an unprejudiced witness, since he failed to notice Ffarington's probable contacts with Strange's Men and did not connect him with Malvolio. "The salient points of his character," says Raines,

> are vividly marked and fully before us. . . . What he would be at the head of Lord Derby's household [may readily be imagined]. It may also be inferred that he was not often found at Whitsun Ales or Wakes of Leyland, and that the pastoral days of pipe and crook and dance and song were little heeded by him. *That he entered not with much spirit into the theatrical representations at Knowsley and New Park*, that the liltings and old ballad music of his sons found small favour with him, *that he had not much delight in comic humour or a particle of imagination or sentiment or romance about him*, may be readily admitted. His life was that of a prosperous man . . . practical

---

any preferm[t] to himselfe obtayned, or yet to the obtayning of any frends thereby, his nowe wieffe being dissended of a base & beggarye parrentadge & she a verye undvtyfulle, vnqwiet & disobedient woman, & came vnto my howse of Worden to enter & to take possessyon in the same w[th]owte my pryvitie & co[n]sente, I beinge then in possessyon of the same,"
— therefore he cuts off his son (*D. H. B.*, pp. lxxxiii ff.). The exact date of the quarrel between father and daughter-in-law is uncertain. Young Ffarington, however, was first married in 1581, and his first wife bore him three children. His second marriage, therefore, would hardly have come before 1586, nor his third before 1590 or later. The quarrel probably developed within a year or two of March 11, 1600, for in a letter of that date Thomas Ffarington reproached his father for the consistently "hard countenance" with which he had refused forgiveness, "neither the submission of myself nor my wife, neither yet the motion of any friend" having availed (*Ffarington Papers*, pp. 142 ff.).

43. See below, p. 131, n. 47.

44. Ffarington's household rules (*D. H. B.*, pp. 20 ff.) expressly provide that the "meaner sort" be kept strictly in their places. In general, these rules confirm Raines's suggestion (cf. n. 45 and text below) that Ffarington was an unconscionable martinet. (Cf. also *Twelfth Night*, II, v, 162.)

and cautious, the mind always on the stretch and the affections perhaps not much in request.[45]

The *prima facie* likenesses between Malvolio and Ffarington, thus viewed, are, I think, fairly evident. Still others deserve attention, but first it will be useful to complete the picture, as Raines draws it, from Ffarington's portrait at Worden Hall:

> *There is great decision and authority, united with more than ordinary sharpness and sternness in the expression,* and *he looks like a man who had been more accustomed to rule than to obey.* . . . His features are handsome and regular . . . face somewhat square, eyes dark, complexion florid . . . forehead high . . . lines across it indicative of thought . . . beard thin, peaked . . . slightly gray. He wears a russet-coloured doublet . . . free from the . . . fashionable 'slashing and jagging' . . . at that period so much affected . . . also a sable fur across his shoulders and a large chain of linked gold . . . in three rounds across his chest. In his right hand he holds a silver-headed cane, or it may be his wand of office . . . and he wears a ring on his little finger. . . . In his left hand . . . a scented glove embroidered with gold, on his forefinger . . . a signet ring. . . .

(The severe elegance of this *tout ensemble*, be it noted, is shot through with more than one indulgent gleam of another sort. Raines's concluding lines will show that the scented glove and "some rich jewels" [46] — the rings and chain and wand — are not the only offset for the *un*slashed restraint of the doublet. Is it altogether fanciful to suggest that all this might make a good serving of red meat for the Freudians? Have we not Hiren here — Ffarington-Malvolio of the yellow stockings and cross garters? And possibly also some reflections of that other glass of fashion — the elegantly finical "neat . . . glass-gazing, superserviceable . . . action-taking . . . base, proud, shallow . . . one-trunk-

---

45. *D. H. B.*, pp. xciv ff. (Italics mine.)
46. *Twelfth Night*, II, v, 66.

inheriting" Oswald? [47] We must look again at Ffarington as he was under his skin, but first I shall let Raines finish his description.)

> He wears the . . . monstrous . . . double cambric ruff
> . . . stiffened or wired, being [according to Stubbs in the
> *Anatomy of Abuses*] 'set three or four times double, and of some
> fitly called three steps and a half to the gallows.' [48]

Other gentlemen too, of course, wore the double ruff; but few of them all, surely, had anything like Ffarington's personal and professional qualifications as a proper model for Malvolio. Very few, indeed, could have enjoyed strategic advantages equal to his as steward to Lord Strange and his father from 1589 to 1594. For one thing, our investigation already has supplied some definite evidence in support of Raines's inferences concerning our steward's lack of humor, imagination, and inclination for theatrical entertainment. Other aspects of the case I have touched upon in another study,[49] in which the reader will find that during the two or three years (1587-1590) actually covered by the *Derby Household Books*, Ffarington names even the least of the many household guests but fails to name even one of thirteen plays by at least four different companies [50] whose appearance at the Lancashire residences of the Stanleys he definitely records in his fragmentary entries for this period. It seems more than likely that the Stanleys and their guests saw more plays than this incomplete record indicates, since Ffarington himself informs us that on one and the same Sunday they had a sermon in the morning and—such was their appetite for drama—"*the same daie* the Quenes Players . . .

47. *Cf. Lear*, II, ii, 15-20, 45.—Those who knew their Ffarington knew also that he had an eye for elegant and gorgeous array. Kellet, for instance, in writing him about his chain (see above, p. 126) added full and glowing details concerning the liveries ("purple in graine Cloake[s] . . . garded with Velvet and . . . gold, . . . black Sattine doubletts & hoese . . . w[th] like garde and lasse") worn by Derby's followers in 1584.

48. *D. H. B.*, pp. xciv ff.

49. "*Faire Em* (and Shakespeare's Company?) *in Lancashire*" (see below p. 141).

50. Leicester's Men, the Queen's, Essex's, and Lord Strange's (see below, pp. 153-156 and notes).

ii severall *nyghtes*"![51] It is certain, at all events, that the Stanleys were traditionally friendly to the players, for they had given them patronage of one sort or another at least as early as 1461, and they called upon them for household entertainment as late as 1606.[52] Ffarington's own record closes in August, 1590, but there can be little doubt that he had to see many another play during the remaining years of his stewardship. For Lord Strange himself remained a generous friend of poets and players [53] until his death in 1594, and Ffarington's entries indicate that Strange missed no opportunity to see his own company in action at his own home.[54] After his death, his widow, the famous Countess of Derby,[55] gave her name and countenance to the company, then certainly including Shakespeare,[56] until Hunsdon, the Lord Chamberlain, took them under his wing.[57] Even then the Stanley family continued to interest itself in plays and players. William Stanley, the next Earl of Derby, was so devoted a patron of theirs that gossip reports him, in 1599 "busye . . . penning commedyes for the commoun players." [58] Even if he did not write plays himself, it is clear, from a letter [59] of his written in 1606, that he had professional players acting for him at the old family seat at Lathom during the Christmas season of that year.

That Shakespeare's company [60] — the company officially under

51. *D. H. B.*, p. 62. (My italics.) See below, p. 154.

52. *Stanley Papers*, I, ii (Chetham Society *Remains*, vol. XXIX; cf. Collier, *Annals*, I, 83, and below, n. 59).

53. Cf. T. Heywood, "Earls of Derby and the Verse Writers," in *Stanley Papers*, I, lii ff.

54. See below, pp. 133, 153-156.

55. As Lady Strange she had frequently seen the players in Lancashire (*D. H. B.*). Like her husband, "she patronized and was praised by the poets," including Spenser, Marston, and Milton.

56. See below, p. 134, n. 64.

57. Cf. Murray, *English Dramatic Companies* (London, 1910), I, 91.

58. Cf. George Fenner's letter in *Calendar of State Papers, Domestic*, V, 227.

59. On December 2, 1606, he wrote the Mayor of Chester to bespeak official favor for the Earl of Hereford's Men, who had "beine wth. mee" and "whose retorne and labor for this Christmas tyme I expecte" (R. H. Morris, *Chester*, London, 1895, p. 353, n.; Murray, II, 234).

60. See below, p. 134, n. 64.

Lord Strange's patronage and later under his widow's—appeared
in the Derby residences during the important years between 1590
and 1594, while Ffarington, presumably, was growing more confirmed in his crabbedness and Shakespeare more certain of his
powers, seems to me altogether likely, for two reasons.

(1) The Stanleys loved plays, and their company (Strange's)
is known to have been at Coventry, Shrewsbury, Leicester, and
perhaps at the nearby Chester,[61] that is to say, within easy range
of its patron's Lancashire residences, year after year between
1591 and 1594. (I cannot prove, to be sure, that Shakespeare was
among the visiting players. The chances are, however, that his
interest in travelling players—*vide Hamlet*—was not altogether
academic or impersonal. Sooner or later few of the tragedians of
the city, beginners or masters, escaped the necessity of travelling
"on the hard hoof." It is all but certain, at any rate, that among
the visiting players in Lancashire during these years were such
men as Kemp and Edward Alleyn, Augustine Phillips and John
Hemings, Shakespeare's fellows and formerly of Leicester's Men,
or the Queen's, or Strange's.[62] In other words, it is at least virtually certain that Ffarington was a character well known to the
players.)

(2) If Shakespeare's company did play in Lancashire during
these years, it was merely living up to its traditions. The reader
will find, by turning to the next chapter, that Strange's Men may
be traced in Ffarington's domain, at Knowsley or Lathom or New
Parke, about 1589 or 1590, and that there is reason to believe
that this company stood lowest of them all in the steward's good
graces. I may note here that these inferences rest upon two sets of
facts. The first is a group of Ffarington's own entries (four in all,
between Christmas, 1587, and February, 1590) concerning a

61. It is certain that Strange's Men intended to play at Chester in 1593, and that they
appeared at Coventry in 1591-2-3-4, at Shrewsbury in 1592 and 1593, and at Leicester in
1593/4 (Murray, I, 89, 108; II, 392, etc.).

62. See lists of company personnel in Murray and T. W. Baldwin, *Organization and
Personnel of the Shakespearean Company*, Princeton, 1927.

company of which he disposes summarily as "*the* [63] Plaiers." Since Ffarington invariably refused to dignify those more or less immediately under his thumb by naming them, I take this company to be that of the household, Lord Strange's Men. In the second place, this interpretation is confirmed, and the presence of Strange's Men in one of the Stanley houses about 1590—probably soon after Shakespeare had joined the company [64]—is virtually attested by two passages in the comedy of *Faire Em*, a Strange's play dating between 1589 and 1591. These passages, which could hardly have been intelligible to any but a Lancashire audience, contain two outspoken compliments to Sir Edmund Trafford, an important associate and friend of the Stanleys, who, as appears below,[65] is thrice mentioned in Ffarington's record for 1587 to 1589 as a household guest of the family while the players were acting.

With reference to the especially scanty notice accorded by Ffarington to the company under the patronage of the house, I have only to repeat that he cherished a particular aversion to "vagrants," always stood tip-toe upon his dignity wherever any household servants were concerned, and never gave a name to any of them except to such dignitaries as "Mr. Comptrowler," "Mr. Receyver Generall," and—"Mr. Steward of the Howsehold." [66] If, being the man he was, players in general seemed a nuisance to

63. My italics.

64. He had become a sharer in Strange's Men at least as early as 1594, and had had a hand in the writing or recasting of *I Henry VI* (including the Talbot scenes), acted by Strange's Men at least as early as March, 1592. Murray (I, 75) and Baldwin (pp. 82, 287) place the beginning of his service—as a hireling—with Strange's Men, in 1588 or earlier. Sir E. K. Chambers (*William Shakespeare*, I, 59) doubts whether Shakespeare's "beginnings . . . as . . . actor and . . . writer" can be safely traced back further than to the Strange-Admiral's combination of 1590/1, but agrees that Shakespeare must have started as a hired man; *i. e.*, in such obscurity as makes difficult the task of dating the beginnings of his career. In any case, Chambers' dates are early enough, for, though Ffarington's entries close in 1590, he certainly retained his stewardship—and the players in all probability continued their visitations—until 1594 (see above, n. 61 and p. 127, n. 34).—Professor J. Q. Adams (*Life of Shakespeare*, pp. 130 ff.) holds that during a part of these four years Shakespeare belonged to Pembroke's Men. If so, the fact remains that he belonged to Strange's before the end of Ffarington's career, and that the steward was well known to Shakespeare's colleagues before and after.

65. See pp. 144, 150-151.    66. *D. H. B.*, p. 23.

him, he might conceivably have cherished a special distaste for the one company of them all which, perhaps, had special claims because it belonged, in a sense, to the family. What other than a churlish welcome, however, could they expect from a crusty official whose most human touches, so far as his entries are concerned, dim the glowing memory of great events — state dinners, pastime and good company, the glories of the chase, a fire which threatened to destroy the house at Lathom, the birth of Lord Strange's daughter — with laconic phrases which *describe* only the man who wrote them: "Mondaie many at din[ner]"; "Frydaie a great companie"; "Wednesday came many Huntesmen & Howndes"; "This night fyre begune in the Buttre"; "on Monday the mydwiffe came." (Two months after writing this last passage, Ffarington explained it by another entry: "Wednesday was the crystening of my L. Strandge's daughter") [67] Some, however, may still wish to press the question why those particular "abstracts and brief chronicles of the time," Shakespeare's company, should have been especially distasteful to Ffarington. *If* they were — for I think my case will stand even without this assumption — I may be pardoned for venturing one final suggestion. If they thought themselves entitled to especial favors, it may be that Ffarington, with whom household familiarity would have bred no less than contempt, used them, like Polonius under similar circumstances,[68] according to his own conception of their "desert." If so, Hamlet's remark a moment later may throw some light upon our question. Perhaps the players, at one time or another, had broken a jest upon the grand steward, by way of giving him an inkling of their feelings toward him? "Look you," says Hamlet to the First Player — "Look you, mock him not." [69]

67. *D. H. B.*, pp. 64, 43, 70, 42, 46.
68. *Hamlet.* "Good my lord, will you see the players well bestow'd? . . . Let them be well us'd."
   *Polonius.* "My lord, I will use them according to their desert" (II, ii, 546).
69. II, ii, 570.

It remains only to recapitulate Ffarington's claims as a Shakespearean original, and to retrace finally the outlines of his likeness
as reflected in Malvolio and perhaps in Oswald. The fact that
these two, almost the only Shakespearean stewards worth mentioning,[70] appear to be two of a kind whom Shakespeare disliked
heartily, would seem to establish some preliminary ground for the
hypothesis that he drew them from some living model whom he
thought worthy to be remembered. As steward to the patrons of
Shakespeare's company during the years 1589 to 1594, while
Shakespeare was winning his spurs and while his company was
almost certainly visiting the Derby houses more frequently than
Ffarington cared to see them, he would appear to be a logical
candidate. Shakespeare might have remembered him for many
reasons. Perhaps it was merely because Ffarington was obviously
no lover of players in general; possibly some particular coldness
on Ffarington's part toward Shakespeare's company was the more
warmly remembered by them. Certainly it is hard to believe
that a character and personality so strongly marked as that of
Ffarington, as he reveals himself in his writings, could have failed
to attract Shakespeare's notice if he knew of him at all. For every
page of Ffarington's papers is full of the man—a man of ability
and substance, but one marked among multitudes by his abysmal
lack of humor and his profound dislike of cakes and ale, especially
for the baser sort. He was well-born, and he achieved honors and
distinction by his own efforts. His pride of place is understandable, but his colossal self-importance would have been no less
trying to his official inferiors. Though he privately gave alms, on
occasion, to the poor and humble, the players would have noticed,
rather, his painstaking—not to say niggardly—[71] frugality, per-

70. Flavius, Timon of Athens' "one honest man" is, like Adam in *As You Like It*, a
faithful servant of the romantic tradition rather than the conventional steward. Davy,
Shallow's factotum in *II Henry IV*, is a real and racy person, but not the steward of a great
house. The steward in *All's Well* is insignificant.

71. "Wouldst thou not be glad to have the niggardly . . . sheep-biter come by some
notable shame?" (*Twelfth Night*, II, v, 5). As steward, Ffarington proscribed "boyes,"
"Doggs," and "vagrant psons." who might nefariously consume his principals' "victualls,

sonal and official. They could not have been unaware of his stubborn integrity, but, while he lorded it over them, they, his superiors in all the man-becoming graces, must have ached to caricature his obstreperous litigiousness, his "neat" and grave pomposity, his lurking vanity, and his unsmiling ambition. If out of these simples Shakespeare's magic compounded Oswald and Malvolio, the whirligig of time brought in its revenges.

bread, or drinke"; and prescribed carefully the exact number of messes and loaves to be cut or baked out of "every vealle, bieffe, mottons . . . and Pecke of Wheat" that came into the household (*D. H. B.*, pp. 21 ff., etc.). "Prudent avoidance of prodigality" (*Id.*, p. xxxix) was a general characteristic of his. Thus, he "avoided the cumbrous office of sheriff"—for the sheriff had to find, at his own expense, an intolerable deal of "wine and venison" for the justices. And he distinguished himself, as early as 1578 "for the frugality enjoined" in a resolution intended to cut down the official allowances of these delicacies to the magistrates. In his will, finally, he forbade "any . . . extraordinarye chardges whatsoever" in connection with his funeral (*Id.*, pp. xlvii, xcvii, lxxix; cf. *Ffarington Papers*, pp. IV-V).

# II

## "COUNTRY" PLAYS
### AND
## STROLLING PLAYERS

# VII

## *FAIRE EM* (AND SHAKESPEARE'S COMPANY?)
## IN LANCASHIRE [1]

THE READER who has followed — in the preceding pages — my quest for the original Malvolio, will agree that there are other personages in Shakespeare and his contemporary dramatists about whose antecedents one would gladly be better informed. Take, for example, the substantial list of neighbors and acquaintances mentioned by the redoubtable Christophero Sly in *The Taming of the Shrew:* [2] old Sly's son of Burton Heath, Marian Hacket, "the fat ale-wife of Wincot," and

> Stephen Sly, and old John Naps of Greece,
> And Peter Turph, and Henry Pimpernell,
> And twenty more such names and men as these,

"Which" — one is bound to admit that Shakespeare's next line is discouraging! — "never were nor no man ever saw." Perhaps not — and yet they sound as though they had been something more than grown-up dream children! Halliwell-Phillipps [3] long ago expressed the hope that systematic research might yet produce fruitful information about personages such as these. "Notices of these individuals," he urged, "would greatly add to the already high probability that Shakespeare . . . was occasionally thinking of his provincial audiences." Recent inquiries by various scholars [4]

1. Reprinted, with additions, from PMLA, XLVI (1931), 647 ff.
2. Induction, ii, 19-23, 95-98.      3. *Shakespeare's Tours*, 1887, p. 48.
4. See, for example, on the subject of old Sly's son, and Wincot, Edgar I. Fripp, *Shakespeare, Man and Artist* (London, 1938), I, 401, 239; and, for other local names and allusions in Elizabethan plays, R. B. Sharpe, *The Real War of the Theaters*, Modern Language Association Monograph Series, 1935, pp. 221 ff.

indicate that Halliwell-Phillipps's judgment was sound. Among others, the preceding study of Malvolio's background points toward the provinces. And this is but one of many leads which emphasize the probability, now generally recognized by students of Elizabethan drama,[5] that further exploration of its provincial roots and byways should yield fresh, and perhaps important, information. In the pages that follow the reader will find a working sketch of various colorful activities of the Elizabethan strolling players and of some of their successors. Here I am concerned, rather, with a single *play* which affords tangible clues for inquiry — local names and allusions such as those to Peter Turph and Henry Pimpernell. Specifically, our subject for study is a "country play" [6] of the Shakespeare Apocrypha — the pleasant comedy of *Faire Em*. This investigation, incidentally, will take us back to Lord Strange's Men (Shakespeare's company), and to Lord Strange's steward, in Lancashire — and so to Malvolio. But we must start by recalling the relatively familiar facts about our play.[7]

"Faire Em, the Millers daughter of Manchester: With the loue of William the Conqueror" was, according to the title page of the (undated) first quarto, "sundrie times publiquely acted in the honourable citie of London, by the right honourable the Lord Strange his seruants" — that is to say, by 1593, when Ferdinando Stanley, Lord Strange, became Earl of Derby, and the company under his patronage assumed the name "Derby's Men." (Shakespeare was a sharer in this company by 1594, and had presumably belonged to it some time before then.) A ballad entitled "The Millers daughter of Manchester" was entered in the Stationers' Register in March, 1581, but no entry for the play has been found. Greg has shown, however, that the first quarto can scarcely be

5. Cf. Tucker Brooke, "Desiderata in the Study of Shakespeare," PMLA, XLIV (1929), Supplement, xxxii.

6. See below, p. 145.

7. As set forth by Chambers, *Elizabethan Stage*, IV, 11, and in the editions by W. W. Greg (*Malone Society Reprints*, 1927), Tucker Brooke (*Shakespeare Apocrypha*), Warnke and Proescholdt, 1883, and Richard Simpson, *School of Shakspere*, 1878, vol. II.

later than 1593. It is virtually certain, indeed, that the play had been acted some years earlier, for Robert Greene had ridiculed two or three lines of it some time between 1589 and 1591, in his Preface to *Farewell to Folly*.[8] On this and other grounds Sir E. K. Chambers dates the play "*c.* 1590," whereas Dr. Greg makes it "between 1589 and 1591," without excluding the possibility that it may have been even earlier.[9]

The most plausible conjecture thus far made as to the authorship of the play is that by Fleay,[10] who ascribed it to Robert Wilson. Charles II's bookbinder, however, had bound it together with *The Merry Devil of Edmonton* and *Mucedorus*, and labelled the miscellany "Shakespeare, vol. 1." Latterday discussion of *Faire Em*, therefore, has centered about two more or less related questions: first, what part did Shakespeare have in the play; second, what is the nature and extent of the "symbolical meaning"—the allegorical-satirical import of the piece—supposed by Simpson and Fleay to have led to Greene's attack upon it? The consensus of critical opinion, has, in effect, supplied simple and definite answers to these questions. To the first it replies, "none at all," [11] despite the devoted but perverse pro-Shakespearean enthusiasm of Simpson and others; to the second, "slight or indeterminate"— witness the mutually destructive allegorical elaborations of Simpson and Fleay.[12] These matters concern us primarily because both

8. Entered in 1587; earliest extant edition, 1591 (cf. Greg, and Simpson, II, 378 ff.).

9. Greg observes that if the piece literally appeared in the 'Citie' "it must have been in 1589 or earlier."—The date, as will appear below, is important in connection with Lancashire's claims upon *Faire Em*.

10. *Life of Shakespeare* (London, 1886), p. 13. For discussion, cf. Chambers and Greg.

11. Here I may note that Fleay, while rejecting Shakespeare's claims to the authorship of *Faire Em*, made one concession to the opposition. "Although I cannot detect Shakespeare's hand as . . . probable author . . . he most likely appeared as an actor" (*Life of Shakespeare*, p. 13). It must be said that, so far as dates are concerned, Fleay's guess is not impossible, especially if we may assume with Murray (*English Dramatic Companies*, I, 73-75) that Shakespeare had joined Strange's Men by 1588. But, while Mr. Fleay was about it, why did he not guess a bit further? *If* Shakespeare acted in *Faire Em, what part* did he play? Most likely, of course (since he liked "kingly parts" with not much acting to do) that of William the Conqueror! (See below, p. 144.) One recalls certain anecdotes about that gentleman and Richard the Third.

12. See below, p. 146.

Simpson and Fleay touched upon certain facts connected with our inquiry as to the status of *Faire Em* as a country play. Unfortunately these writers were so enthusiastic in the pursuit of their allegorical will o' the wisp that they ended by obscuring the facts, with the result, I think, that later writers have discarded some of these facts along with the fancies.

The basic fact, from our point of view, is that *Faire Em* at the outset and again at the end pays tribute to one Sir Edmund Trafford, a mighty man in Lancashire, as we shall see, at the time the play was written, and the head of a family dating back to the time of Canute. Immediately after the opening scene Sir Thomas Goddard introduces himself and Em, his daughter, to the audience. He has disguised himself as a miller to escape the wrath of the Norman conqueror:

> Sir Thomas *Godard* now old *Goddard* is
> Goddard the miller of faire Manchester.
> Why should not I content me with this state
> As good Sir Edmund *Trofferd* did the flaile? [13]
> And thou, sweete *Em* . . .
> To ioyne with mine that thus we may protect
> Our harmless liues? [14]

At the end, when William the Conqueror has somewhat reluctantly agreed to take the Princess of Denmark for himself, and to let the faithful Valingford have fair Em, he turns graciously to her father and makes almost unmistakable the compliment to the Trafford clan (not to add, to "fair Manchester," which had meanwhile been mentioned many times over again in the course of the play):

> Sir *Thomas Goddard* welcome to thy Prince
> And faire *Em*, frolike with thy good father.
> As glad am I to finde Sir *Thomas Goddard*
> As good Sir *Edmund Treford* on the plaines:
> He like a sheepheard, and thou a countrie Miller. [15]

13. See below, p. 145, n. 20.          14. L. 98, Greg's ed.; Brooke, p. 288.
15. Greg, l. 1526; Brooke, p. 306.

That the import of these lines was not lost upon Simpson appears from his suggestion that *Faire Em*, "written perhaps in 1587 . . . was meant for a country play, written for Lord Strange's Men to act in Lancashire and Cheshire. The references to the 'good Sir Edmond Trafford' would be hardly intelligible elsewhere." [16] Simpson, however, seems scarcely to have been aware of the fact (with which I deal below) that Lord Strange's Men, of all companies, had particular reasons for paying their respects to Sir Edmund. Fleay also noticed the allusion to Trafford, but (because he dearly loved to solve a mystery even if he had first to create it) could not resist the temptation to drag the knight into his allegorical scheme of the play. "Sir Thomas Goddard," he writes, "is a thin disguise for Sir Edmund Trafford." [17] Personally I see neither disguise nor allegory here.[18] That part of the plot which concerns the "loves" of Em, the Miller's daughter, is based upon the fact that her noble father played the miller to protect himself against the invader. Now this, according to an ancient Lancashire tradition [19] — which was probably exploited in the ballad concerning the miller's daughter and must have been familiar to any Lancashire audience — is about what Ralph or Randulphus Trafford, Sir Edmund's ancestor, is supposed to have done in Norman times. Hence, according to Baines, the historian of Lancashire (who does not mention *Faire Em* at all), "the peculiar crest" — mentioned in my quotation from the play [20] — of the Trafford family, "a labouring man with a *flail* . . . threshing. This crest," [21] however, "was not granted until about the middle of the sixteenth century" [22] — that is to say, to *our* Sir Edmund himself, or to his father.[23] The lines in the play, then, would ap-

16. II, 372; cf. *New Shakspere Society Transactions*, 1875, p. 176.

17. *English Drama* (London, 1891), II, 282 ff.

18. The name "Goodiard" appears in a Manchester tax-list of 1606 (Chetham Society *Miscellanies*, III, 27).

19. Simpson and Fleay touch upon it, somewhat inaccurately.

20. See p. 144, n. 13, above.         21. Baines prints a picture of it.

22. E. Baines, *History of Lancaster* (London, 1836), III, 235; cf. G. Ormerod, *History of Chester* (London, 1819), I, 588 n.

23. For their dates, see below, pp. 147-148.

pear to be an undisguised compliment to the Elizabethan Traffords. Fleay, meanwhile, does point in the right direction by
reminding us that Em's "fair" Manchester "was in Lancashire,
where L. Strange's chief seat at Knowsley was also situate." At
this point, however, both Fleay and Simpson leave solid ground
and take flight—to explore the "symbolical meaning" of the play.
As Simpson has it, the plot refers

> to events in the history of the stage. William the Conqueror is
> William Kempe . . .[24] the Princess Blanch . . . is . . . the
> Danish stage . . . Mounteney and Valingford are two of his
> company . . . who contend for the prize of the Manchester
> stage,[25]

or, according to Fleay, fair Em herself

> is L. Strange's company,[26] who is married to Peele . . . Greene
> [is] satirized as Manville, Marlowe [as] Mounteney, Peele
> [as] Vallingford.[27]

Manchester and Lancashire, Sir Edmund Trafford and Lord
Strange, are of course, totally submerged in these misty speculations; and it is small wonder that little more is heard about them
in later accounts of the play.[28] For various reasons, I wish to
plead their case further. I hope to be able to establish, in the
order indicated (1) the fact that when *Faire Em* was acted Sir
Edmund Trafford was—in Lancashire at least—a more important
personage than students of the play have realized; (2) that, at
the time of the play also, he was a close official associate and friend
of the Stanleys, Lord Strange and his father, Henry, Earl of

24. Who led a company to Denmark in 1586.
25. *School of Shakspere*, II, 373 ff.
26. In his *Shakespeare Manual* (London, 1876, p. 281) Fleay had written: "Fair Em is
the company of the Queen's Players."
27. *English Drama*, II, 282.
28. A. F. Hopkinson (*Fair Em*, 1895, p. 2) dismisses Lancashire's claims upon the
play; Chambers, Greg, Brooke and others remain silent on the point.

Derby; (3) the probability that Lord Strange's Men were among the many players who certainly came at that time to the various Lancashire houses of the Stanleys to entertain them and their guests, including frequently, Sir Edmund Trafford and his son; and, consequently, the probability that the Trafford allusion was a straightforward compliment, in a Lancashire play, to a distinguished friend of the players' patron.

*Faire Em's* Sir Edmund Trafford, soldier, magistrate,[29] sheriff of Lancaster,[30] ecclesiastical commissioner,[31] and head of the ancient family of the Traffords of Trafford in the parish of Manchester, was born in 1526, and died in Manchester, in May, 1590 [32] —a date which (if my subsequent considerations are valid) checks properly other calculations as to the date of the play,[33] though this fact, like most of the present data concerning him, has escaped the editors of the play.[34] "Sir Edmonde Trafford, miles," is listed as one of three Lancashire knights and gentlemen who, in 1588, contributed the large sum of £100 each (five others giving £50, and fifty-nine £25 each) to the nation's emergency fund, when the Armada threatened. He was for many years one of the Earl of Derby's most active deputies in raising the Lancashire levies for service in Ireland, and, like his son, who commanded the Lancashire troops there in 1584, he had doubtless seen active

29. Baines, I, 231, etc.

30. In 1581 (*Cal. State Papers Dom., Eliz.*, 1581-1590, p. 220; F. Peck, *Desiderata Curiosa*, 1779, I, 120). Peck, and Baines (I, 237) incorrectly make him sheriff of Chester. He is also reported—upon doubtful evidence—to have been "warden of Manchester College" (S. Hibbert-Ware, *History of the Foundations of Christ's College*, Manchester, 1828, I, 115).

31. See below, p. 149, n. 42.

32. See the Trafford pedigree in Baines, III, 238. Trafford Park, Manchester, bears the old family name to this day.

33. See above, p. 143, n. 9, and below, on the date of his visits at Knowsley, p. 151, n. 53.

34. Except for the point referred to in n. 19 above, Simpson's statement that he was "high sheriff of Lancashire and . . . also custos of Manchester Castle," makes up the sum total of information supplied by them.

service.[35]  It is certain that like his father (d. 1564) and his son, Edmund Trafford, Esquire [36] (1561-1620), with whom he is sometimes confused, he was a wealthy and patriotic citizen, and an indefatigable official.  The Privy Council in London conferred trust upon him in matters of no slight consequence,[37] and at home the Earl of Derby named him, as early as 1578, first among his "very loving ffrends," the knights and squires of Lancashire's Salford Hundred.[38]  In short, he was evidently a man of vigorous, outstanding personality, and a power in the county.  Probably he had many friends besides the Earl of Derby; certainly he also made enemies, especially because of his uncompromising attitude in matters of religion.

Sir Edmund, to be more specific, was one of the official leaders in the long and bitter campaign against recusancy and Jesuit intrigue in the pro-Catholic northern counties — a campaign vigorously begun in the sixties, but still unfinished at the time of Trafford's death in 1590.[39]  It seems to have been at its height a decade earlier, before and after the events leading to the execution of Father Edmund Campion, in December, 1581.  This notorious affair had strong repercussions in Lancashire, where Father Campion — who is said to have described Sir Edmund Trafford as "a most bitter enemy of the Catholics" [40] — had preached shortly before his arrest.  But one or two aspects of the matter concern us here, and first of all the fact that Trafford's activities against the recusants brought him close, once more, to the Earl of Derby, and even closer, perhaps, to Lord Strange.

35. See *Names of the Nobility and Gentry*, 1798; Baines, I, 246 ff., 242; *Lancashire Lieutenancy*, Chetham Society *Remains*, L, 136.

36. Knighted by King James *in 1603*, (i.e., he was not *Sir* Edmund at the time of *Faire Em*), M. P. from 1588 to 1592, magistrate, and sheriff of Lancaster in 1602, 1609, and 1617 (*Lanc. Lieut'y.,*—see note above—XLIX, 2, 53; Baines, III, 238, etc.).  Cf. below, p. 149, n. 46.

37. See below, nn. 42, 43, and 46.

38. Chetham Society *Remains*, LXVII, p. cclxxxi.

39. *Crosby Records*, Chetham Society, 1887, pp. v, 90-91; Richard Simpson, *Life of Campion* (London, 1896), p. 190; Baines, I, 236 ff.

40. *Derby Household Books* (hereafter referred to as "*D. H. B.*"), ed. F. R. Raines, Chetham Society *Remains*, XXXI, 99; Baines, II, 104.  Cf. S. Hibbert-Ware *op. cit.*, I, 117.

The Privy Council held these two (as Lord and Deputy Lieutenant, respectively, of Lancashire and Cheshire) and William Chaderton, Bishop of Chester, primarily responsible for controlling recusancy in their district. Even so, a Privy Council letter of February 23, 1584, addressed to

> our verie good lords the earle of Derbie & the lord bishop of Chester, & to our verie lovinge frendes Sir John Biron [41] & *Sir Edmound Trafford*, knts. *& to the rest of the commissioners ecclesiasticall* in the countie of Lancaster . . .[42]

proves that Trafford was intimately associated with them in this onerous business. I believe that Derby for one—though the Council had praised him, together with Biron and Trafford "for their care and paines taken" in apprehending Campion's friends in 1581 [43]—may have thought these duties somewhat onerous. Apparently he was no fanatic. He did what he could, for instance, for his Catholic kinsmen, receiving in his house not a few of them [44] who were at one time or another imprisoned, with other recusants, in Manchester Castle, under the joint wardenship of Trafford and one Robert Worsley.[45] And there are other indications [46] that the Earl was less extreme in these matters than his son, Lord Strange, or Trafford. Lord Strange, if one may judge from certain letters of his written to Bishop Chaderton in 1583 and 1584, must have

41. Then Sheriff of Lancaster.

42. (My italics) Peck, *Desiderata Curiosa*, I, 145. A document signed by the Bishop, Lord Strange, Trafford, and the rest, in May, 1588, proves that they remained actively in control of the "ecclesiasticall commission" for a number of years (Hibbert-Ware I, 121-123).

43. Council letter, Aug. 30, 1581 (Dasent, *Acts of the P. C.*, New Ser., XIII, 184).

44. Sir Thomas Hesketh, Sir John Southworth, and others (*D. H. B.* p. 46, etc.; *Crosby Records*, p. 21, n.).

45. *Cal. St. P. Dom. Eliz.*, 1581-90, pp. 220, 46, 50, 54, 73. (On Worsley, cf. below, p. 150, n. 52.)

46. A curious document, a Privy Council letter of Aug. 31, 1581, "to th' Erle of Derbie" contains an "excuse" (which sounds slightly suspicious) "of yonge Traifford" (see above, p. 148, n. 36) "against whome it was thought that his Lordship *had conceaved some displeasure* for that he *first* delivered their Lordships letters unto Sir John Biron, knight, *and his father*, and *afterwards* sent th' other unto his Lordship"—the excuse being that the Council had thought the matter urgent and that "it was supposed" Derby "might happily be absent . . . huntinge" (*Acts of the P. C.*, 1581, pp. 183-84).

been an enthusiast after Trafford's own heart, for in them Lord Strange expresses his pleasure at the Privy Council's praise for his own part in the recent anti-Catholic proceedings, his zeal to "geve the first blow" in the striking down of "these rebellious minded papists," and his regret of the "backwardnes" of his father, apparently in connection with some matter concerning the ecclesiastical commission.[47]   In the main, however, Derby as well as Strange doubtless approved heartily of the Traffords, father and son.   Though the Earl was no zealot, he stood vigorously for the maintenance of royal authority — witness the report that in 1585 he personally boxed the ear of a recusant who in spiritual matters "acknowledged no authority on Elizabeth's part over him."[48] And the anti-Catholic activities of the Traffords, definitely traceable until 1590,[49] are matched, after all, by evidence of similar activity by Derby himself in the same year.[50]   At all events, and this point is important in connection with what follows, it is clear that both Sir Edmund and his son were on friendly and familiar terms with the Stanleys up to the time of the elder Trafford's death.   I quote below three entries from the *Derby Household Books*[51] which prove that Sir Edmund was repeatedly a household guest of the Earl's at Knowsley in 1587 and 1589:

   1. Entry for week ending July 29, 1587, at Knowsley, Lancashire.

"On Satturdaye Sᵣ Edmund Trayfforth & his Sone & yong Mᵣ Worseley[52] came, Sᵣ Ryc. Shirborne dep'ted home . . ."

   2. Week ending August 5, 1587, Knowsley.

"On Mondaye my L. Bushoppe of Chester & his wiffe & also Sᵣ Edmonde Traifforth did all dep'te away."

47. Peck, I, 142, 147, etc.
49. *Crosby Records*, pp. 90-91.
51. See above, p. 148, n. 40.

48. Baines, II, 97.
50. *D. H. B.*, p. 89.
52. See above, p. 149, n. 45.

3. Week ending July 27, 1589, Knowsley.

"Tuesday M$^r$ Lassels at dinner, S$^r$ Edmond Trafford came . . .
Wednesday S$^r$ Edmond wente . . ." [53]

What is more, a dozen other entries in the same diary, year in year out from 1586 through 1589, record visits at Knowsley, and at Lathom and New Parke, the other Stanley residences, by "yong M$^r$ Trafforth," [54] often in company with Lord Strange and his family.[55]

To sum up so far: we have seen that *Faire Em*, a play probably of the late eighties and certainly belonging to Lord Strange's Men,[56] pays a double compliment to Sir Edmund Trafford, an outstanding Lancashire man and an important official associate and friend of the players' patron. It does not seem likely that these circumstances are to be ascribed to mere coincidence. They suggest, rather, that the play [57] was written for performance, presumably somewhere in Lancashire, in the presence of the Stanleys and the Traffords. This intrinsic probability, I am frank to admit, is stronger than any external evidence I can bring to bear on the point. Indeed, I would be content to rest the case here but for the fact that one document, the *Derby Household Books* already referred to, contains a hint which should perhaps not be ignored since it *may* refer to Strange's Men—Shakespeare's company then or soon after—at the very time when its movements are most shadowy.

The most likely place for our hypothetical performance, I think, would have been Knowsley (or one of the other hospitable residences of the Stanleys) sometime between 1587 and 1590.

53. *D. H. B.*, pp. 35, 34, 63.
54. See above, p. 149, n. 46 and, below, p. 155.
55. *D. H. B.*, pp. 54, 19, 35-37, 56, etc.
56. The only company known to have been under the patronage of the Stanleys in the late eighties (cf. Chambers, II, 118 ff.; Murray, II, 39).
57. Or at least the passages concerning Trafford.

To be sure, a performance in Manchester itself,[58] perhaps at a civic festival of some sort, is not out of the question. Manchester, as we have seen, receives honorable mention in the subtitle and text of *Faire Em*.[59] The Traffords and Stanleys had residences and much official business there.[60] And the Stanleys were in close touch with city officials,[61] were sometimes elected to honorary civic office, and, on such occasions, gave and received sumptuous entertainment,[62] — this within a few years of the time when belated performances of the Chester plays, at least, were still officially given on the Mayor's order.[63] Strange's Men might conceivably have acted *Faire Em* on some such occasion, but evidence is absolutely lacking. As regards the case for a private performance, say at Knowsley, we know definitely at least two things: first, that Sir Edmund Trafford was certainly there between 1587 and 1590; next, thanks to Ffarington, the diarist of the Derby household, that the Stanleys during these years entertained their guests with plays by some of the leading dramatic companies.[64] It is also true, unfortunately, that among these companies Ffarington does not *name* Lord Strange's, but I think they were there for all that.

In this connection it is to be observed, first, that our diarist's entries are lamentably hard-clipped throughout, even where they are not altogether fragmentary.[65] I have already pointed out that he was an honorable man, an able lawyer, and a just magistrate. But, as Steward and Comptroller of the Derby household,

58. Cf. Gibbs, in Simpson, *School of Shakspere*, II, 467 ff.
59. See above, p. 144.        60. *D. H. B.*, pp. 29, 76.
61. "Dyvers Manchester men," "Mr Maire of Chester & some of his brethren," and "the Mayre of Lyverpolle" were among their guests at Knowsley and Lathom (*Id.*, pp. 29, 66, 81).
62. Lord Strange "was made alderman" of Chester in 1586, whereupon he "made a rich banquet" (see J. Hemingway, who also mentions a gorgeous civic reception to Leicester, Derby, and others, in 1583 — *History of Chester*, 1831, I, 152 ff.). Strange was Mayor of Liverpool in 1588 (*D. N. B.*).
63. In 1575 and 1577 "the mayor caused the popish plays of Chester . . . the Shepherds' play . . . and other triumphs . . . to be played" (Hemingway, I, 152).
64. See below, p. 154.
65. Cf. *D. H. B.*, pp. vi, 66, 70, etc., and, on Ffarington's style and character in general, above, pp. 134-135.

he did not wear his "cheane" [66] of office lightly. It is clear, more-over, that he shared, wholeheartedly, Malvolio's dislike for cakes and ale.[67] He wanted no "vagrants" of any sort "kept aboute the house," [68] and was certainly no lover of plays and players.[69] He does not name a single one of the plays given in his domain. And, what is more to the purpose at this juncture, he had high pride of place,[70] and scorned to name in his diary *any servants of the house except the two or three gentlemanly functionaries at the top,* "M^r Receyver," "M^r Recorder," and such like.[71] Since, as I shall show, he does record various performances by a company whom he calls simply "the players," I think it is likely that he refused this company more dignified notice *because he looked upon its members as mere household servants* — of the "meaner sort," and a kind of vagrants to boot. In short, this was probably the company under the patronage of the house — Lord Strange's Men.

To give the entries in question their proper setting, I reproduce below, first, several excerpts from entries concerning other companies:

1. Week ending [72] July 8, 1587, Lathom, Lancashire.

---

66. Cf. *Twelfth Night, II*, iii, 122-128: "Art any more than a steward? . . . Go, sir, rub your chain with crumbs." See above p. 126, n. 26.

67. Witness the stringent "household rules" laid down in *D. H. B.*, pp. 20 ff. See above p. 136, n. 71.

68. *D. H. B.*, pp. 20 ff.

69. According to his editor, "comic humor" did not appeal to him, nor did he have "a particle of imagination or sentiment or romance about him" (see above, p. 129).

70. The rules by which he governed the 150 or more servants in his charge provide that the "meaner sort" be strictly kept in their place (see above, n. 67).

71. *D. H. B.*, pp. 23, 37, 19, 48.

72. Murray (II, 296 ff.) reprints in full, without comment, these and all other entries (including those I discuss below, see p. 155) concerning players at Knowsley, etc.; but errs slightly in dating them, in each case, as of the week "beginning" on the dates mentioned. (See entries of Saturday, Dec. 28, 1588 — "Wednesdaye *was* Christemas daie" — and of Saturday, Jan. 6, 1588 — "Monday being New Years daye" — *D. H. B.*, pp. 56, 46. These and others prove that the diarist's dates are always those of the *last* day of the week covered by his entry.) Murray thereby inadvertently conceals the fact that several of the plays by the unnamed company were given on such special occasions as New Year's and Twelfth Night, when the Derby family might naturally have called upon its own household company for entertainment (see below, p. 155, nn. 76, 78).

"On Thorsdaye M$^r$ Stanley dep'ted & the same daye my L. of Leycesters Plaiers plaied; on Fryday they plaied againe w$^{ch}$ day . . . came . . . also M$^r$ Rec. & on Satterday they dep'ted awaye, & M$^r$ Sorrocolde a Pretcher came."

2. Week ending July 12, 1589, Lathom.   (In the presence of "many . . . gent$^n$".)

"Sonday . . . the Vicker of Ratchedalle pretched, the same daie the Quenes Players plaied ii severall nyghtes."

3. Week ending Sept. 6, 1589, Knowsley.

"Saturdaie my L. . . . & all the rest came home; the Quenes Players came & played at nyght, my Lo. of Essex Players came."

4. Week ending Sept. 13, 1589, Knowsley.

"Sondaie M$^r$ Leigh preached & the Quenes Players played in the afternoone & my L. of Essex$^s$ at nyght; Mondaie my L. and all went away." [73]

All in all Ffarington records, in the period of slightly over two years actually touched by his entries, thirteen plays — by Leicester's Men, the Queen's, Essex's, and the unnamed company.   I suspect that a noble family so hungry for drama as to have a sermon in the morning and *"the same daie* the Quenes Players . . . ii severall *nyghtes"* (!) saw more plays than Ffarington allows; but no one can fill out the gaps in his record.   I must content myself, finally, with a comment or two upon those of his entries, reproduced below, which have to do with the unnamed company.

1. Week ending Dec. 30, 1587, Knowsley.   (The entries for this Christmas week, unfortunately, do not start until the twenty-

73.  *D. H. B.*, pp. 32, 62, 65.

seventh.  Derby had apparently spent Christmas at court, but not so Lord Strange, who had arrived at Knowsley before Dec. 16, with "svndry others," who went hunting with him on the twenty-first, and "all came agayne" the next day, presumably to keep Christmas with him in his father's absence.) [74]

> "On Frydaye my L. the Earle came home from the Cowrte & the same nighte . . . my L. Bushoppe . . . on Saturday S[r] Tho. Hesketh; *Players wente awaie.*" [75]

2. Week ending Jan. 4, 1589, Lathom.  (The preceding entry, of Dec. 28, 1588, once more provokingly meagre, tells us only that there were at least two sermons on Christmas Day and the day after.)

> "Sondaye M[r] Carter pretched . . . on Tvsedaye [Dec. 31, 1588] [76] . . . came . . . the reste of my L. Cownsill . . . *& at nyght a Playe was had in the Halle* & the same nyghte my L. Strandge came home." [77]

3. Week ending Jan. 11, 1589, Lathom (the next week; the play on Twelfth Night Eve — Jan. 5 — being acted, presumably, by the company which had given the New Year's play a few days earlier?)

> "Sondaye [Jan. 5] M[r] Caldewall pretched & *that nyght the Plaiers plaied;* Monday my L. Bushoppe pretched & . . . *M[r] Trafforth* . . . came . . . Wednesday my L. removed . . ." [78]

4. Week ending Feb. 21, 1590, Lathom (Lord Strange being again present, as indicated by notes about his dining *out* on certain days just before and after).[79]

---

74. *Id.*, p. 45.

75. *Id.*, p. 46.  (Italics — here and in the remaining entries — mine.)

76. See above, p. 153, n. 72.  77. *D. H. B.*, pp. 56-57.

78. *Id.* — Some time after the completion of this study, I find that Professor Abel Lefranc (*Sous le Masque*, I, 119-120; see above, p. 120, n. 5) had — independently and on other grounds — identified these "Plaiers" with the Derby family's household company.

79. *D. H. B.*, pp. 74-76.

"This Saturdaie my L. came home, M[r] floxe came & a servant of the B. of Canterbury, *Players played at nyght.*" [80]

My extracts show, for one thing, that Lord Strange was present at all the performances by the unnamed company. It is possible, of course, that the company was not his, or that several different companies instead of one are referred to. Yet it is also noteworthy that all but one of these performances came during the Christmas holiday season, exactly when the Stanleys would, presumably, have been most likely to see plays by their own company. That Ffarington failed to give them a name is vexing, but his laconic notes on the comings and goings of "the players," if he *is* referring to the household company, are not uncharacteristic of a diarist who on one important family occasion could content himself with an entry to the effect that "on Monday the mydwiffe came." [81] In any case, it is all but impossible to believe that Strange's Men, who certainly appeared both at London and in the provinces between 1587 and 1589,[82] would have remained away altogether from Knowsley or Lathom during these years, while all the other companies went there. And, despite Ffarington's inhospitable reticence, Sir Edmund Trafford's prominent place in Lancashire, in the concerns of the Stanleys, and in *Faire Em*, surely stamps that piece a "country play."

80. *Id.*, p. 75.
81. See above, p. 135.
82. Murray (I, 108, 89; II, 221) and Chambers (II, 119; IV, 305 ff.) trace them at Cambridge and Coventry between 1587 and 1589, and at London in November, 1589.

# VIII

## TRAVELLING PLAYERS IN SHAKESPEARE'S ENGLAND [1]

**H**OW CHANCES it they travel?" inquires Hamlet, when "the tragedians of the city" are announced. "Their *residence*, both in reputation and profit, was better both ways." [2] Shakespeare's testimony as to the inferior rewards open to the players "on the road" has had many an echo since, for then as now the reputation and profit of the great metropolitan centers of dramatic activity—the Bankside and the Blackfriars, Broadway and the Strand—have been the goal of "the quality" and the subject matter of students of dramatic history. And yet the humbler Elizabethan actors who travelled "softly on the hoof" [3] through the length and breadth of merry England contributed no small share to the making of the national drama which remains one of the glories of their spacious times.

Many an interesting record has come down to us of the good-humored but irresponsible strolling players who were content to

> travel with pumps full of gravel
> Made of all such running leather
> That once in a week new masters we seeke
> And never can hold together. [4]

It is more important to bear in mind that many of the great tragedians of the city trod the boards in country towns frequently and profitably. Among them were such distinguished actors as

---

1. Revised from *Modern Philology*, XVII (1920), 489 ff.
2. *Hamlet*, II, 2, 352.
3. *Vox Graculi*; see J. P. Collier, *Annals of the Stage*, ed. 1831, III, 310.
4. *Histrio-Mastix* (1599), II, 251.

Henslowe's son-in-law, Edward Alleyn, and his colleagues, Singer and Towne,[5] and Shakespeare's friends and fellow actors, Thomas Pope, Augustine Phillips, William Kemp, and John Hemings, business manager of the Shakespeare-Burbage forces.[6] And there is every reason to believe that Shakespeare played with his company in the provinces, even though his name has not yet been found in the town records. Singer and Kemp, whose names do appear, tried their hand as playwrights as well as in acting. I have shown elsewhere [7] that a very large number of Elizabethan playwrights — Ben Jonson, Heywood, Nathaniel Field, Richard Brome, to mention only a few of the leading names — were recruited from the ranks of the actors. These actor-playwrights profited magnificently by their opportunity of viewing the life of their time in the large, of examining with equally open eyes the hucksters of Bartholomew Fair and the rustic philosophers of Stratford and Gloucestershire.

And yet many of the curiously interesting circumstances and conditions of the provincial drama have been neglected or ignored by earlier students of the period. Miss Gildersleeve, for example, failed to include in her "hierarchy of dramatic rulers" — the Privy Council, the Lord Chamberlain, and the King [8] — an almost equally important element: "Mr. Mayor" and the town councils. Many useful compilations of the dramatic records of various towns and localities have been produced, but nothing approaching a synthetic study of the extant materials has yet appeared. Meanwhile Professor John T. Murray's compilation of materials in the second volume of his *English Dramatic Companies* (1910), and his earlier article [9] on some of these materials are still the basic sources of information in this field. Mr. Murray's article, however, was written before he had completed his investigation, and its conclusions were necessarily, as he says, "more or less tentative."

5. *Henslowe's Diary*, ed. Greg, I, 4 and 6.
6. Halliwell-Phillipps, *Illustrations*, 1852, p. 33.
7. In *Shakspere to Sheridan* (Cambridge, 1922), p. 27.
8. *Government Regulation of the Elizabethan Drama* (New York, 1908), p. 19.
9. See *Modern Philology*, II (1905), 539-59.

His later collections and additional materials which I have gathered from other sources make available much information not hitherto accessible to the general student. It is my purpose here to present in short compass some of the conclusions derivable from these materials.

We may begin with a glance at the strollers and vagabonds of Elizabethan drama. These players were frequently made the butt of contemporary jibes, and it appears that they paced the open road humbly enough. One of the earliest extant records of them, an entry from the exchequer accounts of Henry VII, suggests something of their low estate. In the year 1493 the King gave largesse of 6s. 8d. "to the players that begged by the way." [10] Nor did the strollers of the next century fare much better, if we may believe Thomas Dekker. The poet of *The Gentle Craft* did not always deal gently with the misfortunes of his fellows, and yet his picture of their indigent condition makes good contemporary evidence. In his *Belman of London* (1608), Dekker takes a fling at certain "Players . . . who, out of an ambition to weare the Best Ierkin (in a Strowling Company) or to Act Great Parts forsake the stately Cittie Stages to trauel upon ye hard hoofe from village to village for chees and buttermilke." [11] Again, in his *Newes from Hell* (1606), he transcribes a leaf from Charon's account book: "Item, lent to a Companie of country players, being nine in number, one sharer & the rest Iorneymen that with strowling were brought to deaths door, XIIId. ob., upon their stocke of apparell, to pay for their boat hire, because they would trie if they could be suffred to play in the diuels name." [12] The last phrase of the passage obviously refers to the Statute of 1572, by which unlicensed players were threatened with branding as "rogues, vagabonds and sturdy beggars." [13] It is interesting to note further that Dekker's nondescript company of nine, "one

10. Malone's *Shakspeare*, ed. Boswell, III, 43.
11. Grosart's *Dekker*, III, 81.     12. *Id.*, II, 146.
13. Gildersleeve, *op. cit.*, p. 27; A. H. Thorndike, *Shakespeare's Theater* (New York, 1916), p. 204.

sharer & the rest Iorneymen," is paralleled by other evidence, later and more specific. Richard Bradshawe, one-time servant of Gabriel Spencer, the actor who enjoyed the distinction of being killed by Ben Jonson,[14] forsook the city stages sometime before 1633. In that year his company of seven was arrested at Banbury because its license was believed to be fraudulent, and all its members testify that Bradshawe alone was "master," the rest being apprenticed to serve him for seven years for "nothing but meat and drink." [15] And yet even the more soundly constituted companies — organizations that boasted full complements of "sharers" [16] — were sometimes in almost as heavy case as Dekker's hopeless crew. Pembroke's Men, for example, travelled happily into the provinces in 1593, only to be stranded on the road and forced to pawn their properties.[17]

The passage from *Histrio-Mastix* quoted above points at one of the difficulties experienced by the strollers — that of "holding together." Even the best of the London companies — Shakespeare's among them — had to use elaborate safeguards to keep their members from seeking all too frequent changes of scene.[18] The road companies, having fewer advantages to offer, must have found this problem much more difficult to solve, and their managers were frequently embarrassed by the tardiness or disappearance of actors entrusted with important parts. The lateness of Bottom the Weaver, and the non-appearance of one of the important actors in the play of *Sir Thomas More* [19] probably had many a counterpart on provincial stages.

Nor were the absent members always to blame, for sometimes their non-appearance was brought about by causes beyond their control. The strollers, even if they avoided the letter of the statute against masterless men, were ready victims for the recruiting offi-

14. *Henslowe's Diary*, II, 243, 313.          15. Murray, *E. D. C.*, II, 163.
16. I.e., actors who had graduated from the "hireling" or apprentice stage and had become investors in the capital of their company and sharers in its profits.
17. Collier, *Memoirs of Edward Alleyn* (London, 1841), p. 32; Murray, *E. D. C.*, I, 65.
18. Compare Thaler, *Shakspere to Sheridan*, p. 28.
19. *Midsummer-Night's Dream*, IV, 2; *Sir Thomas More*, IV, 1.

cer's press gang. "Press money!" exclaims a sadly surprised player in *Histrio-Mastix*, "alas, sir, press me? I am no fit actor for the action!" But the recruiting officer is not to be denied. "Text-bills," he insists, "must now be turned to iron-bills." [20] The licenses of the great London companies specifically protected them from interference of this sort,[21] but their humbler brethren had no recourse except to suit the word even to this sort of action. Again, the strollers were subject to retributive justice — or malice — dispensed by petty local functionaries whose officiousness they delighted to ridicule in their plays. Justice Clack, in Brome's *Jovial Crew* (1641), cools his wrath at the players and illustrates our point. "They can act Justices, can they?" he suggests; "I'll act a Justice among 'em: that is to say, I will do justice upon them." [22]

In fairness to Justice Clack and his kind we are obliged to add that certain elements among the strollers were a sore burden to the constituted authorities. Beggary was not the sole offense of the strollers. The actors in *Histrio-Mastix* describe a rival company as an aggregation of "coney catchers that cousen mayors," [23] and the merry crew of "comedians, tragi-comedians, comi-tragedians, pastorists, humorists, satirists," who hold forth in Middleton's *Mayor of Queenborough* (*ca.* 1602), meet the description to a nicety. They throw flour into Mr. Mayor's eyes and, having stolen his purse, leave His Honor to derive such comfort as he can from his clerk's explanation: "You are cozened, Sir; they are all professed cheaters. . . . They only take the name of country comedians to abuse simple people with a printed play or two which they bought at Canterbury for sixpence." [24] Similar exploits enacted by other "roguish players" might be recounted,[25] but we must leave the strollers here to look into the affairs of the companies that had more reputation and profit to lose.

20. Act V.  21. See Thaler, *op. cit.*, pp. 169-170.
22. V, 1.  23. Act V.
24. V, 1. Cf. Percy Simpson, *Shakespeare's England* (Oxford, 1917), II, 240.
25. See T. S. Graves, *Modern Philology*, IX, 431, on the famous *England's Joy* episode at the Swan Theatre in 1602, and compare p. 177, below, on a similar exploit ascribed to Peele.

We have seen that the names of some of the most distinguished Elizabethan actors appear in the provincial records. It is safe to add that without the resource of going into the country when acting in London was unprofitable or impossible, even the best of the city companies could hardly have survived. The conditions which periodically forced the players to travel are well known, and a rapid summary will suffice to recall them to the reader. The ravages of the plague again and again led to an inhibition of acting in the metropolis, and brought about a steady exodus of actors, sometimes for periods of many months in successive years.[26] The closing of part or all of the London theatres at times when the Puritan opposition was able to dominate the situation led to the same result, as did also the very frequent occurrence of theatre fires in London.[27] Another driving force was the keen competition among the companies in London — such competition, for example, as that between the children's companies and the adult actors to which Shakespeare alludes in *Hamlet*.[28] More important, perhaps, was the sharp rivalry for public favor among the adult companies themselves.[29]

Nor was competition eliminated when the players left the city. Managers anxious to steal a march upon their rivals were none too scrupulous in their methods. Certain playwrights also — Robert Greene and perhaps Thomas Dekker among them, if contemporary allusions may be trusted — were sometimes guilty of sharp practice. A familiar passage from *The Defense of Conny Catching* (1592) would seem to indicate that on one occasion Greene profited by the synchronous absence of copyright protection and of a certain company with which he had had business relations:

> Ask the Queens Players if you solde them not *Orlando Furioso* for twenty Nobles and when they were in the country sold the same play to the Lord Admirals men for as much more? Was not this plaine Connycatching, Maister R. G.?[30]

26. See Murray, *E. D. C.*, I, 155, etc.
27. Fires at the Globe, the Fortune, the Rose, and the Blackfriars are recorded.
28. II, 2, 361.          29. See *Shakspere to Sheridan*, pp. 22 ff.
30. See Grosart's *Greene*, XI, 75.

Somewhat later the Admiral's Men may have been concerned in a similar transaction, in which Thomas Dekker and Shakespeare's company also appear as principals. On January 30, 1599, Henslowe significantly records a loan of 3l. 10s. to the Admiral's Men "to descarge Thomas dickers from the a reaste of my lord chamberlens men." [31]

A more serious abuse than the stealing of plays, however, was the stealing or forging of licenses. A notable dispute at Leicester in 1583, between Worcester's Men and those of Edmund Tilney, Master of the Revels, may serve as a case in point. Tilney's Men reached the mayor first, and were permitted to play. The other company received a gratuity of 10s., and orders to leave the town. Thereupon they marched "with drum & Trumppytts thorowe the Towne in contempt of Mr. Mayor," and then calmly put on their play, Mr. Mayor to the contrary notwithstanding. By way of excuse for their action Worcester's Men urged that their rivals "were not lawfully aucthoryzed & that they had taken from them there comyssion." Tilney's company categorically denied the charge, but the Mayor settled the controversy by accepting the apology of Worcester's Men and authorizing them to stay on.[32] Whatever the merits of this particular case may have been, it is clear that many similar irregularities occurred. Their causes are not far to seek. After 1581 each and every company was required by law to obtain a license from the Master of the Revels, and that official made heavy demands upon the financial resources of the players, his fees being limited only by his judgment of what the market would bear.[33] Bartholomew Jones, one of the witnesses in the Bradshawe case at Danbury in 1633, testifies that "the Master of the Revels will give allowance to the raising [of the license] if he be paid," [34] so that the trouble there seems to have resulted only from the manager's inability to pay the five or ten pounds which

31. *Henslowe's Diary*, I, 101.
32. William Kelly, *Notices of the Drama at Leicester*, 1865, p. 213.
33. See *Shakspere to Sheridan*, pp. 198 ff.
34. Murray, *E. D. C.*, II, 164; Collier, *Annals*, II, 48-49. "Raising" means "renewal."

were probably required.[35] By 1633, however, licenses were not to be had freely, even though the applicants were able to pay. In that year witnesses stated that the Bradshawe license had been sold in turn to at least three different managers, and that Bradshawe "gave 20s. in earnest for this commission, and was to pay either 10l. or 20l." [36] It must be remembered that in order to gain legal standing, a company besides paying its license fee had to find some nobleman willing to lend it his name or "countenance." Minor companies doubtless experienced difficulty in finding such patrons. At all events, more or less illegitimate trading in players' licenses had come to be a considerable annoyance to the authorities at least ten years before the Bradshawe case, for in 1622 we find Pembroke, the Lord Chamberlain, writing to provincial officials to forbid transactions whereby irresponsible companies, for "whome such grants & lycences were nevr. intended . . . are suffered to have free passage." [37] The stealing of plays and licenses was symptomatic of the keen competition among the travelling players. Some allowance for the sharp practice then in vogue may well be made, however, in view of the fact that the players had not only to compete with rivals of their own "quality," but also with hordes of jugglers, exhibitors of puppet-shows, dancers, sleight-of-hand artists, and miscellaneous performers of all kinds. And there were other difficulties.

It was formerly believed that the Puritan opposition was not serious in the provinces,[38] but the contrary is true. The documents prove beyond a doubt that many towns made holiday when the players came, and supported them in something of the spirit that used to find expression in the receptions accorded to Chautauqua organizations in our own rural districts. But the documents prove

35. If we may judge from the rates charged the city companies. The sum in question (between $200 and $400 in our money, allowance being made for the greater purchasing power of Elizabethan money) was no small item for those days and circumstances.

36. Murray, *E. D. C.*, II, 165.

37. *Id.*, II, 351-52.

38. Murray (*Modern Philology*, II, 557) held this view, and took sharp exception to Courthope's position in this connection (*History of English Poetry*, IV, 391).

just as clearly that from about 1600 to the closing of the theatres in 1642 the Puritan opposition in the provinces as well as in London became increasingly troublesome. Indeed, certain notoriously puritanical towns had come to be bywords among the players even in the first decades of the seventeenth century. Banbury, the scene of Bradshawe's troubles, was so prominent an offender that Ben Jonson in *Bartholomew Fair* (1614) freely labels Zeal-of-the-Land Busy "a Banbury man." Later in the play, when the elder feels called upon to rehearse all the stock arguments against tolerance for the players, the poet scathingly enlarges upon Busy's "Banbury vapours." [39] The University of Cambridge, as early as 1592, protested to the Privy Council because certain players, in defiance of orders prohibiting their appearance within five miles of the University, "sett vp their bills" upon the very gates of the colleges.[40] In 1604 the Duke of Lenox wrote to "all maiors and Justices of the peas" to urge forbearance of opposition to his "servants . . . in the exercise of their plays," [41] but in that very year the town of Cambridge once more forbade all plays, in order to put a stop to the corruption of manners "in the younger sort." [42] Exeter in 1618 took similar action on the ground that "those who spend their money on plays are ordinarily very poor people," [43] and so did Norwich in 1623, "by reason of the want of worke for the poor & in respect of the contagion feared and for many other causes." [44] In short, it is clear that such towns as Exeter, Dover, Barnstaple, Canterbury, and Plymouth, which until about 1610 had supported visiting players with numerous grants from their town funds, practically closed their doors to them thereafter. In some cases, however, the towns were still willing to pay them

39. V, v, 26 (Herford and Simpson, *Jonson*, Oxford, 1938, VI, 12, 133).
40. *Malone Society Collections*, I, 2, 191-202. Both universities, of course, furnished dramatic entertainment from time to time to Elizabeth and her successors, but the authorities did not take kindly to the professional players until Restoration times. Cf. *Mal. Soc. Coll.*, I, 3, 247, and W. J. Lawrence, *Elizabethan Playhouse*, II, 192.
41. G. F. Warner, *Catalogue of Dulwich College MSS.*, 1881, p. 27.
42. Murray, *E. D. C.*, II, 220 ff.
43. Collier, I, 369; Murray, *E. D. C.*, II, 6, 253-54.
44. Murray, *E. D. C.*, II, 347.

gratuities "for putting them off," that is, "for not suffering them to play" [45]—in short, to speed them on their way elsewhere with a fee meant to express the town's respect for the patron who had lent his name to the players: "for their L. and Mr. his sake," as a Norwich entry has it.[46] Barnstaple between 1618 and 1637 allowed but two companies to play, whereas eleven companies were bought off "to ridd the Towne of them." Dover after 1610 made payment for but two town plays, though it records thirty-five gratuities "upon benevolence . . . to dept. the cittie & not to play," and Canterbury took much the same action.[47] Many towns remained open to the players until the close of our period, but the evidence here cited certainly indicates that in its later decades the Puritan opposition made the struggle for existence much severer for the travelling companies than it had been.

These were the decades also when they felt most strongly the competition of showmen not connected with the legitimate drama. In some of the town records the payments to the regular companies are almost entirely crowded out by rewards granted to manipulators of "Italian motions" or puppet-shows—the "movies" of Elizabethan times—and to miscellaneous tricksters and jugglers. The Coventry records for the years 1624 to 1642 are particularly illuminating in this connection. During these years the town allowed payment for many interesting entertainments on the occasion of the first appearance of the artists in question. Thus it granted 3s. 4d. to one Richard Thompson, "who had a commission to play the Worlds wonder," and 12s. to three performers "who had a motion to shew expressing the worlds abuses." Still better fared Christopher Thomson, who "came with Commission to shew the Creation of the world" and won an official reward of 13s. 4d. "Walter Neare that went about to show a child borne without armes," and "a soldier that tossed a Pike at the Crosse before Mr.

45. *Id.*, II, 270, 258.                              46. *Id.*, II, 25, 337.
47. *Id.*, II, 197-200, 258-67, 221-34.

Maior and his Bretheren," made a less favorable impression and got but 2s. 6d. and 18d., respectively. Other performers did better. "An Italian that thrust himself under the side to make experiment of his oyle," Bartholomew Cloys "for shewing a musical organ with divers strang and rare motions," and "one John Shepheard . . . who came wth. commission to shew a sow with 6 hoggs," drew five or six shillings each, whereas during the same years the town repeatedly paid but two or three shillings by way of reward for official first performances by regular dramatic companies. Between 1636 and 1642 Coventry made thirteen payments to tricksters such as the gentleman with the sow and hogs and divers other strange and rare motions, and but ten payments for legitimate plays.[48]

The actors, however, were quick to respond to the demands of their public, and soon began to appear with certain "special" or "added" attractions of their own. Thus "the Kings Players and hocus pocus" arrived in Coventry in 1638 (the year of Mr. Richard Thompson and the World's Wonder, and but one year before John Shepherd and his hogs) and the King's Men and their assisting artist led all the rest, for the town fathers gave them a reward of 20s.[49] Meanwhile the players "of the Earle of Essex & the Turk"—without question another redoubtable tumbler or juggler—had earned a fee of 40s. elsewhere.[50] From Marlowe to Shakespeare and Jonson, the playwrights rebelled at the low conceits which clownage keeps in pay—the antics of the clowns and buffoons which the astonishing elasticity of Elizabethan taste applauded and supported almost as liberally as it did its Tamberlaines, its Alchemists, and its Hamlets. It was left for Ben Jonson to express most clearly the playwrights' objection to the growing taste for jugglery and buffoonery which signalized the period of the decline. "Do they think this pen can juggle?" inquires Damn-

48. For the materials quoted see Murray, E. D. C., II, 235-54, and II, 340 for similar items at Norwich.

49. Murray, E. D. C., II, 253.        50. Id., I, 313.

Play in *The Magnetic Lady* (1632); "I would we had Hokos-pokos for 'em, then, or Travitanto Tudesco." [51]

The players learned to meet in still another way the difficulties created by the ever increasing competition for the favor of the public. We have seen what happened when Worcester's Men and Tilney's simultaneously claimed the plaudits and the shillings of the city of Worcester in 1583. Later companies realized that co-operation may at times be more profitable than competition and court proceedings. They hit upon the simple expedient of joining forces, doubtless with an eye to the advertising value of an arrangement which may have been forced upon them by sheer necessity. Such arrangements had, indeed, high precedent in their favor. Thus the two leading companies of London, the Admiral's Men and the Chamberlain's Men, are known to have played together before Queen Elizabeth in 1586.[52] From the records of Newcastle-on-Tyne we learn that its town fathers enjoyed a similar distinction not long after, for in 1593 they granted the sum of 30*s.* "to my Lord Admiralls plaiers and my Lord Morleis plaiers being all in one company." [53] So too when on March 20, 1616, trouble threatened between the advance agents of Queen Anne's Men and the representatives of "the Prince's servants," who came on the same day to book their companies with the authorities of Norwich, the matter was compromised, "and theise two companys" together were given "leave to play ffower days this next weke." [54] Other cases of this sort are on record, but sufficient evidence has been cited to establish our general point—that competition was keen, that the players had at times to face sharp rivalry from non-legitimate performers and strong opposition from the authorities, but that, on the whole, they learned to adapt themselves to new situations. It remains to examine the evidence concerning the expenses and the

51. I, I. Tudesco was a famous Italian juggler. For another allusion to Hokos-pokos, see *The Staple of News*, II, I.
52. Halliwell-Phillipps, *op. cit.*, p. 31.
53. See Richard Welford, 10 *Notes & Queries*, XII, 222.
54. Murray, *E. D. C.*, II, 340.

income of the provincial companies, their methods of financing their trips, and the manner of their reception by the towns they visited.

Since the provinces had no playhouses properly speaking, the travelling players were not required to find money for the building and upkeep of theatres, as were their London colleagues.[55] Like them, however, their sharers had to provide capital for the expenses of production—costuming, playwrights' fees, lighting, the wages of the inferior actors or "hirelings"—and for travelling expenses. We have already seen that in such humble organizations as that of Bradshawe the whole burden rested upon the single manager and owner, who likewise appropriated any profit that might be earned. *Henslowe's Diary* indicates clearly, however, that when the stronger companies went on tour their actor-sharers raised money toward the company equipment fund much as they sometimes did on preparing for a London season. On May 3, 1593, Henslowe notes that his nephew, Francis Henslowe, borrowed from him the sum of 15*l.* "for *his share* to the Quenes players when they broke & went into the contrey." [56] Two years later came a loan of 9*l.* "for *his halfe share* with the company wch. he dothe play wth.," [57] and still a third entry, probably of the year 1604, shows Henslowe lending his nephew 7*l.* to "goyn wth. owld Garland & symcockes & sauery when they played in the duckes nam at ther last goinge owt." [58] This entry does not necessarily indicate that only Garland, Simcock, and Savery were young Henslowe's fellow-sharers when the Duke's Men went on tour in 1604. We shall see in a moment that the stronger travelling companies averaged some six or eight full sharers. Since Francis Henslowe borrowed 15*l.* and 9*l.* for his "share" and "half-share" respectively, it would follow that the travelling companies of which he was a member started with a capital of 100 to 150*l.* or its equivalent in properties. From other sources it appears that a single share in

55. For a full discussion of London playhouse and company finance see chapters VI and IV, *Shakspere to Sheridan.*

56. *Diary*, I, 4.          57. *Id.*, I, 6.          58. *Id.*, I, 160; II, 267.

the stock of Worcester's Men, a travelling company in 1589, sold for 37*l.* 10*s.*[59] — in other words, that the total stock of that company may have been worth some 200*l.* Provincial playgoers in their own degree were as fond of gorgeous costume and expensive show as the gallants and groundlings of the metropolis.[60] Moreover, the cost of Elizabethan theatrical apparel was so high [61] that a capital of 100 to 200*l.* would have been none too much to provide the necessary equipment and to leave a working reserve for travelling expenses. "Our companie is greate," complain the Lord Chamberlain's Men in 1592, "and thearbie *our chardge intollerable in travellinge the countrie,* and the contynuance therof wilbe a meane to bring us to division and separation." [62]

Not the least difficult of the problems to be faced by the managers of the travelling companies must have been that of limiting expenses by keeping down the number of actors. Their plays required such large casts — Shakespeare's, for example, averaging twenty-five speaking parts — that it must have been difficult to draw the line between the conflicting demands of the stage and business managers. Murray puts the usual number of actors in a travelling company of any importance at about ten or eleven,[63] and this estimate will serve as well as any that could be reached. It may be worth while, however, to give some indication of the evidence on the subject. The earliest companies, naturally, were the smallest, unless we except the obscure strollers of later times. Thus we learn from the Household Book of Lord Howard, afterward Duke of Norfolk, that this nobleman "on Crystemas daye [1482] gaff *to IIII players* of my Lord Gloucestres" the sum of 3*s.* 4*d.*,[64] and the strollers who entertain More and Erasmus in *Sir Thomas*

59. Collier, *Memoirs of Edward Alleyn,* p. 4. Cf. *Henslowe's Diary,* II, 130.

60. See *Malone Soc. Coll.,* I, 247-59; J. C. Dibdin, *Annals of the Edinburgh Stage,* 1888, pp. 8-9; Collier, *Annals,* I, 9; Kelly, *Notices of the Drama at Leicester,* pp. 19, 24, 61. On silk robes used by travelling players, see quotation from Peele's *Jests,* below, p.177.

61. See *Shakspere to Sheridan,* pp. 253 ff.

62. Warner, *op. cit.,* p. 11; Murray, *E. D. C.,* I, 88; II, 127-28.

63. *Id.,* I, 88.          64. Kelly, *op. cit.,* p. 74.

*More* (*ca.* 1599) manage with "Foure men and a boy." [65] An equal economy of means is practiced by Sir Oliver Owlet's Men in *Histrio-Mastix.* Sir Oliver's Men number "but four or five" — whereby, as the poet Posthaste remarks, "they are the liker to thrive." [66]

Posthaste to the contrary notwithstanding, the town records prove that the more thriving companies had larger resources in man power, though the number of actors varies from town to town and from year to year. "My lorde Sussexe players, *being VI men,*" appeared at Ludlow in 1570,[67] and the travelling license of the Chamberlain's Men for 1593 enumerates seven performers, though the list is probably incomplete.[68] Worcester's Men at Norwich in 1583 had at least ten "Players & servants," and "the lady Elizabeth's Players" at Plymouth in 1618 employed the respectable number of "20 persons, wch. had the King's hand for playing as well by night as by day." [69] Other entries place the number of actors at 6, 8, 10, 13, 15, 16, and 18, respectively,[70] and the average lies between 10 and 12. We may add that the Lady Elizabeth's Company of twenty probably included six or eight hirelings, whose demands upon the company treasury would have been moderate even if they received something more than bread and meat by way of remuneration. Henslowe once more helps us here, for Edward Alleyn's transcript of one of his father-in-law's entries shows that in at least one case a hireling expressly agreed to accept, while playing in the country, one-half of his London wages of 10s. a week.[71]

Our materials make possible a somewhat more definite view of the income than of the expenses of the provincial companies. We shall see that in spite of the "intollerable chardge" they had to meet, when conditions were favorable their sharers had something

---

65. IV, 1, 53.     66. I, 1, 154.     67. Murray, *E. D. C.,* II, 324.
68. *Id.,* I, 88; Halliwell-Phillipps, *op. cit.,* p. 33.
69. Murray, *E. D. C.,* II, 336, 385.     70. *Id.,* II, 333, 103, 254-55.
71. Henslowe agreed to give William Kendall (Dec. 8, 1597) "everi week of his playing in london Xs, & in ye cuntrie Vs" (*Diary,* I, XLIX).

to look forward to besides the "chees and buttermilke" at which Dekker scornfully put their part in the gains.[72]

The evidence, in fact, proves conclusively that the players frequently enjoyed much more substantial cheer, and with it certainly more comfort than fell to the lot of Dekker in his all too frequent sojourns in the prisons of London. "Wine & chirries," "junkets & bankets," "dynner wth beere & bysketts" and "musyck" and much good "sacke"—such items appear with pleasing regularity in the expense accounts of the town fathers who provided the players with these sound refreshments at the public charge "to welcome them to towne" or to wish them God-speed with "a breakfaste at their depture."; all this perhaps after making additional provision for the purchase of certain "loads of coal" and "links for lights"—"to keep the actors warm"—and properly illuminated, one is tempted to add, in case the sack ran short.[73] The custom is worth something more than passing notice. These "junckets with Mr. Mair and his brotherne" [74] did not in themselves perhaps represent a large credit item on the books of the company business manager, but they speak eloquently of the hearty reception accorded the players in normal times. Possibly these feasts did not provide for more than an occasional change from Dekker's "chees and buttermilke," and yet they came often enough to win the notice of still another redoubtable commentator upon the life of the times. Ben Jonson has Cokes in *Bartholomew Fair* score a point for the puppets, the actors of the "Italian motions," over "the great players": "I like 'em for that . . . *there goes not so much charge to the feasting of them, or making them drunk,* as to the other, by reason of their littleness." [75]

The drinkings and banquetings, however, made but a part of

72. See above, p. 159.

73. See Dibdin, *op. cit.*, p. 9; Richard Welford, 10 *Notes & Queries*, XII, 222; G. T. Watts, *Theatrical Bristol*, 1915, p. 4; G. D. Rendel, *Newcastle-on-Tyne*, 1898, p. 10; and Murray, *E. D. C.*, II, 259, 380, 392, 362, 365, 324, 228-31, etc. Murray (*Modern Philology*, II, 548) notes that the towns "sometimes" paid for the players' ale or wine, but does not indicate that the practice was widespread and well established.

74. Murray, *E. D. C.*, II, 220.          75. V, 3.

the substantial advantages derived by the players from the public receptions given them by the towns they visited. Many years ago Malone called attention to the fact that the town fathers regularly attended the opening performance in state, and rewarded the actors from the public funds. The documents bearing on this point have been repeatedly discussed,[76] but they may be made to yield more information than has yet appeared. Malone's quotation from R. Willis' *Mount Tabor* (1659) deserves repetition here:

> In the city of Gloucester the manner is (as I think it is in other like corporations) that when players of enterludes come to towne, they first attend the Mayor, to enforme him what nobleman's servants they are, and so to get license to play their first play before himself and the Aldermen and Common Counsell of the city, *and that is called the Mayor's play: where everyone that will comes in without money, the Mayor giving the players a reward as he thinks fit to shew respect unto them.*[77]

The passage is indispensable — but not altogether trustworthy, nor does it tell the whole story. It may well be supplemented by an entry from the Leicester records of the year 1553, which indicates that Mr. Mayor and the aldermen did not always stand upon ceremony, but on at least one occasion were quite ready to honor the players at a moment's notice, even though they had to sacrifice an official dinner of good venison upon the altar of Thalia or Melpomene. In that year the Council made allowance "for the expences that went to the buck that my lady of Huntyngton gave to the XLVIII,[78] which was ordeyned at the hall for the Company & they cam not because of the play that was in the Church." [79]

It is well to bear in mind the advertising value of these public receptions and official first performances over and above the rewards in pounds, shillings, pence, and food. Indeed, a further

---

76. Cf. Murray, *Modern Philology*, II, 539-59.
77. Malone, *op. cit.*, III, 28.  78. I.e., the town council.
79. Kelly, *op. cit.*, p. 193.

word on theatrical advertising in the country may be in order
before we seek to estimate the earnings of the players from official
grants and popular "gatherings."

I have already referred to the custom of sending advance
agents to make the necessary arrangements, and to that of posting
bills to advertise plays.[80]  A more spectacular part of the Elizabethan publicity man's work was to arrange for circus processions
through the towns to announce the presence of the players.
Many a hireling in his time "led the drum before the English
tragedians" [81] in their travels through provincial England, sometimes against the wishes of the authorities.  We have seen that
in 1583 Worcester's Men went with drum and trumpet through
the town of Leicester in defiance of its mayor,[82] and there is
evidence of the same sort of high-handed procedure in Dover and
even in London itself.[83]  The advertising methods of the travelling
company in *Histrio-Mastix* are of particular interest because in
this case the instrumentalists of the company are not the only ones
called upon to trumpet forth the quality of its wares.  The players
have just arrived in the market-place of a small town, where a
crowd is gathered to bargain for country produce.  One of the
actors "steppes on the crosse and cryes 'A Play.' "  He then
illustrates our point and enables us to pass from the consideration
of advertising methods to the counting of the gains, as follows:

> All they that can sing and say
> Come to the Towne-house and see a play,
> At three o'clock it shall beginne—
> The finest play that ere was seene;
> Yet there is one thing more in my mind:
> *Take heed you leave not your purses behind.*[84]

80. See above, pp. 165, 168, and cf. W. J. Lawrence, *op. cit.*, II, 55.
81. *All's Well That Ends Well*, IV, 3, 300.  Maurice Jonas, *Shakespeare and the Stage*,
p. 233, states that this passage "puzzled" him, but its significance is obvious after all.
82. See above, p. 163.
83. Cf. Halliwell-Phillipps, *op. cit.*, pp. 31-32; Murray, *E. D. C.*, II, 342.
84. Act II.

The last line of this passage indicates that a first performance —a "town-play," as it is called in *Histrio-Mastix*—with all its official sanction and reward was not necessarily a performance "where everyone that will comes in without money," as the *Mount Tabor* passage has it. That it was sometimes free to the public appears from such records as those of Newcastle-on-Tyne for the year 1593, when the town granted 3*l.* to Sussex's Men "in full paymente . . . *for playing a free play.*" [85] On the other hand, Murray has properly called attention to several entries covering official payments at Leicester which distinctly state that these were "over and above that was gathered" from the public at the doors.[86] And there is other evidence to the same effect.[87] We shall try to determine in a moment just what amounts the players derived from these town fees and public gatherings. Meanwhile we must note that Murray's attempt to decide this point on the basis of the Leicester entries for 1590 leads to unacceptable conclusions. One of these entries reads as follows: "Received of John Underwood, the Mayor's Sergeant, which was by him received *of the Mayors Brethren* [88] for 6 plays and one Bear Baiting—44*s.*" From this and certain other entries Murray infers that such items as the 44*s.* represent *the public gathering* over and above the town fee, and he concludes that the average takings at the door "seem to have been about 7*s.*," while the official rewards "vary from 10*s.* to 40*s.*" [89] It is difficult to believe that the players could have managed with such small average takings as 7*s.*, for we must bear in mind that the extra town fee was paid only for the first performance. Moreover, a highly advertised first performance must have drawn at least as large a public gathering as any that might be expected at subsequent plays, so that if we are to accept Murray's interpretation of these entries it would follow that a 7*s.* house was the best the players might expect at any time. But

85. See Richard Welford, 10 *Notes & Queries*, XII, 222.
86. See *Modern Philology*, II, 547, and Kelly, *op. cit.*, pp. 194, 227.
87. Murray, *E. D. C.*, II, 202.     88. The italics are mine.
89. *Mod. Phil.*, II, 553-54.

this interpretation is not valid. Murray for the moment over-looked the Leicester ordinance of 1566, which provided that "everyone *of the Mayors brethren* and of the forty-eight, being required to be [at the town play] shall bear everyone of them his . . . portion." This ordinance was passed because "the town stock has been much decayed by giving of great gifts." [90] Later council orders reiterated the provision that the aldermen must raise the town reward from their own pockets, and other towns took the same action.[91] There can be no doubt that the entries Murray has mistaken for the totals of the public gatherings, repre-sent merely certain contributions of "the mayor's brethren" toward the town fee. The town officials had no interest in the public gatherings, and their records throw no light upon that part of the players' income.

A passage from *Ratseis Ghost* (1606), a pamphlet celebrating the adventures of the redoubtable Gamaliell Ratsey, highway-man, does contribute certain information on this subject. Ratsey, we are told, fell in one day with a travelling company — "heard their play and seemed to like that . . . and verie liberally . . . *gave them fortie shillings*, with which they held themselves richly satisfied, *for they scarce had twentie shilling audience* . . . for a play in the countrey." [92] Ratsey, to be sure, immediately after relieved the players of their 40s. and also forced them to make him "a desperate tender of their stock," yet it is comforting to reflect upon the margin of difference between their usual 20s. receipts and the seven of Murray's estimate. Indeed a gathering of 40s. was probably by no means beyond the ken of the players. One of the *Jests* of George Peele (1607) may serve for further testimony on this point. According to the story, Peele had stayed in Bristol "somewhat longer than his coin would last him," his hard-hearted landlord thereupon attaching the poet's horse for

90. Kelly, *op. cit.*, p. 95.
91. Bridgenorth did, for example. See Murray, *E. D. C.*, II, 206.
92. Halliwell-Phillipps, *op. cit.*, p. 85.

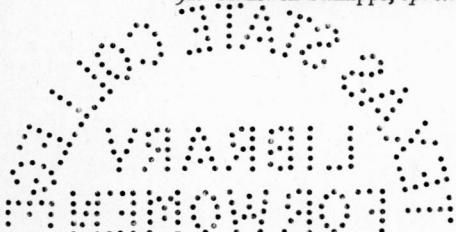

security. A fortunate turn of circumstance enabled Peele and his Pegasus to beat a strategic but very successful retreat:

> It so fortuned that certain players came to the town . . . to whom George Peele was well known, being in that time an excellent poet. . . . There were not past three of the company come . . . the rest were behind . . . so that night they could not enact, which George hearing had presently a stratagem in his head. . . . He goes directly to the Mayor, tells him he . . . had a certain history of *The Knight of the Rhodes*, desiring the mayor that he with his presence . . . would grace his labours. The mayor agreed to it . . . but for himself he could not be there being in the evening, but . . . very liberally gave him an angel. . . . About his business [Peele] goes . . . hired the players' apparel to flourish out his show, promising to pay them liberally, and withal desired them they would favor him so much as to gather him his money at the door. . . . George in the meantime, with the ten shillings he had of the Mayor, delivered his horse out of Purgatory. . . . By this time the audience were come *and some forty shillings gathered*, which money George put in his purse, and, putting on one of the players silk robes after the trumpet had sounded thrice . . . *down stairs goes he*, gets to his horse, and so with forty shillings to London: leaves the players to answer it.[93]

Even a gathering of 40s. was only about a quarter of the average takings at the London playhouses,[94] and the probabilities are that the travelling companies occasionally drew much more.[95] The records of Bristol, the scene of Peele's fabled exploit, prove, at any rate, that they sometimes succeeded very well indeed in their efforts to attract a full audience. In 1576 the town paid 5s. 1d. for repairing the guildhall door and replacing "the cramp of yren wch . . . was stretched wth. the press of people at the play

93. See A. H. Bullen's *Peele*, II, 389; Watts, *op. cit.*, pp. 10-11.
94. See my article on "Shakspere's Income," *Studies in Philology*, XV (1918), 89.
95. A play produced in Malden, Essex, brought total receipts of over 7l. in 1540 (A. Clark, 10 *Notes & Queries*, VII, 182). See also Murray, *E. D. C.*, II, 388, on average receipts of 2l. 16s. at St. Ives, Cornwall.

of my Lord Chamberleyns survts . . . before Mr. Mayor and thaldermen." [96] Again, though travelling charges may have been "intollerable," the cost of living was much lower in the country than in London. [97] We shall see presently, moreover, that the travelling players frequently doubled their earnings by giving two performances a day. And they had no playhouse charges to meet, for the town-hall, or sometimes the church, was to be had gratis. Queen Anne's warrant to her players in 1605 specifically commands all officers of towns and municipalities to "affourd them your Townehalls" or other suitable quarters for acting, "that they may be in better readiness for our service," [98] and the licenses of the King's and the Prince's Men call for the same privilege. [99] Some of the towns objected to the custom. Chester, for example, in 1615, took exception to "the common . . . scandall . . . of late incurred . . . by admittinge of Stage Plaiers to act their obscene and unlawful plays . . . in the comon hall of the Citie, thereby convertinge the same, beinge appointed . . . for the judicial hearinge . . . of criminal offenses, into a stage for players and receptacle for idle persons." [100] Southampton and Worcester likewise objected,[101] and Mayor Simon of Queenborough, whom we have met earlier in this study, was also of the opposition party. The players have asked his permission to give the usual official performance. "In the town-hall?" he queries; " 'tis ten to one I never grant them that. . . . If my house will not serve their turn I would fain see the proudest he lend them a barn." [102] Most of the towns, however, did not object at all. The communities which delighted to entertain the players with good ale and wine and substantial dinners felt no hardship in welcoming them to their town-halls. At worst, when the business of the town preëmpted

96. Watts, *op. cit.*, p. 8.
97. On comparative costs and wages see the extensive materials in John Nichols' *Progresses* (Elizabeth and James) and cf. Albert Feuillerat, *Revels Documents, Elizabeth*, p. 257; Murray, *E. D. C.*, II, 214.
98. Murray, *E. D. C.*, II, 400.
99. *Malone Soc. Coll.*, I, 268-69, 281.
100. Murray, *E. D. C.*, II, 235.
101. *Id.*, II, 395, 409.
102. *The Mayor of Queenborough*, V, 1.

its hall, most of them probably followed the example of Coventry and Leicester and allowed the players special grants to cover their expenditure in providing quarters elsewhere.[103]

Our summary of the evidence concerning the size of the public gatherings, and the non-chargeable item of playing facilities brings us back to the question of the receipts from official fees at first performances. The town treasurers scrupulously record the amounts they expended for this purpose, and we are not compelled to seek our information in out-of-the-way places, as in the case of the unofficial but really much more important item of public gatherings. We have seen that the gifts of the city of Leicester, about 1590, ranged from 10s. to 40s. Naturally, as one surveys the whole of the provincial accounts, a much larger variation appears. The lowest payments on record are two of 4d. each — the rewards of the town of Gloucester to Sir Andrew Fortescue's Players in 1560, and of Plymouth to Lord Mounteagle's Men in 1575.[104] Other small fees, of 11d., 2s., 3s. 4d., 5s., and 6s. 8d., are recorded,[105] but as a rule these payments either came comparatively early in our period or went to companies of small repute. The great majority of the town rewards ranged from 10s. to 2l.[106] At the other end of the scale we find such towns as Newcastle-on-Tyne, Plymouth, Norwich, Worcester, and Coventry, occasionally granting the large [107] fees of 3l., 3l. 6s., and even 4l.[108] One of the Bristol entries indicates that this town on one occasion allowed a

103. See Murray, E. D. C., II, 254, and Kelly, op. cit., p. 226. It is interesting to note that the town-hall of Leicester was used for the presentation of plays until 1722, when a statutory prohibition put an end to the custom (Kelly, p. 273).

104. Murray, E. D. C., II, 276-86, 383.

105. Id., II, 200-205, 196, 197, 220, 256, 273. Murray, who collected much of this material, doubted the authenticity of an entry for the payment of 3s. to Lord Willoughby's Men at Coventry in 1612. He believed this sum too "niggardly" to be accurate, but the weight of his own evidence throws this view absolutely out of court. See Murray, E. D. C., II, 75.

106. See the records of Dover, Bristol, Doncaster, Worcester, York, or any of the towns, in Murray's collections, E. D. C., II, and compare Kelly, Watts, and other collections of extracts from the town records.

107. See above, p. 164, n. 35.

108. Murray, E. D. C., II, 335, 358, 380, 412-13, 235.

definite amount for each actor in the company which entertained the council. In the year 1581 the treasurer paid Lord Oxford's Men "being i man and ix boys at ii*s*. a piece the sum of xx*s*.," [109] but this rather blind method of fixing the reward of artistic endeavor does not appear elsewhere in the records. Both Collier and Kelly believed that the town rewards to the players were minutely graded according to the rank and prestige of their patrons.[110] Murray qualifies this view by noting that the records show no particular differentiation between the payments to companies patronized by the greater and the lesser nobles, but he follows Kelly to the extent of holding that "those companies patronized by royalty and one or two of the more famous noblemen always received the greatest amount." [111] This was generally but not "always" the case. I find, for example, that the reward of the King's Men at Coventry in November, 1627, was but 2*s*. 6*d*., whereas the same town fifty-two years earlier had paid Warwick's Men, an organization of much less prestige, the sum of 30*s*.[112] Again, the accounts of Smithils, Lancashire, for 1612 record a payment of 50*s*. to Lord Mounteagle's Players, the same company which had drawn but 4*d*. from Plymouth some years earlier.[113] Smithils, further, paid Strafford's Men 40*s*. in 1612, and but 3*s*. 4*d*. when they returned five years later, and Doncaster, which had granted Leicester's Men 20*s*. for a performance in 1574, gave but 10*s*. to the King's Men in 1633.[114] As a rule the companies under the patronage of the royal family or the great nobles fared best, but the evidence indicates that many of the towns practiced a refreshing eclecticism in apportioning their rewards — that on occasion at least they paid most liberally the companies whose acting pleased them most, irrespective of their patrons. The evidence indicates also that town fees increased gradually in the course of our period, and that in the ordinary

109. *Id.*, II, 215.    110. Collier, *Annals*, I, 84; Kelly, *op. cit.*, pp. 226-27.
111. *Modern Philology*, II, 553.    112. Murray, *E. D. C.*, II, 235 ff.
113. *Id.*, II, 220.    114. *Id.*, II, 256.

course of events local prosperity or hard times were reflected in the rewards granted the players.

A word may be added concerning the gratuities often paid by the towns when for one reason or another they did not permit the players to "enact." [115] The amounts cover about the same range as the payments for official first performances. Thus "Lord Dakers his Players who did not playe" at Leicester in 1592 received 5s., "the King's Players who played not" drew 20s. there in 1621, and in the same year Queen Anne's Men were bought off with a gratuity of 30s. [116] The records of Leicester contain thirty-seven entries for the payment of similar gratuities, but the players were not always to be bought off. In 1585, for instance, Norwich refused Essex's Men permission to act "for fear of . . . infeccon," but "for their L. and Mr. his sake" allowed them a gratuity of 26s. 8d. The actors pocketed the money — and then calmly proceeded to play at the inn. The city fathers thereupon solemnly voted to withhold all future rewards from the culprits, only to prove a little later that they knew how to forgive and forget. Within four years the offending company received another reward of 20s. by order of the mayor. [117] Curiously enough, the gratuities paid "for sending them out of the city" were sometimes larger than the fees for the official performances. Barnstaple, for example, allowed the Prince's Men 40s. "for not playing" in 1621, and only 30s. for a town play the next year. [118] Certain of the poorer companies seem to have been quite content to pocket their gratuities and to go on their way rejoicing. The Norwich records of 1614 make mention of certain players who, "being demaunded wherefore their comeinge was, sayd they came not to ask leave to play But to aske the gratuetie of the Cytty." [119] Even substantial gratuities, however, could have offered but small compensation to the better companies for the loss of the takings of an extended

115. See above, p. 166.    116. Kelly, *op. cit.*, pp. 226, 255.
117. Murray, *E. D. C.*, II, 336-37.    119. *Id.*, II, 339.
118. *Id.*, II, 199. See also II, 341-42, etc., for gratuities of *2l., 3l. 6s.*, etc.

stay. Indeed the records show that several companies absolutely refused to accept the gratuities offered them. Instead, on the strength of their licenses they defied the authorities and "enacted." [120]

Another matter deserves attention here—the number of performances the companies gave on an average visit,[121] and this involves the question of evening performances. Murray noted that the players sometimes gave their entertainment in the evening, but he believed that "their usual time of performance was in the afternoon, as in London." [122] The weight of the evidence indicates, however, not only that evening performances were the rule rather than the exception, but that the companies often played twice a day. Pembroke's Men at Norwich, for example, in the the year 1598, got "lycens to use their facultie *two days and two nights* and not to use the same after nyne of the clock on either night." In 1610 this town allowed the Queen's Men to stay for one week on condition that they keep the Sabbath "nor [give] *more then one play a day.*" [123] Again, the Plymouth records for 1618 testify that the Lady Elizabeth's Men "had the King's hand for playing *as well by night as by day,*" [124] and Richard Heton's draft for his patent as governor of the Queen's Men in 1635 provides for the same privilege. Heton stipulates that his company when in the country shall be free to perform "at all tyme or tymes (the tyme of Divine Service only excepted) *before or after supper.* . . ." [125] Many of the towns objected strongly to the disturbances which frequently accompanied evening performances. "Consideringe . . . the many disorders which by reason of plaies acted in the night time doe oftentime happen"—more particularly the

---

120. *Id.,* II, 347, 356.

121. Murray (*Modern Philology,* II, 555) states that he was unable to determine "how long a company would remain in a town" and "how many performances it would give . . . as the town records deal almost exclusively with the single performance in which the . . . authorities were financially interested." His later documents, and others, answer the question.

122. *Id.,* II, 551.          123. Murray, *E. D. C.,* II, 337-39.          124. *Id.,* II, 385.

125. Peter Cunningham, *Shakespeare Society Papers,* IV, 99.

rioting of apprentices—the town of Chester in 1615 felt obliged to forbid acting after six o'clock at night.[126] It is interesting to note that Canterbury, which in 1636 complained that its citizens were unable to "restrain their servants from being at the plays till near Midnight," some sixty years earlier had gone so far as to allow certain companies extra money to pay for "candells & torches . . . at the play." [127] Such allowances were made from time to time also at Dover, Newcastle, and Bristol.[128] In short, it is clear that the custom of giving evening performances—or, in many cases, two a day—was very well established indeed.[129]

Some of our citations have touched not only upon the matter of double performances but also upon the length of the company's stay for any one visit. Considerable additional information on this point is available. We know, for example, that the companies occasionally played at great private houses for but one or two performances,[130] that the Norwich authorities in 1587 paid Leicester's Men 40s. on condition that "they play not above II times," and that the Queen's Men in 1600 successfully petitioned for leave to play there four days, whereas Huntington's Men and Hertford's were allowed three days each in the same town that year, the Lady Elizabeth's three days in 1617, and the Duke's Men eight days in 1614.[131] The 1618 patent of the Queen's Men authorized them to "play in any one place [not] above fourteen days together." [132] Twenty-three years earlier Canterbury had passed an ordinance which allowed but two performances to any one company, no company to visit the town more than once a month.[133] Restrictive measures of this sort sometimes caused trouble. When the Lady Elizabeth's Men came to Norwich in March, 1617, with the king's authority to play for fourteen days

126. Murray, *E. D. C.*, II, 235.
127. *Id.*, I, 275; II, 222, 227; cf. *Cal. State Papers*, 1636.
128. Murray, *E. D. C.*, II, 261, 335, 214.
129. Cf. T. S. Graves, *Studies in Philology*, XIV (1917), 103.
130. See above, pp. 154 ff., and cf. Murray, *E. D. C.*, II, 296.
131. *Id.*, II, 337-40, 344-45.      132. Collier, *Annals*, I, 413, note.
133. Murray, *E. D. C.*, II, 233.

in any one town, the city fathers demurred, for this company had been in town earlier that year. They compromised by giving the players "one whole weke & no longer . . . and they pmise . . . not to come agayne duringe this whole yeare." [134]  Our evidence warrants the conclusion that the average stay of the companies was probably three or four days, though occasional visits lasted for a week or even two weeks, and that many of the companies played twice on each day of their stay.

But one question remains to be dealt with. How many plays and companies did the provincial towns of England see in the course of a year? Once more the records may be permitted to speak for themselves. Bath paid for at least four town plays each year from 1577 to 1598 — that is to say, its citizens probably had the opportunity to see fifteen or twenty plays a year during this period.[135] From 1590 to the close of Queen Elizabeth's reign in 1603 Leicester was visited by four, five, or even six companies each season, and an average of four companies came during the reign of King James.[136] Coventry paid for 304 official first performances between 1574 and 1642, distributing its largesse to some five different companies each year, with not a single year missing. And Stratford-on-Avon in 1587, about the time of Shakespeare's arrival in London, was entertained by four different companies.[137] The list might be extended indefinitely. No additional figures or illustrations are needed, however, to show how great a hold the drama had upon the provinces, nor to drive home the fact that from them the players and their playwrights derived a very substantial part of the support that enabled them to live in their own day, and so, in the last analysis, for all time.

134. Murray, *E. D. C.*, II, 345.
135. *Id.*, II, 200 ff. The calculations and summaries are my own.
136. See Kelly, *op. cit.*              137. Murray, *E. D. C.*, II, 235, 402.

# IX

## STROLLING PLAYERS AND PROVINCIAL
## DRAMA AFTER SHAKESPEARE [1]

IN THE preceding chapter I have written of the actors who travelled "softly on the hoof" through the length and breadth of Shakespeare's England. Here I propose to deal with their successors of the seventeenth and eighteenth centuries. They make part—perhaps a more important part than is generally understood—of the history of the drama and theatre in a period that is full of life and interest even though the greater glory had departed. To the student of Elizabethan times the ways and means of these "weather-beaten weary travellers" [2] are significant because the strollers were, and are, the most conservative of all players. They continued the ancient and honorable traditions of the Elizabethans long after the patent theatres, the new scenes out of France, the new comedy of manners, and, finally, the new sentimentalism, had dimmed the very memory of the days of the Globe and the Blackfriars and stamped the customs and devices of those great times as subjects for mockery. [3] But the later strollers are worthy of study in and for themselves, or at least in the light of their practical contribution to the stage history of their time. To be sure, their predecessors at Stratford-on-Avon who gave Shakespeare his first glimpse of the puppets dallying, came at a more opportune moment; but those who followed made the most of their opportunities. Bright-plumed "birds of passage"

1. Reprinted, with additions, from *PMLA*, XXXVII (1922), 243 ff.
2. See below, p. 211.
3. For illustrative documents and further discussion of this subject see the writer's *Shakspere to Sheridan*, 1922.

were they,[4] and wheresoever they passed most men were glad of
their coming.   They left long trails of debt behind them, and
played more than one rather scurvy trick upon their hosts, but
they brought the old plays and the new away from the cramped
quarters of London's theatrical monopoly into the furthest corner
of the provinces.   They kept England merry England still, besides crossing the ocean and establishing the theatre in the colonies
—including America.[5]

From start to finish their rewards were poor and their life was
a hard one.   Elizabethan jibes at the strollers are legion, and later
commentators were as uncharitable as ever.   In Thomas Nabbes's
*Covent Garden*,[6] a play printed shortly before the closing of the
theatres in 1642, there is the usual girding at "the ragged fellows
. . . that borrowed the red blanket off my bed to make their
mayor a gown," and no detail of their "progress with the anatomy
of a sumpter horse, laden with the sweepings of Long Lane in a
dead Vacation, and purchased at the exchange of their owne whole
wardrobe," is omitted.   And Wright's *Historia Histrionica*,[7] one
of the documents which bridge the gap between the closing of the
theatres and early Restoration times, at once re-emphasizes "the
ill character of vagrant Players, or, as they are now called,
Strolers."

But ill character or no, the generality of men were glad to
have the strollers come to town.   As early as April 22, 1661 — the
day before the coronation of the Merry Monarch—Sir Thomas
Browne wrote his son Thomas that the strollers had come back
to Norwich, a town which had long been friendly to the players
and long remained so.[8]   Norwich celebrated the coronation, according to the author of the *Religio Medici*, with great feasts,

4.  See below, p. 218, n. 122.
5.  See below, p. 220, n. 128, and cf. O. S. Coad, *Journal of English and Germanic
Philology*, XIX (1920), pp. 201 ff.; B. Sprague Allen, *PMLA*, XXXV (1920), 358 ff.
6.  1638; Bullen's *Nabbes*, I, pp. 8-9.    7.  Cf. Hazlitt's *Dodsley*, XV, p. 430.
8.  See J. T. Murray, *English Dramatic Companies*, II, 335 ff., and Sybil Rosenfeld,
*Strolling Players, 1660-1765* (Cambridge, 1939), pp. 35 ff.   (This book has valuable new
material also on theatricals at York, Bath, Bristol, and other towns.)

sermons, "becon bonfires, speeches, *and a little play by the strollers in the market-place* . . . Cromwell hanged and burnt every where." [9]   At Oxford, too, the students received the strollers with open arms almost as soon as King Charles had come back to England.   Anthony Wood at Oxford saw them give sixteen plays, "wherein women acted," in nine days.[10]   And Wood was but one of a multitude of students who had long been waiting for the return of the players.   Tradition has it that the career of young Thomas Otway at Christ Church came to an untimely end because the lure of the footlights proved too strong; it is said that he and Elkanah Settle, who was then at Trinity College, "ran away from Oxford together with a company of strolling players." [11]   And some of the students of the other great university were scarcely less enthusiastic.   According to one account,[12] Jo Hayns—later the inimitable epiloguist of the King's Men—"takes his M. A. at Cambridge, which scarce had he performed, when down comes certain strowling Players . . . induce him to become [their] fellow Companion . . . and no sooner proposed but Hayns embraces."   The great Macklin, too, ran away from Trinity College, Dublin, to turn stroller.   In short, young gentlemen runaways from school and college to the open road and the stroller's barn seem to have been plentiful,[13] but the strollers won recruits from

9. *Works of Sir Thomas Browne*, ed. Simon Wilkin (London, 1852), III, 393; cf. Thaler, *Shakspere's Silences*, pp. 107-108.

10. *Life and Times of Anthony Wood*, ed. A. Clark, I, p. 405.   For additional materials on Commonwealth and early Restoration strollers see Hyder E. Rollins, *Studies in Philology*, XVIII (1921), 267 ff., XX (1923), 52 ff., and Leslie Hotson, *Commonwealth and Restoration Stage* (Cambridge, 1928); on later strollers, Elbridge Colby, *PMLA*, XXXIX (1924), 642 ff.

11. See W. Cooke's *Memoirs of Samuel Foote*, 1805, II, pp. 137-38; cf. F. C. Brown, *Elkanah Settle* (Chicago, 1910), p. 9.

12. *Life of Jo Hayns*, London, 1701, p. 4; John Doran, *Their Majesties' Servants*, 1865, II, pp. 185-86.

13. Cf. John O'Keeffe's *Beggar on Horseback* (1785), Act I: *Scout* (to *Horace*)—Sir, I guessed what would come of your last scamper from Oxford.   Your uncle has heard of all our frolics.

*Horace*—The Devil!

*Scout*—All out, Sir,—your excursion to Abingdon and acting Captain Plume in the barn. . . .

all classes and professions.  The famous Anthony Aston, of whom we shall hear more anon, left the law to "strain forth a comedy" and try his fortune in the provinces; and Richard Estcourt, one of the best of the later Restoration players and author of several good acting plays, "stole from his father's House with a country company . . . in the fifteenth year of his age." [14]  And so did many of the actors and not a few of the playwrights who won fame in their time.  Among the writers who learned something of their business in this way there were, besides Otway and Farquhar, such others as Mrs. Inchbald and Thomas Holcroft, John Cunningham, Shield (the composer), Samuel Foote, Tom Davies, and, later, Thomas Dibdin and Sheridan Knowles.[15]  As for the players, there were comparatively few of any consequence in the seventeenth and eighteenth centuries who did not begin their careers in that best of all "nurseries" for great actors, the hard training school of the road.  Estcourt, Jo Hayns, and Tom Dogget, Macklin, Quin, Garrick, Mrs. Siddons, Henderson, and Edmund Kean, —all tried themselves in the country before they conquered London.[16]  A few there were who, like Colley Cibber, managed to work their way up painfully from the ranks in London, but they also took to the road sooner or later in their careers.

Before considering what they did and how they fared, we must observe that in Post-Restoration times as well as during the Elizabethan period there were greater and lesser strollers.  The "great players from the city," duly licensed and sometimes strongly recommended to the kind consideration of the provinces by kings and potentates in London, continued to go on tour when sickness of body, purse, or state, diminished their city audiences too severely.  The poorer strollers, unlicensed vagabonds in the eyes of the law, subject to prosecution, impressment, and hunger, and

---

14.  W. R. Chetwood, *General History of the Stage*, 1749, pp. 87-90, 140.

15.  Thomas Holcroft's *Memoirs*, ed. William Hazlitt (London, 1816), I, pp. 246-258; Waldron's *Miscellany* (London, 1802), p. 47; Cooke, *op. cit.*; Doran, *op. cit.*, II, 382.

16.  Cf. Genest, *Some Account of the English Stage*, 1832, X, p. 307; Watts, *Theatrical Bristol*, pp. 65, 83; Cibber's *Apology*, ed. Lowe, II, p. 318; Doran, II, pp. 185, 242, 381, etc.

many of them without hope of ever making their bow on "the statelie cittie stages," are the more picturesque and interesting for all their obscurity, and it is they who best illustrate the survival of Elizabethan traditions.  But their more opulent brethren from the city in some respects also did much what Shakespeare and the King's Men had done before them, and so they are worthy of a preliminary glance.

In Shakespeare's time and later, players great and little often met with decided opposition from puritanic town councils,[17] but the well established companies under the patronage of the royal family were properly fortified against this sort of thing.  They came properly accredited and were able to show the town authorities that they "had the king's hand for playing"; indeed they frequently brought royal orders requesting the provincial authorities to "affourd them your Townehalls" or other convenient quarters, that they might be in "better readiness" for the royal service.  At Cambridge between 1592 and 1604, first the university authorities and then the town fathers had objected strenuously because the players had "set vp their bills" on the very gates of the colleges and generally brought about a corruption of manners "in the younger sort."[18]  But the players continued to come to Cambridge and Oxford during the last decades before the closing of the theatres—and to play, possibly at the universities themselves, certainly within the town limits, where students could find them without trying too desperately.[19]  We have seen how assiduously Anthony Wood worshipped the dramatic muses when the players came to Oxford in 1661, and it is worth while to notice, with Mr. W. J. Lawrence,[20] that when the Duke's Men came from Lincoln's Inn Fields to Oxford eight years later, their Guild Hall performances brought them £1,500, the

17. See the preceding chapter, and below, pp. 201, 217.
18. See above, p. 165.
19. Professor F. S. Boas (*Fortnightly Review*, August, 1913, and May 1920) holds that the plays were given in the towns but not within the universities.  Mr. W. J. Lawrence (*Fortn. Rev.*, August, 1919) takes the contrary view.
20. *Elizabethan Playhouse*, II, p. 192; cf. Anthony Wood, II, p. 165.

students pawning "books, blankets, and bedding" to raise the wherewithal to see them. Lawrence has called attention to still other Oxford visits,—by the King's Men in 1674, and by Irish companies in 1667 and 1677, in which year they are said to have netted six or seven hundred pounds.[21] So far as I know, however, two very interesting documents which have a decided bearing upon this matter of the dramatic activity at the universities in Restoration times, have never been noticed at all. They are the more significant because they show that Charles II, like his father and grandfather before him, did what he could for his players when they went on tour, even to the extent of safeguarding them against competition.[22] The documents in question are two letters under date of May 15, and June 5, 1680, respectively, written by Arlington, the Lord Chamberlain, to the Reverend Timothy Haughton, Vice Chancellor of Oxford. They appear in the manuscript records of the Lord Chamberlain for 1680:[23]

[May 15, 1680]

Reverend S$^r$

His Ma$^{tis}$ Comoedians having obteyned His leave to go and aire themselves in the Country now wee have no need of their Attendance at Court and beleiving no aire better than that of Oxford, having likewise prevailed with His Ma$^{tie}$ to comand mee to recomend them to yo$^r$ protection, That they may represent some of their good Playes, for some convenient time before the Universitie: I do heartily do it, assuring myselfe that for the Character and Priviledge they have of being his Ma$^{ties}$ sworne Servants, and for being men of letters, you will be pleased to afford them all the favour that shall be necessary towards their security whilst they are there, which they promise they shall not abuse in any degree. I am with much truth

Reverend S$^r$

Yo$^r$ most affectionate and humble Servant

ARLINGTON

21. II, p. 195.
22. See above, p. 185, n. 3.
   23. London Public Record Office, L. C. 7/1, f. 9 (cf. *Shakspere to Sheridan*, pp. 293-294).

[June 5, 1680]

Reverend S[r]

I wrote to you on May the 15th recommending to yo[r] favour and protection His Ma[tis] Comoedians, who haveing since complained to him that there is another Company of the same profession, whose admittance in the Universitie will frustrate them of the proffitt they promised themselves under His Ma[ties] name, His Ma[tie] hath comanded mee to lett you know His pleasure that Hee would have his owne Comoedians onely gratified with this favour they needing such an Extraordinary Encouragement to repaire them for some misfortunes lately befallen them, and perswadeing himselfe they can singly afford the university as much divertisement as their vacancie from their studies will admitt off   I am

S[r]

Y[r] most Affectionate humble Servant

ARLINGTON

The Stuarts, it would seem, believed in monopoly even on the high road. Doubtless many companies besides the King's Players came to Oxford none the less, but that company continued to enjoy great prestige and profit there for many decades to come, — particularly on the occasion of the "public Acts." These "academical jubilees," were, according to Colley Cibber,[24] "look'd upon as a kind of congratulatory compliment to the Accession of every new Prince to the throne." Students and visitors crowded in upon the actors on such occasions: two plays a day were the rule, the actors drew double pay, and their managers earned substantial profits.

As for the Stuart family, its own "vacancie" from its studies admitted of sufficient leisure to engage the service of more than one travelling company, particularly when the king or princes were away from London. James I and Charles I had on several occasions employed actors to beguile the *taedium vitae* during a progress of the court,[25] and just so did their two successors. In

24. *Apology*, II, p. 134, n.   25. Cf. *Shakspere to Sheridan*, Chapter V.

1670, for example, Charles II took the Duke's Men with him to play for the court at Dover,[26] and in 1684 he paid a round sum to certain French players "for attending his Majestie at Windsor and Winchester and returning to London." [27]   It is reported, further, that the Merry Monarch's tristful queen once sent for a company of comedians when life at Tunbridge Wells grew too dull to be endured.[28]  Other royal ladies followed the precedent. Thus we read that in 1728 the Princess Amelia, "attended by the Dutchess of Marlborough . . . and many other Persons of Quality" (including the poet Gay) were "agreeably entertained" at Bath by a company of comedians who played *The Beggar's Opera* first for them and later in the private houses of other "persons of quality." [29]   And at Bath, somewhat later, the Princess of Wales saw Rowe's *Tamerlane*.[30]  We must not leave Charles II, however, without noting that his brother, James II, also encouraged the players to venture forth from London,— even so far north as Edinburgh.

The records of that city are silent as regards dramatic performances from 1633 to 1663, in which year certain royal officials were entertained with a play given by a company of gentlemen, while some professionals were allowed to build a stage for public exhibitions, "they acting no obscene thing." [31]   By 1668 a professional company under the management of one Thomas Sydserf had more or less established itself in the favor of Edinburgh's lovers of the drama.  Its recurring visits, or those of other companies, must have enjoyed at least a fair amount of patronage; else it would be difficult to account for the fact that within five years the crown had appointed a Master of the Revels [32] for Scotland. The town council of Edinburgh protested vigorously against this

26. Downes, *Roscius Anglicanus*, ed. Knight, p. 29.    27. Lawrence, I, p. 151.
28. Cf. *Mémoires du Comte de Grammont*, 1713 (ed. 1792, p. 259).
29. *The Gloucester Journal*, June 18, 1728.
30. B. S. Penley, *The Bath Stage*, 1892, pp. 23-26.
31. This and the material immediately following is based upon J. C. Dibdin's *Annals of the Edinburgh Stage*, 1888, pp. 26 ff.; cf. also Doran, *op. cit.*, I, 412.
32. Or rather, two joint Masters, Edward and James Fountanes.

official recognition of plays and players, but to no effect. The King of England and Scotland had slight sympathy with them. and his brother, then Duke of York, showed his position in the matter unequivocally. When he came to hold his court at Edinburgh in 1679 the Duke brought with him a company of players from London, and two years later he and his Duchess welcomed another company from Dublin. At the same time, also, the Princess Anne and other great ladies and gentlemen of the Duke's court staged private performances of their own, with the aid and advice of the professionals. It was well for the latter that the court smiled upon them, for the town authorities maintained their uncompromising opposition to all theatrical activity throughout the reign of Charles II, and it was only the support of the court and nobility that gave the players the necessary encouragement to journey northward from time to time.

In other parts of the country, meanwhile, conditions were somewhat more favorable, though the humble, unlicensed strollers were always in danger from the constable and the beadle. For the moment our concern is not with them, but rather with the provincial activities of the stronger companies, who left London only on occasion and for their own purposes. Still, I may note here that from time to time the King's hand and seal was exhibited also by certain harum-scarum travellers, who had no headquarters in London, nor anywhere else, for that matter. (Sharp practice of one sort or another probably helped some of them to obtain their royal "licenses.") It was with just such a company of jolly "rascals" that Jo Hayns is said to have associated himself when he first forsook Cambridge in favor of the itinerant sock and buskin. In singing of their adventures later, he explains that on reaching Greenwich, —

> Then up they all march'd to the Sign of the Bull
> Where asking for Lodging, says the Folks 'we are full
> But we'll see for some for ye,' and so, with that wheedle
> Exit the Landlord and Enters the Beadle.

With that the Chief Actor begins for to Bristle,—
'Pish . . .' quoth he, 'let the Beadle go whistle,
For I can' (and he did too) 'produce strait a Patent
That has the King's Hand, and his seal, and all that in't.' [33]

And so this "rub of fortune" was smoothed out. It will appear presently that the Greenwich Strollers and others of their ilk, did not always fare so well; but we must stop for a moment longer with their more fortunate colleagues of the city. Three points are to be noted in this connection. In the first place, the companies from Drury Lane and Covent Garden continued to go into the country from time to time when for one reason or another conditions in London were unpromising—or less promising than in some of the flourishing towns near the capital. In the *London Daily Courant* of October 4, 1703, for instance, we read that "Her Majesty's Servants of the Theatre Royal, *being returned from the Bath*, will open Drury Lane on the 6th with the Comedy of *Love Makes a Man*," and this is but one of many notices [34] which testify to the fact that this fashionable watering place had strong attractions for the metropolitan actors. [35] Secondly, it is worth observing that other towns, preferably, again, those very close to London, were often favored by *week-end visits*. Thus, the *London Journal* of June 20, 1724, hears that "a select Company of Comedians from the Theatre Royal design to perform Saturdays and Mondays at Mr. Penkethman's Theatre in Richmond. They begin on Monday next, with a play of Sir John Vanbrugh's called *The False Friend*, with a Choice Band of Musick, and Entertainments of Dancing." Even more important to the country towns—and more profitable to the actors—were the longer tours often undertaken by star

33. Hayns's "Lampoon on the Greenwich Strowlers,"—*Covent Garden Drollery*, Malone Collection, Bodley.

34. Others, from *Heraclitus Ridens*, August 24-25, 1703, etc., are cited in Smith's MS. *Collection towards an History of the English Stage* (British Museum).

35. See also Sybil Rosenfeld, *op. cit.*, chapter VIII.—Such towns as Birmingham and Bristol were also on the London actors' visiting list. (See *Shakespeariana*, 10 ser. XI, 30, etc.)

performers from London [36] during the summer months, when the city theatres were, as a rule,[37] closed. It must be said that some of these summer excursions scarcely paid for themselves. In the late summer of 1779, for example, a company headed by Mr. and Mrs. Lewis of Covent Garden dismissed an audience at Wakefield because "there were but thirty shillings in the house"; [38] and some twenty-five years earlier John Lee, of Drury Lane and Edinburgh, had lost £500 in a summer's travelling.[39] Other summers, however, helped to balance accounts. The Lewises had bad luck at Wakefield, but they were "liberally rewarded" at Birmingham, York, and Liverpool; and better known performers won golden rewards as well as opinions wherever their summer tours led them. Thus, Victor [40] tells us that Woodward, "having obtained Leave from the managers of Drury Lane" in the summer of 1755, gave nine performances in Dublin and "cleared something more than £200 by the expedition." Garrick likewise earned huge applause and handsome profits at Dublin, though he was less responsive to the lure of the road than most great actors, and refused flattering invitations to play before certain great monarchs of continental Europe.[41] Dublin, moreover, opened wide its portals to Mrs. Siddons (who made a thousand pounds there on a summer trip in 1782) — and so did such cities as Edinburgh, Glasgow, Reading, and Bath. Mrs. Siddons, above all the great players of her time, had the will and ability to travel far and fast. "In four days," says Doran,[42] she "achieved the (then) incredible task of acting in three theatres so wide apart as London, Reading, and

36. Or, later, from Edinburgh and Dublin, when the theatre had become well established there.

37. Genest (IV, p. 616) notes that in 1761 Foote and Murphy in partnership rented Drury Lane from Garrick for the summer season "at a moderate price." Murphy wrote several new pieces, and with Foote acting some of the best of his old parts, the partners had an eminently successful season, "each man clearing over £300."

38. Genest, VI, p. 119.       39. Dibdin, *op. cit.*, pp. 72, ff.

40. *History of the Theatres of London and Dublin*, 1761, I, p. 206.

41. The Czarina Catherine offered him 2,000 guineas for four performances. Cf. Doran, *op. cit.*, II, p. 85.

42. *Op. cit.*, II, p. 251.

Bath." The important thing to note here, however, is not merely that these trips were profitable, but rather that they brought home to the whole country the great actors and the new plays. And we shall see shortly that the provinces saw the new plays, such as they were, almost as soon as did London.

The third and last point to be made concerning the extramural activities of the great players has to do with their appearances at the fairs. Bartholomew Fair, of course, had been a joyously uproarious show-place in Ben Jonson's day, and a document of the year 1641 [43] states that in that critical time there were still "more motions in a day to be seene" there "then are in a terme in Westminster Hall to be heard." Tricksters, hucksters, and puppetshowmen ruled the Fair as Jonson knew it, but later times brought more ambitious entertainers and entertainments. In 1689 Tom Dogget, later Colley Cibber's fellow-patentee at Drury Lane, played at Bartholomew Fair, [44] and at Bartholomew and Southwark Fairs the best and the worst of the players disported themselves now and again for fifty years to come. Bullock and Penkethman, Anthony Aston, Booth, Quin, the Spillers, Mrs. Cibber and Mrs. Pritchard, Shuter, Yates, Ryan, Mills, Hippisley, and Theophilus Cibber,—these are but a few of the names one meets in the checkered pages that tell the story of the great fairs. Churchill, in *The Rosciad* (1761) laughed at the city comedians in the fair booths. Shuter, he says,

> Keeps open house at Southwark Fair
> And hopes the friends of humour will be there;
> In Smithfield Yates prepares the rival treat
> For those who laughter love instead of meat.

But it is not difficult to understand why they chose to play there. During the closing decades of the seventeenth century the younger players of the two patent houses repeatedly tried to get the town

---

43. *Bartholomew Faire, or Variety of Fancies* (Douce Collection, Bodley). Extracts printed in Henry Morley's *Memoirs of Bartholomew Fair*, pp. 144-147.

44. Cf. T. A. Cook, *Tom Dogget, Deceased*, and Morley, pp. 268, 283.

to come to their theatres during the summer months, — but, as James Ralph wrote in 1731,[45] "at that dead Time of year . . . Business and Diversions in London sink under the weight of a long Vacation. . . . Trade lies dead and Pleasure languishes." At the fair, however, things were different. Town and country flocked thither, and the players were not slow to follow the main chance. Edward Ward, in the *London Spy* of August, 1699,[46] comments forcefully upon what he saw and heard when he and a friend went to Drury Lane:

> We steer'd our Course into Bridges-Street, with intention to see a Play. But when we came to the House found (upon enquiry) that all the Wiser part of the Family of Tom Fools has Translated themselves to Bartholomew Fair. After struggling with a long See-Saw, between Pride and Profit; and having Prudently consider'd the weighty difference between the Honourable Title of one of her Majesties Servants and that of a Bartholomew Fair Player, a Vagabond by the Statute, did at last with much difficulty conclude that it was equally Reputable to Play the Fool in the Fair for Fifteen or Twenty Shillings a Day as 'twas to Please Fools in the Play-House at so much per Week. And indeed, I think they make a very commendable Result for I think there's no more distinction between a Queen's-House-Player and a Country Stroler than there is between a Bull-Dog Bred up in Clare-Market and another educated in her Majesties Bear Garden, and he is the most valuable Dog that runs furthest and fairest. . . .

Elkanah Settle, poet laureate, would not have stooped to adapt Drury Lane plays for presentation in the theatrical booths of Bartholomew Fair if his necessities had not forced him to earn his bread as best he might; but he might have taken comfort had he lived till 1722, when Royalty honored Southwark Fair with its presence.[47] By this time Mayfair had been demolished and

45. In *The Taste of the Town*, pp. 230-231.
46. 2nd ed., pp. 235-36. Cf. Morley, pp. 264, 281 ff., 329.
47. Cf. T. A. Cook, *op. cit.*, p. 13; F. C. Brown, *op. cit.*, p. 35; Morley, pp. 264, 277. The *Daily Journal* of September 15, 1722, states that "On Thursday their Royal Highnesses, the Prince and Princess, honored with their Presence Southwark Fair."

"Bartholomew's wings close-clipp'd," according to James Ralph, —but that writer lived to see Southwark Fair equal the glories of its predecessors. He has left a vivid picture of the fair, its visitors, and its stages: "There," he says,[48]

> Scepter'd Kings and long-tailed Queens fill the capacious Stage to awe with their tinsel Grandeur the admiring Populace. There Love-sick Heroes and sighing Princesses, too, in friendly Murmurs break the Hearts of amorous Prentices and draw Floods of Tears from good-natur'd Chambermaids. There the humourous Clowns and cunning sharpers display their Talents of Joke and Trick, till tickell'd Cockneys stretch their Sides with immoderate Laughter. There the Beaus and Belles (who have only breath'd the dusty air of Hide Park all summer) may find themselves lost in the Middle of the Fair, and not discover where they are, or what they have been about, till the Mist is clear'd from their Eyes and the agreeable Vision vanish'd.

Victor[49] admits that Southwark Fair was "much frequented by persons of all distinctions," but holds that it lasted but two weeks. It would seem, however, that this time limit was sometimes exceeded. At all events, certain newspaper advertisements of those days show that the comedians of the fair were sometimes bold enough to keep right on playing after the patent houses had opened. Thus, it is interesting to find side by side (in the *Daily Post* of September 10, 1724) first, an advertisement of Drury Lane Theatre, and then, among others, two which describe the entertainment at "Penkethman's Great Booth, Southwark Fair,—by the Company of Comedians from both Theatres" and at "Lee's and Harper's Great Theatrical Booth,—Comedians from both theatres." Between the strollers come to town, the many novices anxious for a trial, and the steady supply of experienced but disgruntled actors from the patent houses which those troubled days afforded, the fairs found plenty of players. Not infrequently, indeed, the several booths between them boasted as fine an array

48. *The Taste of the Town*, pp. 230-231.    49. II, p. 74.

of talent as any that Old Drury or Covent Garden had to offer. In the summer of 1717, for instance, one booth at Southwark Fair enlisted the services of Bullock, Leigh, and their company, while Penkethman and his elephant, not to mention Quin, Spiller, Mrs. Spiller, Ryan, and others, were drolling it at another.[50]   In 1733, again, there were four great booths, with Hippisley, Lee, Mills, and Theophilus Cibber, respectively, in charge,—and *Alexander the Great, Tamerlane, Jane Shore*, and other popular plays on the bills.[51]   One does not wonder that those most concerned protested vigorously a couple of years later when Parliament was considering a bill to suppress all theatricals in and about London except the enterprises of the patent houses.   At that time a certain Mrs. Lee told Parliament that she had successfully carried on her business at Southwark Fair for thirty years, that her companies had been "the nurseries of the greatest performers, particularly Mrs. Boutell and Mr. Booth, as well as a great number of the players of Drury Lane and Covent Garden," and that she had "erected annually two booths," at a cost for "scenes, decoration, and erection" of £2,000.[52]

Another quotation from James Ralph,[53] whose report of the lively activities at the fairs I have just laid under contribution, will serve to show that the humbler strollers had not risen in public esteem with the coming of the eighteenth century.   His kind words for them are few and far between:

> To form a true Idea of these itinerant Players and un-deceive that Part of the World which may expect mighty Matters from them, I am inclinable to think that most of them were got under Hedges, born in Barns, and brought up in Houses of Correction: nor should they ever dare to shew their faces in any Place but a wooden Booth.
>
> For undoubtedly, the buskin'd Ragamuffins that Thespis

50. Genest, II, pp. 603-604.          51. *Id.*, III, p. 401.
52. Quoted from P. Fitzgerald, *New History of the English Stage* (London, 1882), II, p. 102.
53. P. 223.

first carted about the World, must have been Demi-gods and Heroes, to these Pedlars in Poetry and Gipsies of the Stage.

It is impossible to enter into a regular Criticism either on their Action or Drama; to get thro' such Heaps of Rubbish would require more than Herculean Help: the Confusion of such Nonsensical Scenes cannot be view'd forwards, they will not bear the least Light; nor have they the Merit even of a Witch's Prayer to be read backwards.

The unpleasantest aspect of all this is that Ralph — like Dekker, who had said harsh things of earlier strollers [54] — was befouling his own nest. But Ralph was nothing if not scurrilous, and the humbler members of his own profession were not the only persons he maligned. (Witness the testimony of his one-time friend, Ben Franklin, and Pope's in *The Dunciad*.) We have already seen that he did the strollers something less than justice, but there is no denying the fact that their official status, or rather their lack of official status, left them open to general contempt and often added untold difficulties to a profession already sufficiently precarious in and by itself. The Elizabethan statute of 1572 by which unlicensed players were threatened with branding as "rogues, vagabonds, and sturdy beggars," was mitigated but slightly or not at all during the next two centuries. In Queen Anne's time an act of the year 1713 declared anew that "all Fencers, Bear-wards, common players of interludes," etc., were punishable as "rogues and vagabonds," and twenty years later an attempt was made to enforce the act even against popular metropolitan actors who were in revolt against the managers, — this in the capital itself, where by this time the old puritan opposition to the stage and the renewed assault of Jeremy Collier had spent themselves.[55] Of course, the act was not universally enforced, for the simple reason that most country towns counted on

54. See above, p. 159. Ralph was a second-rate playwright at one time associated with Fielding, and a voluminous pamphleteer.

55. Victor, I, p. 22; Colley Cibber, *Apology*, I, p. 229. The act of 1713 was renewed, and in some respects sharpened, in 1737.

the players to help make life enjoyable.  The Country Mayoress in Fielding's *Pasquin* (1736) bemoans the fact that she "has been confined these twelve months in the country, where we have no entertainment but a set of hideous strollers"; but "the towns-people," says a late eighteenth century writer who graduated from the ranks of the strollers,[56] "constantly were railing against them, yet are exceedingly unhappy if they fail to return at the appointed time."  For a long time, however, certain places were closed to them.  In Betterton's day, for example, Newbury and Reading would tolerate no actors,[57] and so late as 1730 a "Citizen of London" urged in a printed *Letter to the Lord Mayor of London* "how fatal it must be to the Nation if such Places as Norwich, Coventry, Leeds, etc., whose Labour and Industry are so bene-ficial, should be debauched and corrupted by Stage-Players and their constant Attendants, lewd Strumpets."  Let it be noted here that certain other attendants of the strollers continued to travel with them.  The recruiting officer and the press-gang had preyed upon them in Shakespeare's time, and "text-bills" had then to be "turned to iron-bills" on more occasions than one.[58]  This old affinity between player and press-gang held good for generations, for Doran[59] reports that Edmund Kean, who was a very young stroller when the eighteenth century came to a close, used to good effect his excellent ability as a swimmer, — "particularly when a press-gang was near."

The strollers had still other difficulties to overcome — of which more anon.  It is time to glance at their business organization and methods, and to observe from the outset how closely these approximated those of the Elizabethans.  In Shakespeare's time practically the whole business of the theatre, — acting, play-writ-ing, producing, and the general business of management, — was in the hands of the players.  In that highly democratic age of the theatre each actor, except the mere beginners or "supers," drew

56. Holcroft, *op. cit.*, I, pp. 228-31.  *Pasquin*, ii, 1.     57. Doran, *op. cit.*, I, p. 88.
58. See above, p. 161.     59. *Op. cit.*, II, p. 381.

his remuneration from his share of the daily takings, and as a member of a shareholding company he had a full voice in the election of the officers who looked after the business management.[60]  This was the system of the great London companies as well as of the strollers, and this system, with certain modifications, was kept alive by succeeding strollers for the better part of the next three centuries, though in London itself the theatrical monopoly from the very beginning of the Restoration deprived the actors of their ancient liberties and made them merely the paid employees of managers who enjoyed absolute power by virtue of royal authority.  In the provinces, too, the manager became more and more powerful, but the old sharing system held over.  It was the established order before the Commonwealth tried to put an end to playing in city and country, and it had come into its own once more in early Restoration times, — for we know from Anthony Aston that Tom Dogget, early in his career, managed a company of sharing strollers, Aston among them.[61]  The anonymous author of the *Memoirs of the Countess of Derby* (1797), describes the situation soon after 1700, when Farren, the father of the Countess and former actress, was a stroller.  "The companies out of London," says the biographer, "were what are called sharing companies, every Performer partaking equally of the profits. There are generally in each of them, including the manager, sixteen persons.[62]  The profits are divided into twenty shares, of which the manager, for Scenery, Wardrobe, &c., takes four, and one as a performer; of the remaining Fifteen Shares, each member takes one; and it is to be observed that every Actor takes an equal share, whether he performs first, second, or third-rate parts.  Thus Macbeth and the Murderer, Hamlet and the Sentinel, Lear and one of his knights, all take an equal division of the spoils."  (Here was equality with a vengeance!  The younger Elizabethan actors,

60. Cf. *Shakspere to Sheridan*, pp. 70 ff.
61. Anthony Aston's Brief Supplement to Cibber's *Apology*, II, p. 318.
62. I.e., just about as many as the Elizabethan companies carried.

unlike Hamlet,[63] had sometimes been content with "half a share" or a quarter or three-quarter share, according to their merits.)

This account of things in Farren's company is confirmed by Thomas Holcroft, author of *The Road to Ruin* (1792), and *A Tale of Mystery* (1802), who began life as an itinerant shoemaker's son and worked his way up from stable boy and strolling player to success as a dramatist. In his *Memoirs* [64] Holcroft set down much information that has its bearing upon our study. Thus, he noted — apropos of the company managed by the elder Kemble, Mrs. Siddons's father, about 1765 — that

> A company of travelling comedians is a small kingdom, of which the manager is the monarch. Their code of laws seems to have existed with few material variations since the days of Shakespeare, who is, with great reason, the god of their idolatry. The person who is rich enough to furnish a wardrobe and scenes, commences manager and has his privileges accordingly . . . four 'dead shares' in payment for the use of his dresses and scenes . . .

besides the one to which he was "entitled as a performer." The younger Dibdin, a contemporary of Holcroft's, also won his way to London and successful authorship through a stroller's apprenticeship. He began his career with the Dover company in 1789, and it appears that the manager of that company had even a better bargain of it than most. "The manager," writes Dibdin,[65]

> took six portions for his trouble and the use of his scenery and wardrobe, and every other member of the corps took one. The prompter had something additional, and, if any actor had interest or address to procure a night's patronage from any family of rank, he claimed an additional share for what was a very important service.

Genest [66] states that country actors continued to "play on shares" in the nineteenth century, but it is clear that long before

63. III, ii, 289-296; cf. *Shakspere to Sheridan*, p. 71.    64. I, pp. 228-33.
65. Thomas Dibdin, *Reminiscences*, (1827) I, pp. 80-81.    66. I, 8.

then certain individual players, and sometimes entire companies, were on a salary basis. Holcroft himself,[67] soon after he became a stroller, had an offer of set wages of a pound a week, — which he foolishly refused, only to fare worse thereafter. Dibdin,[68] too, mentions a company which enjoyed much popularity in Canterbury, Rochester, Tunbridge Wells, and other Kentish towns in the 1780's, and which, "being on a salary establishment and not a joint-stock concern, ranked considerably above the Dover association." Fixed salaries may have had their advantages, but the strollers who enjoyed them did not necessarily roll in wealth by that token. *"For salary* of my famous Harlequin," Mist, the country impressario in Frederick Reynolds's comedy of *Management* (1799) [69] paid "only twelve shillings a week and fare of slow waggon." I shall present a little later certain additional figures covering the receipts and earnings of some of the sharing strollers, but the reader will be glad to have me anticipate the evidence here long enough to say that some of them at times had better luck than Mist's harlequin.

Meanwhile, we must not leave the country managers without another word. Towards the close of the eighteenth century, when a number of provincial towns began to boast playhouses of their own, and the players' barn gradually fell out of favor, there arose certain astute managers who controlled entire theatrical circuits of their own. Such an one was Mrs. Baker, the lady who managed the successful Kentish company just referred to and owned the several little theatres in which it played. Perhaps it was she to whom John O'Keeffe referred in his *Beggar on Horseback* (1785),[70] as "Mrs. Mummery, a great manageress of three or four country playhouses . . . and a special good customer she is!" With substantial provincial managers of this sort the London managers seem to have maintained more or less amicable relations, — at least to the extent of ridding themselves of unseasoned aspirants for fame on the boards by recommending them to the country at

67. *Op. cit.,* I, p. 183.    68. *Op. cit.,* I, 91-92.    69. Act I.    70. ii, 4.

large. One of the characters in the play just mentioned puts it this way:

> Waited above half an hour before this King of shreds and patches wou'd condescend to grant me an audience; then, after asking me to favour him with a speech — he stops me before I've got three lines, told me I had a fine voice — was a good figure — therefore, Sir, says he, I'd advise you to go into the country for a few summers — hey — oh — Cumberland or Birmingham, or stay, I'll give you a line to the manager of Coventry.[71]

Some of the earlier country managers who had no playhouses of their own were none the less enterprising and resourceful. There was Booth, for example, with whose company Holcroft [72] strolled for several years. The first thing this manager did when he came to any town, we hear,

> was to wait on the magistrate, to ask leave for his company to play, or, if this was refused, that he might have the honor of painting his picture. If his scenes and dresses were lying idle, he was the more busy with his pencil: and that tempting bait hung out at the shop-windows, *Likenesses taken in this manner for half a guinea*, seldom failed to fill his pockets while his company were starving.

When the company was acting, this manager — and other managers — got the lion's share of the takings: not merely the four or five "dead shares" but sometimes half a dozen living ones in addition. Anthony Aston's company, Farren's, Kemble's, — in fact most of them — [73] counted among their players the numerous sons and daughters of their managers, and the head of the family duly collected their shares. Thus it was that in one of the companies in which Holcroft served, "near half the profits" went into the manager's pocket every night. This, says Holcroft,[74] was

71. *Id.*  72. I, pp. 255-58.
73. Cf. Chetwood, pp. 87-90; *Memoirs of the Countess of Derby;* and next note.
74. I, pp. 228-31.

a continual subject for discontent to the rest of the actors, who are all, to a man, disaffected to the higher powers. They are, however, most of them in debt to the manager, and of course chained to his galley, a circumstance which he does not fail to remind them of, whenever they are refractory.

In justice to the managers, however, it should be said that their task was not an easy one, and that most of them probably earned what they got. Theirs, after all, was the initial outlay; theirs also the difficult problem of preserving order and discipline,[75] of training their players, and of keeping them together. These problems were difficult of solution in the first place because the strollers were always a more or less happy but irresponsible lot. Again, when a country manager had discovered or developed a really first-class performer there was always the theatrical scout from the capital to entice him away, — or, indeed, to call in country actors by the wholesale when the regular city players revolted against their managers: a situation which arose more than once while the patent monopoly held sway in London.[76] The provincial managers, in short, had their troubles as well as their profits. Before we draw the curtain upon them and their companies we must look into certain additional details of their methods and procedure, — their advertising, their circuits, the plays they used, their costumes and properties, and last, but perhaps not least interesting, the pleasant tricks they played upon their audiences and the world at large when the pinch of adverse circumstances was upon them, and only stout hearts and the indomitable will to keep smiling were between them and absolute destitution.

Students of the Elizabethan theatre will recall the familiar picture of Richard Tarlton in which that great clown is shown

75. "First call, new pantomime," says Mist in Reynolds's *Management*, "and not an actor come to rehearsal" (Act IV). This piece alludes also to the fact that certain players were notoriously fond of strong drink.

76. When Cibber, Wilks, and others, revolted from Drury Lane in 1709, Christopher Rich, "to compleat his company bethought himself of calling in the most eminent of strollers from all parts of the kingdom" (Cibber's *Apology*, II, p. 77).

merrily beating his drum.[77] The picture, I take it, either harks back to an early stage in Tarlton's career as a player, or else it shows him burlesquing one of the functions of the young "hireling" actors when he himself had become a public favorite. Certain it is that the Elizabethan players literally and energetically drummed up trade, — sometimes in London itself, but particularly when they travelled into the provinces, whose less sophisticated inhabitants dearly enjoyed the drums and trumpets and such other pomp and circumstance as the players' circus processions afforded when they came to town. Many an actor then, as Shakespeare put it, "led the drum before the English tragedians" [78] in order to advertise their wares, and many another did the same thing during the next two centuries. In Shakespeare's time, too, the strollers had supplemented the work of their drummers and trumpeters by sending advance agents ahead "to set vp their bills." This additional publicity work, of course, was likewise continued later on. Miss Farren's biographer [79] says his say on both these advertising devices as employed in the eighteenth century. With the strollers, he observes, "Prudence compels strictest economy"; hence,

> a very small number of Bills are made to answer the purpose of announcing the intended Representations. . . . To make amends for this defect . . . they distribute their Bills by beat of Drum, in order that their arrival and intentions may be known to every inhabitant. A Drum, on this account, always makes a part of the Property of a Country Company.

He adds that "some companies which wish to appear very respectable add at the bottom of their printed Bills, 'N. B., The Company does not use a Drum'," and this statement is supported by other evidence, for it appears that in the year 1751 a company of "His Majesties Servants from the Theatres Royal in London" announced on its arrival at Birmingham that it

77. Cf. Thorndike, *Shakespeare's Theater*, p. 374.
78. *All's Well*, iv, 3, 300; see above, p. 174.
79. *Memoirs of the Countess of Derby*, pp. 12-13.

"hoped the public would excuse the ceremony of the drum as beneath the dignity of a London company." [80]  Other good companies, however, did not consider the ceremony beneath their dignity,—as witness the flourishing strollers in O'Keeffe's *Wild Oats* (1791), who, as one of them remarks,[81] "trumpeted" the fame of their plays and players "ten miles round the country."  Trap, the treasurer of this company, personally wrote the playbills, and the chances are that he was none too modest in doing it.  James Ralph [82] gives the following mock extract from the strollers' playbills as he knew them:

> This evening *Argentina will represent a particular Fatigue call'd* the Hobgoblin; *with a Prologue by all the Devils in Hell: a Comedy of that Variety of Incidents, that she personates all Nations upon Earth,* with *Singing and Dancing in all their different Manners.*

For once Ralph did not shoot far beyond the mark, for one can almost match this effusion by advertisements which may still be read in the newspapers of the period.  Anthony Aston, for instance, when he came to London on April 20, 1724, boldly advertised in the papers, side by side with the offerings of the Theatre Royal in Lincoln's Inn Fields, as follows: [83]

### TONY ASTON

> In Hell, alias the Exchequer Eating-House in the Palace Yard, Westminster.  This present Monday the 20th of April, performs his Medley, viz. Lorenzo, Gomez, and Elvira in the Spanish Friar, Sauney, Petruchio, and Peg, in the Taming of the Shrew.  Belmour, Fondlewife, and Laetitia in the Old Batchelor, Woodcock, Hillaria, and Squib, in the Yeomen of Kent, Roger and Aesop, Sir Toby and Philosophers, in Love's Contrivance.  With comical Songs, Prologue and Epilogue.  Beginning at seven o'clock.

80.  Cf. Maurice Jonas, *Shakespeare and the Stage*, p. 234, and *Shakespeariana*, 10 Ser., XI, p. 30.
81.  Act II.      82.  *Op. cit.,* p. 223.      83.  *London Daily Post*, April 20, 1724.

N. B. We perform on Thursday next at the Three Tuns Tavern in the Borough, all New.

At Bath, again, he humbly gave Notice to "the Quality and Gentry" of certain added attractions, which remind one of the extra forces sometimes carried by the Elizabethan players when they went on tour with "hocus pocus" or Travitanto Tudesco, or some other notable trickster: [84]

> He hath brought to Town from Wales an admirable Curiosity, Viz. a Mock Voice. . . . He imitates with his Voice Domestic Animals as Cocks, Hens, Ducks, Turkey-Cocks, and Turkey-Hens, Swine, Horses, Dogs, also Ravens, Lap-Wings, Sea-fowl, Sheep, Lambs, Bulls, Cows, Cats, &c: and that too after a Comical Manner, following them through their different Passions: as Surprize, Fear, Anger &c: in their Eating, Walking, Converse, &c. . . . Any Person of Quality, or others, may Command him to their House &c by sending word. . . . Note, Tony Aston's Medley, consisting of select parts of Comedies, new Songs, Prologues, Epilogues &c. Mr. Purcell's and other comical English Dialogues is performed every Monday, Wednesday and Friday . . . beginning at 6 o'clock. Pit 1 s. 6 d. Being new each night.[85]

Doubtless Aston wrote his own bills. In other companies, also, the writing and even the printing of playbills was part of the day's work for one of the regular actors. Thus, in the Dover company with which Dibdin made his début, there was one "little Jerrold," who was "both actor and printer, and prepared fresh play-bills at least every so often, by no means too modest in their announcements." [86] It is worth noting, in passing, that this multiplication of functions was not an exceptional aspect of the interior economy of strolling companies. Their resources, in man power and otherwise, were never very great, and each player in his

84. See above, p. 168.
85. Reproduced from a clipping in Smith's *Collection* (see above, p. 194, n. 34).
86. Dibdin, *Reminiscences*, I, pp. 70, 85.

time had perforce to act many parts. When they had time to prepare, and no accidents, doubling or trebling of parts solved the problem after a fashion; but in emergencies they were sometimes sadly put to it. "I have seen a Play acted in the country by Strollers," says a writer of the year 1748,[87] "where, from a Scarcity of Players, one of the Dramatis Personae has been oblig'd to act his own Part, and read the other concern'd with him in the same scene." Equally exacting, perhaps, but surely less embarrassing, were the labors of the functionary (appropriately named Stopgap) in one of Reynolds's comedies,[88] who combined the offices of "Prompter, treasurer, box-book-keeper, and deputy manager," — but as a matter of fact plenty of actors worked even harder than he. We learn from Dibdin,[89] once more, that Gardner, the stage manager of the company with which Dibdin first took the road, "played all the heroes, Falstaff, and the violoncello, set accompaniments for the orchestra, taught the singers, and sometimes copied the parts." And Holcroft's *Memoirs*,[90] provide us with a sketch of the activities of a player whose hours were even more crowded, if possible, than those of Gardner. When Holcroft joined Booth's travelling company in 1774, he

> engaged to perform all the old men and principal low comedy characters; he was to be *the music*, that is, literally the sole accompaniment to all songs, &c. on his fiddle in the orchestra; he undertook to instruct the younger performers in singing and music, and to write out the different casts or parts in every new comedy.

Finally, he was to furnish the company

> with several new pieces never published . . . and for all these services, various and important as they were, he stipulated that he should be entitled to a share and a half of the profits.

---

87. *D-ry L-ne P-yh-se Broke Open.* A Letter to Mr. Garrick, London, 1748, p. 21.
88. *Management*, Act I.      89. *Op. cit.*, I, p. 108.      90. I, pp. 241-42.

These profits, says the editor of the *Memoirs*, "generally amounted to between four and five pounds a night" whenever they played, — "that is, three times a week." The proposed salary, therefore, "could not have amounted to more than seventeen or eighteen shillings weekly."

I have already suggested that the strollers' resources were not limited as regards man power alone. Certainly most of the provincial companies were none too well supplied with those rather essential tools of their trade, — costumes and properties. The Greenwich Strollers, for example, acted in a tumble-down barn, with but a few modern conveniences. As Jo Hayns put it, — [91]

> I confess *they had never a Scene* at all,
> They wanted no copy, they had th' original,
> For the windowes being down, and most part of the roof,
> How could they want Scenes, when they had prospect enough?

So, too, the "Prologue for Wandering Players" printed in the 1680 quarto of an obscure play called *Love Lost in the Dark*, or *The Drunken Couple*,[92] pictures their costumes and other impedimenta as of the thinnest and humblest:

> Our habits and our Acting such appears
> Like weather-beaten weary Travellers
> Who have endured more than may here be told
> From Eastern blasts and sharper Northern cold. . . .

Yet the strollers were doubtless well aware of the fact that good scenes and costumes counted for much with the play-going public, — especially in the seventeenth and eighteenth centuries, when the London theatres made up for the comparative inferiority of their new plays by brilliant acting and by an unheard-of lavishness and splendor in all the fittings and trimmings of their productions.

91. See above, p. 194, n. 33.     92. Malone Collection, Bodley.

In Spence's *Anecdotes* [93] there appears a "Prologue for the Blandford Strollers" in which those gentlemen lament their lack of such equipment:

> To aggravate the case we have not one
> Of all the new Refinements of the Town.
> No moving Statue, no lewd harlequins,
> No pasteboard play'rs, no Actors in machines,
> No rosin to make lightning; ('twould exhaust us
> To buy a Devil and a Doctor Faustus);
> No millers, Windmills, Dragons, Conjurers,
> To exercise your eyes and spare your ears,
> No witches to descend, no stage to rise,—
> Scarce *one* for *us*, the actors.　We can set
> Nothing before you but mere sense and wit.

We may be reasonably sure, however, that no company of them all would have hesitated to supplement sense and wit with expensive costumes and properties—if it could have afforded to do so.　Indeed, if an allusion of O'Keeffe's may be trusted, certain provincial managers emulated Drury Lane and Covent Garden to good effect.　"You must know," says Mrs. Mummery, in the second act of *A Beggar on Horseback*, "our gentlefolks down in the country have got mad after camels, birds, horses, musical hares, balloons, and such things; and so in compliance with these new fancies my business . . . in London was to engage the dancing dogs for them."　And the lady goes on to say that she has all her stage properties "made in London by Mr. Combes of Covent Garden, a very ingenious man, and I even have my scenes painted by Mr. Hodgins.—Here's a cargo of crowns, scepters, daggers, bowls, and truncheons."

But the earlier strollers rarely enjoyed such opulence.　Holcroft,[94] for instance, tells of an early Scotch company which when it started played nothing but Allan Ramsay's *Gentle Shepherd*,—and this, he says, "they continued to do for several years, *without either scenery or music*."　At first there were no actors except the

93. Ed. 1858, p. 294.　　94. *Op. cit.*, I, pp. 246-51.

immediate members of the manager's family, and not until time, marriage, and stern thrift had brought new actors and some capital into the company, did it undertake to enlarge its programs and acquire a supply of stage fittings.   Allan Ramsay's good friend Anthony Aston also began his managerial career in a very small way, and he too at first employed only his wife and children to assist him.   He prospered in time, and Ramsay reports that in 1727 Aston had "paid out above £200 for fine clothes and other things proper for his business," — but that was only because he had worked very hard and thus laid up some store of worldly goods. It is pleasant to read, by the way, the excellent character Ramsay gives this stroller of the strollers.   "Mr. Aston and his family," he wrote,[95] "live . . . to my certain knowledge with sobriety, justice and discretion, he pays his debts without being dunn'd, is of a charitable disposition, and avoids the intoxicating bottle." We shall see presently that other writers did not altogether share Ramsay's views as to the sobriety and general trustworthiness of Aston and his comrades of the road.   For the moment it is in order to repeat that most of them had but little superfluous equipment. Dr. Doran [96] tells of an Irish company which, on its arrival at Edinburgh in 1681, managed to get a royal exemption for the duty they would otherwise have had to pay upon "the gold and silver lace of their wardrobe."   Most strollers, whatever their troubles, would have had no such embarrassment, for the simple reason that few had any wardrobe to speak of other than that which they carried on their backs.

95. For the document see Dibdin, *Annals of the Edinburgh Stage*, p. 37; cf. Doran, I, 413, and Watson Nicholson's *Anthony Aston, Stroller and Adventurer* (1920).   The Aston notices quoted above (cf. pp. 208 ff.) do not duplicate Nicholson's, whose chief contribution is a new and interesting document, *A Sketch of the Life &. of Mr. Anthony Aston*, written by himself and found by Nicholson.  The *Sketch*, however, does not mention, and Nicholson seems not to have been aware of the details of Aston's career in Scotland, nor of his association with Ramsay, for Nicholson writes that beyond Aston's "bald statement . . . in the *Sketch* that Ireland and Scotland were included in his itinerary . . . we know little or nothing of the details of his life for some years following his adventure in London," i. e., roughly, from 1717 to 1735 (Nicholson, pp. 33-34, 36).

96. *Op. cit.*, I, p. 412.

As regards plays they were much better off. To be sure, not
a few companies must have started with a repertory scarcely
larger than that of the Scotchmen who played *The Gentle Shepherd*
and nothing else for several years. But those who stuck to a few
old plays did so because this procedure required little study or
scenic equipment, for new plays were neither expensive nor difficult to obtain. To say that no copyright nor acting right was
sacred during the seventeenth and eighteenth centuries is to put
the case mildly; the fact is that pirating was boldly and openly
practiced: was, in short, the established order of the time. So
well established it was that so late as 1795 the London managers
could win no redress in the courts when they sued certain provincial managers for stealing their plays.[97] Again, as regards
pirated prints of plays, there is an unbroken line of protests from
the playwrights — from Thomas Heywood's time and Dryden's
through John O'Keeffe's.[98] Under the circumstances the meanest
strollers were almost as free to use the latest London successes as
were the great city players when they went on tour. The provinces surely were the gainers, whatever may be thought of the
point of equity involved.

This situation, at all events, accounts for the fact that one
strolling company brought to Edinburgh *Sir Salomon* or *The
Cautious Coxcomb*—one of the very successful productions of the
Duke's Men in the London season of 1671 —[99] in less than a year
after its first appearance on the boards; and for the same reason
both Edinburgh and Bath saw *The Beggar's Opera* within a few
months after its first triumph at Lincoln's Inn Fields.[100] Sometimes such "borrowings" were made even more rapidly, for it is
recorded that *Pamela* (a dramatization, of course, of Richardson's

97. The younger Colman sued the manager of the Richmond company in 1795, for
appropriating O'Keeffe's *Son-in-Law*, but got no satisfaction at all (O'Keeffe, *Recollections*,
II, London, 1826, pp. 312-15).

98. Cf. Neilson and Thorndike, *The Facts about Shakespeare* (New York, 1931), pp.
132 ff.; Scott-Saintsbury, *Dryden*, V, p. 112; O'Keeffe, *op. cit.*, II, pp. 2, 305-37.

99. Downes, *Roscius Anglicanus*, p. 29; Dibdin, *Annals*, p. 27.

100. Dibdin, *Annals*, p. 42; see above, p. 192 and n. 29.

novel) was put on at Edinburgh in December, 1741,—one month after Garrick had made his first appearance in that play at Goodman's Fields Theatre in London.[101]  Ordinarily the provinces had to wait more than a month, but the records show specifically that the strollers brought them the plays of Dryden, Southerne, Rowe, Congreve, Vanbrugh, Farquhar, Addison, Steele, Colley Cibber, and Fielding, as well as the then popular revivals of Elizabethan plays, very soon after London saw them.[102]  One of my earlier quotations from Holcroft,[103] moreover, indicates that certain new plays first saw the light in the strollers' barn or in the little country theatres of later days.  Frederick Reynolds [104] explains, in a measure, how this came to be: having had one or two of his early plays rejected by the London managers, he was able to find at Bath a company enterprising enough to risk producing them for the sake of the novelty.  But slight importance attaches to such provincial first performances "on any stage" of insignificant pieces by young playwrights; on the other hand, if one is to understand the real growth and appeal of the later drama it is essential to bear in mind the fact—scarcely noted hitherto—that the strollers brought to the remotest corner of England practically all the plays that counted in London.

One or two further details and we have done.  Reference has been made repeatedly in this study to the immediate physical background of the provincial drama.  The word "barnstorming," be it noted, had a much more literal significance a hundred years ago than it has now, and for two centuries after Shakespeare most provincial players were true barnstormers in every sense of the word.  "The ringleader of the shew-folks" in O'Keeffe's *Strolling Gentlemen* [105] comes ahead from Andover to find them "a barn to

101. Dibdin, *Annals*, p. 53; Genest, IV, pp. 17-18.
102. Dibdin, *Annals*, pp. 38-41; Penley, *Bath Stage*, pp. 23-26; Dibdin, *Reminiscences*, I, p. 57.
103. See above, p. 210.
104. *Life and Times of Frederick Reynolds* (London, 1826), I, pp. 302-05.
105. *Wild Oats*, or *The Strolling Gentlemen* (1791), Act II.

play in," and a substantial farmer hastens to accept a deposit, lest "they should engage the great room at the inn,"—for the inns also, as of old, served the players when no barn was handy. Some of the barns, it may be hoped, were less tumble-down than the one which Jo Hayns described,[106] but even the best of them were dangerous, and not a few accidents occurred. In September, 1727, for example, "a most dismal fire broke out in a barn in which a great number of people were met together to see a puppet-show," —of whom seventy-eight lost their lives in the fire and subsequent panic.[107] In the year 1576 the town of Bristol had had to appropriate certain funds from its treasury to repair its guildhall door and to make good other damage caused "by the press of people" who had come to see the Lord Chamberlain's Men act before the mayor and council.[108] Some one hundred and fifty years later, according to a newspaper clipping of July 12, 1733,[109] much more serious damage was done when "a company of comedians were performing a Comedy . . . at the County Hall" of Nottingham. This "melancholy accident" was caused by the fact that "the upper Gallery, being much crowded, fell down upon those below," whereby one spectator was killed and many were badly injured. In Leicester as in Nottingham the townhall served as the players' headquarters at least so late as 1736, when "Mr. Herbert's Company of Players" acted there, after paying five pounds for the use of the poor.[110] The ever-ready barn, however, was much more generally used, since it could be had without appeal to the public authorities. Long before the last decade of the eighteenth century, the provincial drama had entered upon a new phase: with the establishment of a number of duly licensed "theatres royal" in certain of the larger towns it had begun to acquire something like a local habitation and a name. But the strollers' barn still held

106. See above, p. 211, and cf. Sybil Rosenfeld, *op. cit.*, p. 22.
107. A servant had set a candle and lantern near a heap of straw in the barn.—I quote from a newspaper clipping—which I have been unable to trace further—in Smith's *Collection*, vol. IV (B. M.).
108. See above, p. 177.　　　　　　109. In Smith's *Collection*, vol. IV.
110. William Kelly, *Notices of the Drama at Leicester*, p. 273.

its own. Dibdin [111] informs us that when his company played at Eastbourne in 1789, "the theatre was formed in a very large barn and adjoining stables."

The story of the long fight for the establishment of duly licensed provincial theatres is not one that can be told in detail here. The facts are set forth in sundry books which sketch the history of the drama in such cities as Edinburgh, Bath, Bristol, Leicester, and Norwich; and only a few outstanding points can be noted here. It is clear, in the first place, that the efforts of the enterprising showmen who undertook to build playhouses in the provinces, met with threefold difficulties. There was determined opposition from the London patentees, who felt that the extension of the royal license and authority to the country at large would mean a loss of prestige and profit to themselves. Further, there were equally strong objections from certain town councils, — like that of Bristol, for instance, which declared in 1704 that the recognition of the "public stage" would "eclipse the good order and government of the city, corrupt and debauch our youth, and utterly ruin many Apprentices and Servants already . . . Unruly and Licentious . . . and with great difficulty kept under any reasonable order." [112] And these two difficulties were in part responsible for the third, — that of finding the money for playhouse building, a problem made more difficult still by the keen competition between rival entrepreneurs and companies.[113] Even so, inexpensive "theatrical booths" were built in a number of towns during the first two or three decades after the Restoration, and small playhouses made their appearances soon after 1700, though none was "patented" by the crown for another half century. Thus, the first Bath theatre was built in 1705, at a cost of £1,300,[114] while Edinburgh patronized two or three little makeshift houses successively during the next two decades.[115] By 1729 Bristol, in spite of its city fathers, had a rather pretentious theatre

111. *Reminiscences*, I, p. 74.     112. Cf. Watts, *Theatrical Bristol*, pp. 17 ff.
113. Cf. Penley, *Bath Stage*, p. 31.     114. *Id.*, p. 17.
115. Dibdin, *Annals*, pp. 37 ff.

which is said to have cost £5,400; [116] and Leicester opened its first regular playhouse in 1750.[117] A few years later the first royal patents for provincial theatres were issued. Bath still disputes with Edinburgh the honor of having been the first to win the king's hand and seal for its stage and players, and, whichever scored first, it is clear that both cities secured patents in the year 1767-1768.[118] Liverpool secured its patent three years later, Bristol followed in 1778 — and thereafter the gates were thrown open to all the rest.[119]

But while the new temples were rising the strollers still worshipped in their barns, and before we leave them we must observe how they managed their tours and circuits from one to another. The Lord Chamberlain's Men complained in 1592 that their company was very "greate . . . and thearbie our chardge intollerable in travellinge the countrie." [120] This item of travelling charges remained a grievous one in later times. Since it frequently happened that company funds were "so low as not to furnish the necessary funds for the hire of any kind of vehicle to convey their live and dead stock from town to town," the actors had sometimes to do the next best thing: each player "took a portion of the scenery or wardrobe on his back, and trudged on to where they next intended to establish themselves." [121] Under the circumstances long trips were, as a rule, quite out of the question. We have already seen that there were exceptions to the rule, — that great players like Garrick and Mrs. Siddons, and especially favored companies such as the King's Men from London, sometimes travelled as far as Edinburgh or Dublin, while Irish companies occasionally returned the compliment. But these were distinctly exceptional cases. So late as 1759, if we may believe Tate Wilkinson,[122] "birds of passage from London to Scotland were experiments

---

116. Watts, pp. 65-83; *London Weekly Journal*, June 28, 1729.
117. Kelly, *op. cit.*, pp. 297-98.
118. Penley, pp. 31-32; Dibdin, *Annals*, pp. 132, 145-48. Doran (II, p. 222) reports that the Edinburgh Theatre Royal cost £7,000.
119. Genest, V, p. 338; Watts, pp. 65-83.     120. Cf. above, p. 170.
121. *Memoirs of the Countess of Derby*, p. 12.     122. *Memoirs*, II, p. 72.

unknown, for it was judged impossible for a London theatrical sunflower to survive the chillness of such a barbarous northern clime." In the year 1683 no less a company than the King's Men found itself stranded on the road between Edinburgh and London, and had to raise a forced loan of twenty pounds to get home.[123] Naturally, therefore, they preferred, in general, to limit their travels to such comparatively safe and accessible points as Bath—and the travels of the lesser strollers were, of course, even more circumscribed. They established themselves, accordingly, in reasonably small districts such as that of the Kentish company already mentioned,—whereby they saved travelling expenses, and, by returning frequently to fixed points, built up a clientele that knew them and welcomed their visits. By the middle of the eighteenth century, moreover, the companies who made their headquarters in the several provincial theatres then growing up, made periodical trips to other towns near them. The Bath players, for example, appeared regularly also at Bristol, the Dublin companies, similarly, at Cork and Limerick, and those of Edinburgh, at Glasgow, Newcastle, Scarborough, and other points.[124] Their visits, of course, varied in length; they stayed from three days to two weeks, and played sometimes every night, sometimes only on alternate evenings.[125]

In this matter of finding their orbit and avoiding collisions with other wandering stars of small magnitude, the humbler strollers again had the worst time of it. Once more, however, their experiences were not the least interesting of all. Chetwood says of Anthony Aston that he

> pretended a Right to every Town he entered; and if a Company came to any Place where he exhibited his Compositions, he would use all his Art to evacuate the Place of these Interlopers,

123. Lord Chamberlain's Books, 7/1, f. 10, London Public Record Office; cf. *Shakspere to Sheridan*, p. 294.
124. Penley, p. 40; Genest, X, p. 481; Dibdin, *Annals*, p. 72.
125. Dibdin, *Reminiscences*, I, pp. 86, 57; Holcroft, *Memoirs*, I, pp. 241-42. (See also p. 211 above.)

as he called them. . . . His general Conditions of Peace were
that they should act a Play for his Benefit, that he might leave
the Siege and march with his small Troop to some other Place.
And as he was a Person of Humour, and of a proper Assurance,
he generally, like a Cat, skimm'd off the fat Cream, and left the
lean Milk to those that stay'd behind. . . . He is as well
known in every Town as the Post Horse that carries the Mail.[126]

Dekker [127] observed long ago that it was the stroller's lot to
"trauel upon ye hard hoof from village to village for chees and
buttermilk," and the evidence goes to show that even Anthony
Aston did not get more fat than his system could properly assimi-
late.  At any rate, one sympathizes with him and those of his
fellows who were clever enough to enrich their diet occasionally.
There are, to be sure, stories which ascribe fabulous earnings to
certain strollers, particularly to those who brought the drama to
India and other colonies.[128]  Again, a Drury Lane play written
soon after the close of the eighteenth century,[129] suggests that a
stroller might sometimes attain to the solid fortunes of a "squire"
or a "bank director."  But there were not many such, for the
golden showers fell but seldom.  Mist's chief stroller, in Reynolds's
play,[130] boasts benefit profits of "four pounds over expences,"
but he was lucky.  "The mightiest Kings and Queens we keep in
pay," said the Blandford Strollers,[131] "support their pomp on
eighteenpence a day."  And even this irreducible minimum was
frequently but an ideal to strive for.  Since even the King's Men
sometimes felt the slings and arrows of outrageous fortune, it is
small wonder that lesser companies should have found themselves, now and again, confronted with an audience of "three

126. *History of the Stage*, pp. 87-90.        127. See above, p. 159.
128. An English company is said to have cleared £1,500 at a single benefit in Bengal in
1782, and others are reported to have earned huge sums in Jamaica (cf. Chetwood, *op. cit.*,
pp. 40-41; *Percy Anecdotes*, XVII, p. 145).
129. Genest (VIII, p. 595) quotes from *Touchstone, or The World as it Goes,—
Cropley*—Blessy, he be turned Squire.
*Probe*—Squire! What do you mean?  A bank director or a strolling player?
130. *Management*, Act IV.                131. See p. 212, above.

people," [132] or with total receipts such as those which Tate Wilkinson once collected at Maidstone:—"two pieces of candle and eighteenpence." [133]

"The Tunbridge Wells Theatre," writes Doran,[134] "was of such dimensions that the audience part was in Kent, the stage in Sussex, and between the two ran a ditch, which players in debt found convenient when bailiffs were after them, as they speedily evaded jurisdiction by escaping into another county."   One hopes that most of them escaped safely; indeed it is difficult not to take the poor strollers' part when it comes to judging of other tricks charged against them.   There is the story of Jo Hayns, for example, who found a way out when, by reason of his company "having but a small stock of plays and those so often acted that no one would come to see 'em," the actors were fallen into a "deplorable condition."   On the promise that half the receipts should be his, Jo undertook to get a full and understanding auditory,—by advertising a performance of *The Merry Wives of Windsor*, though that play was not in the company's repertory.   He did fill the house, and then made good his colleagues' shortcomings by persuading "a great lady in the audience" to object to *The Merry Wives* on the ground that she had seen it too often in London; whereupon the audience agreed to let them substitute their regular performance.[135]   Anthony Aston in his time was publicly charged with "deserting from his Majesty's Company of Stage Players at Bath, with all his Cloaths and Accoutrements, after having receiv'd Advanc'd Money," and then "entering himself among the socks and buskins of Bartholomew Fair," [136]—but this unsupported charge may well be ignored in view of another episode of Aston's career, for which Chetwood [137] vouches.   It would seem

132. Frederick Reynolds (*Life and Times*, I, p. 97) reports this occurrence as of the year 1780; the audience was "mercifully dismissed."

133. Cf. Doran, II, p. 315.            134. *Id.*, II, p. 315.

135. *Life of Jo Hayns*, pp. 43-45.

136. Smith (*Collection*, vol. IV) quotes to this effect from a lampooning advertisement in *Heraclitus Ridens*, August 24, 1703.

137. *Op. cit.*, p. 90.

that the good Anthony once found himself something in debt to his landlord, but, instead of paying, managed to raise an additional loan on security of his wardrobe, "which he shewed him in a large Box, ten times the value of the debt owing or the sum borrowed." When the borrower had moved on, the landlord discovered that the box was filled up "with cabbage-stalks, Bricks, and Stone, cloath'd in Rags to prevent moving," but—and herein lies the redeeming grace—we are assured that when Anthony's finances were "cured of the consumption," he honestly paid his debt. Without seeking to multiply anecdotes of this sort, I may venture to illuminate old truth by one modern instance more. In the preceding chapter I have recounted how George Peele, good Elizabethan stroller as he was, once attracted a great audience at Bristol by advertising the production of a spectacular new play, and how he then, after making only a preliminary bow to the audience, disappeared with the takings. The following quotation from James Ralph [138] suggests once more that age cannot wither the pleasant and ingenious devices of the players:—

> The Prince of a Tribe of *Dramatick Wanderers* once fix'd the seat of his Empire in the largest barn of one of the Hans-Towns: his vast Equipage of tatter'd Scenes, various Instruments, tarnish'd Tinsel, and empty Bandboxes delighted the Populace, and gave wonder to the Magistrates. After a week's necessary Preparation, he promis'd the City a most entertaining and magnificent Play upon the Story of St. Peter's following our Saviour into Galilee. The Play-Bills gave the Town Hopes of fine Machinery, gay Scenes, and exquisite Musick, surprizing Dancing, and all those additional Ornaments of the Stage which are requir'd to coax a *High-Dutch Audience* into swallowing Wit.
>
> The long-expected Night comes, the House quickly fills, Crowds that could not enter were so unfortunate as to be oblig'd to carry back their Money. Prodigious was the expectation of the happy Mortals within, as great the Vexation of the Wretches excluded. At last, the wish'd for Minute comes, the Curtain flies up, and he who personated our Saviour appears with good

138. *Op. cit.*, p. 61.

St. Peter at his Heels, whom with an Air of Majesty he commands to follow him into Galilee; then quits the Stage . . . and St. Peter follows.  From behind the Scenes they immediately convey their Persons with the Treasure of their Wit. . . . The Audience with unspeakable Impatience waited their Return to proceed with the Business of the Stage — but all in Vain — Moment succeeds to Moment; no Tidings, no Appearance . . . to finish the Play.  The Audience, enquiring into the Reasons of their Delay, were inform'd that indeed they had taken Post-Horses and were by that time got out of the Territories of the said Town on their way to Galilee.

To some extent, however, it was only a case of the cheaters cheated.  "It is a saying amongst us," wrote one of the strollers,[139] "that a player's sixpence does not go as far as a town-man's groat; though the latter are continually abusing them . . . they take good care to indemnify themselves, and are no great losers if they get ten shillings in the pound."  The strollers' sins, at worst, were venial sins.  They brought the drama home to Dutch burghers and English country folk alike, and so they deserved to rest at ease in Zion.

139. Holcroft, *op. cit.*, I, pp. 228-31.

# X

## SHAKESPEARE, STRATFORD, AND SIR THOMAS BROWNE [1]

SOME years ago I undertook to establish the probability that "the poet of Stratford exerted upon the sage of Norwich a remarkable attraction and an unmistakable influence." [2] The *evidence*, as I then remarked, could not, in the nature of the case, claim finality. Some of it, however, has commended itself to other readers—notably the fact that Sir Thomas Browne was clearly a lover of the theatre and drama, and, specifically, the almost unmistakably close echoes, in the *Religio Medici, Hydriotaphia*, and elsewhere in his writings, of such plays as *Macbeth* (in Browne's words, "I . . . begin to be weary of the sun" and "Sleep . . . that death . . . we . . . die daily"), *Julius Caesar* ("Men have lost their reason"), *Richard III* ("God and good angels"), and *Hamlet* (the spurns that "patient meekness takes" and the "strumpet . . . fortune.") The least satisfactory aspect of the case, it seemed to me, was my inability to find a more direct link between Shakespeare and Browne. Shakespearean echoes I heard clearly, and, I think, in unvanquishable number; but their music did not reconcile me to the deafness or blindness to which I should have liked to charge my inability to find even a single direct mention of Shakespeare's name in the whole length and breadth of Sir Thomas Browne's writings. To be sure, Sir Thomas himself reminds us, in the *Vulgar Errors*,[3] that others besides him have tantalized students in this way. "Virgil," for

1. Reprinted, with additions, from The Shakespeare Association *Bulletin*, VI (1931), 60 ff.

2. "Shakspere and Sir Thomas Browne," *Shakspere's Silences* (1929), pp. 97 ff. Details here are drawn from this essay. (See also the next chapter of the present volume, and, for references to Browne, the *Works*, ed. Wilkin, 1835.)

3. I, vi; cf. above, n. 2.

instance, "so much beholding unto Homer, hath not his name in all his works." And the present writer — by way of proving himself not totally blind — has previously called attention to the fact that if Browne does not actually *name* Shakespeare, he does *allude* to him [4] or at least to *A Midsummer-Night's Dream* — "the tale of Oberon." I return to the subject here to add a small link to the chain, for I think that anyone who may be interested in the literary relations between Shakespeare and Sir Thomas Browne will also be interested to learn that in one of the Browne manuscripts in the British Museum there does appear a mention of Shakespeare's name, and something more. Unfortunately it is not by Sir Thomas himself. And yet it is virtually his own — for it appears in the memorandum book of his best-beloved pupil, one whom he taught with scholarly zeal and paternal devotion: his eldest son, later the distinguished Dr. Edward Browne, traveller, member of the Royal Society, physician to the king, and President of the College of Physicians. Let me add at once that the younger Browne makes honorable mention of Shakespeare's Stratford, and of at least one "country play" not hitherto noticed, which he and his brother enjoyed about the year 1663.

Dr. Norman Moore's *Medicine in the British Isles* [5] contains a well-informed essay on Edward Browne. A conjecture which makes part of this essay is, I think, substantially confirmed by the hitherto unpublished manuscript entries with which I shall conclude this chapter. "I can imagine," writes Moore, that as Sir Thomas Browne "took his boy to school . . . he pleasantly pointed to the figure [of] Sir Thomas Erpingham, a hero of Agincourt . . . within the gate of the Norwich Grammar School . . . and quoted the words of King Henry V in Shakespeare,

> Good morrow, old Sir Thomas Erpingham."

The painstaking, affectionate, and voluminous pages of Sir Thomas Browne's published and unpublished letters to his sons

4. In *Vulgar Errors*, IV, xi; cf. above, p. 224, n. 2.    5. Oxford, 1908, pp. 70, 81 ff.

prove beyond the shadow of a doubt that Edward Browne's education followed closely the lines laid down by his father. And it may be observed incidentally that he constantly advised his sons where to go, what to see, and what to read. In short, as Moore noted, Sir Thomas guided not merely Edward Browne's *professional* training but also the particulars of that "sound literary education" which preceded and accompanied his study of medicine. Edward Browne, I may add, was also an enthusiastic student of the drama! His memorandum book [6] indicates that he saw almost two-score plays — probably between 1662 and 1663 — at London, Cambridge, and Norwich. Certain portions of this memorandum book which have escaped the notice of previous investigators suggest that Shakespeare was among the masters of whom Sir Thomas Browne had taught his children at their sitting down and at their walking by the way.

From MS. Sloan. 1900, Simon Wilkin printed in his 1835 edition of Sir Thomas Browne's *Works*, Edward Browne's Journal of a "Tour in Derbyshire" — a journey of 344 miles — which he and his younger brother Thomas undertook in September, 1662. At the end of this Journal young Browne promised to be "once again a vagabond" [7] in his own country. Students of Sir Thomas Browne, and his son's biographers, have apparently not known that Edward Browne kept his promise — for Wilkin did not print a series of entries — undated, but probably of the year 1663 — in the same manuscript, which cover a 400 mile circular journey by the two brothers through the rest of the Midland counties. In the course of this journey they travelled southeast from Norwich to Northamptonshire, and then south and east again through Warwickshire, Worcester, Gloucester, Oxford, Cambridge, back to

6. British Museum MS. Sloan. 1900. The plays mentioned immediately below have been discussed by W. W. Greg, *Gentleman's Magazine*, July, 1906, W. J. Lawrence, *Englische Studien*, XXXV (1905), 279, Leslie Hotson, *Commonwealth and Restoration Stage*, p. 178, and others. — On earlier plays at Norwich, see above, pp. 186–187.

7. Wilkin, I, 22 ff.

Norwich. Like the gay young travellers they were, they stopped to enjoy the amenities of town and country: *"a play* and Mr. Howard's hunting," for instance, "at Thetford" — where their host was probably the Mr. Henry Howard, later Duke of Norfolk, in whose company Edward Browne danced (in January, 1664) with the "greatest beauties" and "dranke out of pure golde." [8] Being their father's sons, the young men missed no places of scientific, historic, or literary interest by the way. We have Edward Browne's notes for it that they allowed themselves ample time to gaze leisurely and seriously upon "these things" which were most "remarkable." In Warwickshire it was, naturally, according to the manuscript, the "Shakspear tombe in Stretford." [9] From it we learn, further, that "Y^e Clark^e at Stretford" had a shilling from them, and mine host another ten shillings for "Reckoning," "horses," and "fruit." Before the reckoning, however, and the brothers' subsequent departure for Worcester (and its Cathedral, with King John's tomb and Prince Arthur's) the clerk at Stratford seems to have given them their money's worth, for Edward Browne paused long enough to copy out, in full, from the tombstone, the "Good friend, for Jesus' sake forbear," and, altogether, more than a dozen lines of the familiar inscriptions in the chancel of Stratford Church.

Before printing my excerpts from Edward Browne's notes, I may add a word as to the date of the tour which they record. I think it is almost certainly 1663. This journey would naturally have suggested itself as an early sequel to the long Derbyshire tour in the autumn of 1662. It is known, moreover, that the two brothers were together in residence at Cambridge for the greater part of 1663,[10] whereas in 1664 their roads divided — permanently, so far as the records show — for in that year Edward Browne

8. Wilkin, I, 45. — This is the *country play* to which I have referred above.

9. In their earlier tour, similarly, they had stopped at the Tomb of Sir Philip Sidney's friend, Fulke Greville, in Warwick (*Id.*, I, 40). See below, p. 240.

10. Cf. Wilkin, I, LXXV, 42, etc.

started upon his busy course of foreign travel and professional study, while (Lieutenant) Thomas Browne the younger began the short but gallant career in the Navy which came to a close with his premature death a few years later.[11]

It remains only to append the following extracts from Edward Browne's

*Memoranda of a Tour through the Midlands (ca. 1663)*
by *Edward and Thomas Browne.*[12]
[MS. Sloan. 1900, f. 32 v.]

[1. Itinerary]

| | |
|---|---|
| "From Norwich to Thetford | 20 [miles] |
| From Thetfr. . . . to Hadnam | 24 |
| From Hadnam . . . to Heigham ferries | 23 |
| From Heigham Ferries . . . to Daventry | 17 |
| *From Daventry to Stretford upon Avon* [13] | 18 |
| From Stretford to Worcester | 28 . . ." |

[Thence, by Hereford, Gloucester, Barclay, Abington, Oxford, Newport and Cambridge, to Norwich—about 400 miles, in 21 stages.]

[2. "Sights" and Entertainments *En Route*]

[*Id.*, f. 15 v.]
"A play & Mr Howards hunting at Thetford
Ely minster
Wellingborough
Northampton Brinton tombes
Daventry ye hill and soape well
Shrugbury Starre stones
Sr Edward Peto's windmill

---

11. *Id.*     12. I have supplied the square-bracketed material.     13. My italics.

*Shakspear tombe in Stretford*
Worcester Cathedrall in which is King Johns tombe . . .
Prince Arthurs tombe & Chappell, Littletons tombe . . .
Glocester Colledge, in which these things are remarkable,
the cloisters, yᵉ roof of the Quire. . . ."

[3.  Expenses]

[*Id.*, f. 14 v.]

| | | | |
|---|---|---|---|
| "Thetford supper | o — | 19[?]— | 6 |
| *Yᵉ Clarkᵉ at Stretford* | o | 1 | o |
| fruit | o | o | 4 |
| Reckoning | o | 5 | o |
| Horses | o | 4 | o |
| & see Worcester Colledge | o | 2 | o |
| at yᵉ Castle | o | o | 6 |
| fruit | o | o | 3 |
| To my brother [14] | o | 1 | 6 . . . |
| to yᵉ Butler at Hereford Colledge | o | 1 | o . . ." |

[4.  Copies of the Stratford Church Inscriptions] [15]

[*Id.*, f. 64 v.]

"Judicio pyliu[m] Genio Socrate[m] arte Marone[m]
terra tegit populus maeret olympus habet

\* \* \*

Stay passenger why goest thou by so fast
Read if thou canst whom envious death hath plac'd
Within yⁱˢ monument Shakespear with who[m]
Quick nature died whose name doth deck this tombe
Far more than cost sith all yᵗ hee hath writ
Leaves living art but Page to serve his wit

14.  This entry proves that both brothers made the journey.
15.  Cf. the transcripts in *Shakespeare Allusion Book*, ed. Munro, I, 267.

Good friend for Jesus sake forbear
To dig yᵉ dust inclosed here
Blest bee yᵉ man yᵗ spares these stones
& curs'd bee hee yᵗ moves my bones

John of Stratford Archbishop of Canterbury founder of this chancell."

# III

## POETS, PLAYS, AND ACTORS

# XI

## SIR THOMAS BROWNE AND THE ELIZABETHANS [1]

IN A previous volume I have pointed out that Sir Thomas Browne certainly knew and liked his theatre, and, almost as certainly, his Shakespeare.[2] My first purpose here is to show that Browne's interest *in the Elizabethans in general* was more lively, his contact with them more far-reaching and probably more significant, than has yet been realized. The Baconians will be entitled to get all the comfort they can from the second part of this study — for there, though I have but recently dealt with Browne and Shakespeare, I shall bring together much evidence old and new which indicates that one of the Elizabethans whom Browne especially remembered was Francis Bacon. The reader will quickly recognize the difficulties inherent in the nature of much of this evidence. Browne himself protested [3] against the easy assumption that "coincidence" in letters is necessarily ascribable to borrowing.[4] He would have agreed with Gibbon that the language of nature may be the same in Cappadocia and in Britain; and in studies of this sort he would certainly have urged due caution and a proper discount of *chance likenesses* between the many dialects into which nature translates the mother tongue of the human spirit. I am equally confident, however, that he would have welcomed any reasonable quest for such truth as may remain — for the indications in his own work, for instance, of the

1. Reprinted, with additions, from *Studies in Philology*, XXVIII (1931), 87 ff.
2. "Shakspere and Sir Thomas Browne," *Shakspere's Silences* (1929), pp. 97 ff.
3. With reference to the supposed indebtedness of the *Religio Medici* to Montaigne (see n. 4).
4. I.e., to "imitation" or "plagiarism" or what not. See Wilkin, *Works of Sir Thomas Browne*, ed. 1835 (referred to hereafter as "W"), II, p. 218; IV, p. 386.

flux and reflux, the eternal renewal of the creative imagination from the deep well-springs of old. For Browne's own unfailing quest for truth and excellence is not least in evidence in the life-long enthusiasm he himself brought to the study of literature.

## I

Mr. Saintsbury, indeed, asserts that Browne ("though his literary knowledge was certainly not small") *"never touches"* upon "pure literature." [5] I cannot help thinking that if Charles Lamb could have heard this pronouncement he would have responded with a whistle — or an indignant stutter, and that Coleridge (who also loved the "delicious" savor of Browne) would have joined him in more eloquent if no more energetic rebuttal. Let us stand with the angels — and recall but one remark of Browne's upon a subject surely not far removed from "pure literature":

> How unhappy great poets have been in versifying their own epitaphs: wherein Petrarca, Dante, and Ariosto have so unhappily failed that if their tombs should outlast their works posterity would find so little of Apollo in them as to mistake them for Ciceronian poets. . . .[6]

I, for one, regret that Browne did not carry out a "purely" literary project of his own which he jotted down for future reference in an unpublished commonplace book note: "To make a poem or epigramme upon this subject, a windmill built upon a mount of dead men's bones." [7] Of course it is not to be denied that Browne's achievements as a stylist still commend themselves to the critics. Saintsbury, like Pater and Lytton Strachey,[8] is by no means unsympathetic toward this side of Browne, but he is one of the modern majority who deal with him primarily as an antiquary, and, for one reason or another, deny him something of his birth-

5. *Cambridge History of English Literature*, VII, p. 272.
6. *Letter to a Friend*, W, IV, p. 48.
7. MS. Sloan. 1843 (British Museum), f. 33.
8. Cf. *Appreciations* and *Books and Characters*, respectively.

right as a man of letters. One reason, perhaps, is the general failure to appreciate the studied catholicity of Browne's reading — that is to say, not only in the classics but in the literature of his own time, and not least in the literature of England. Curiously enough, the tendency to pigeonhole Browne as a classicist (who ignored English literature!) seems to date from the very time that should have brought more light instead of less. Wilkin's edition of Browne's *Works* (1835) made available for the first time a fairly complete *corpus* of Browne's writings. In it there are, as I shall show, many allusions to the Elizabethans; but it contained also one somewhat crusty note on *Hudibras* and the much more "ancient . . . inventor[s] . . . of burlesque poems." [9] The critics seized avidly upon this remark, and upon their facile assumption that this small part equals the whole rests, I think, most of the general notion still prevalent as to Browne's supposed indifference to modern literature.

In this connection I must let the critics speak for themselves. Bulwer-Lytton, reviewing Wilkin for the *Edinburgh* in 1836, struck the keynote. Browne, he held,

> probably read little of the works of his younger contemporaries, for in his correspondence he scarcely observes upon what made the current literature of the day. Even Hudibras . . . appears only to draw from him an erudite comment upon the antiquity of burlesque poems.[10]

We shall see presently that the correspondence also alludes — in no mere dryasdust vein — to English writers so diverse as Michael Drayton and Sir Thomas North, Dr. Donne and Sir John Denham. Meanwhile, it is to be noted that Sir Edmund Gosse, in his influential *Life* (1905) [11] repeats Bulwer Lytton's large assertion, illustrating it, once more, by the allusion to *Hudibras*. The assertion is, in fact, more sweeping and has proved to be proportionately more misleading to later students. Gosse found in Browne

9. W, IV, p. 253.      10. *Edinburgh Review*, CXXIX, pp. 1-35.
11. *Browne*, English Men of Letters, p. 55.

little sympathy with the current literature of his country or the modern vernaculars . . . [but] *superb neglect of all contemporary poetry and prose* . . . [and] *scorn of the poets in particular.* . . . The great English writers from Chaucer down to Milton, from Wycliffe down to Dryden, might never have existed for all the attention they receive from Sir Thomas Browne. Almost the only reference to a living imaginative author which is to be found in the length and breadth of his works is a note written at the time that *Hudibras* was published . . . a mere pellet of sun-dried pedantry. . . .

Here I must pause for a moment to summarize from my earlier study the *prima facie* objections to these large assumptions. To begin with, Browne himself [12] states clearly that his love for the ancients did not blind him to the claims of the moderns, including his own countrymen. Next, as regards his "neglect" and "scorn" of the poets in particular: the simple fact is that Browne himself was a poet, and that he knew it. He wrote poems in verse and prose—both in the *Religio Medici*; and many stately prose-poems in the *Urn Burial* and *Christian Morals.* In his letter "Of . . . Gradual Verses" [13]—and in other places noted below [14] he speaks of poetry as one who cherishes excellence therein. Let it be remembered, finally, that Browne did not scorn to describe his own youth as "a piece of poetry" [15] and that he did not neglect Shakespeare. And though my study of Browne and Shakespeare could take no close account of the other Elizabethans, it did suggest that he had probably read such good Elizabethans, among others, as Raleigh, Spenser, Sidney, and Donne.[16] I am now able to confirm this conjectural list in its entirety, and to add to it the names of Ben Jonson, Drayton, Thomas Lodge, Purchas, Sir Thomas North, and Francis Bacon. There is reason to believe, further, that he *read* (and therefore that he did *not* contemn) many another old master and new: Chaucer and Jeremy Taylor, Occleve

12. In the *Pseudodoxia*, I, vi; W, II, pp. 222 ff. (quoted below, p. 263, n. 134).
13. W, IV, pp. 193-194.    14. See below, pp. 247-248.
15. *Rel. Medici*, II, xi; W, II, p. 110.    16. See above, p. 233, n. 2.

and Thomas Fuller, Lydgate and Lord Herbert of Cherbury. Before citing chapter and verse, however, I must indicate how the traditional criticism has blinded students to the significance of these facts.

In a series of notes published nine years after Gosse's *Life*, Mr. Malcolm Letts [17] called attention to a source of information which is still too little known. This important document is the 1711 sale "Catalogue of the Libraries of the Learned Sir Thomas Brown and Dr. Edward Brown, his Son." [18] Mr. Letts's notes on this Catalogue, though, as he says, "by no means" exhaustive, are distinctly useful in all respects but one. Unfortunately he begs entirely the question of the significance of the list of English classics in the Catalogue; witness the fact that he begins with a generalization straight from Gosse and his predecessors. "Browne," we hear once more, "is not a writer who is much in touch with English imaginative literature." Somewhat later Letts observes that the works of Spenser, Beaumont and Fletcher, Jonson, Milton, George Herbert, and others [19] are listed in the Catalogue. Immediately after the remark about "English imaginative literature," however, *Hudibras* is once more served up as proof of the pudding: "He seems to have read *Hudibras* . . . but Part III only is in the Catalogue"!

Much of the fresh evidence here to be presented concerning Browne's reading is based upon this Catalogue, particularly in so far as it is supported by significant utterances in Browne's published writings and in his manuscripts. Before proceeding, however, I must attempt to dispose of a difficulty connected with the use of the Catalogue. The problem—which has never been ade-

17. *Notes & Queries*, 11 Ser. (1914), X, pp. 321, 342, 361 ff.

18. (Hereafter referred to as "S. C.") Published by Thomas Ballard, Bookseller. But two copies (British Museum and Osler Collection) are extant. More recently Sir Geoffrey Keynes (*Bibliography of Sir Thomas Browne*, Cambridge, 1924, p. 183) and Professor A. C. Howell ("Browne's Knowledge of Languages," *Studies in Philology*, XXII, 1925, pp. 412 ff.) have borne witness to the importance of this document.

19. I.e., Daniel, Cowley, Walton, Evelyn, and Selden. In so far as I can supplement Letts's findings, I shall return to these and other writers, below.

quately dealt with—is simple enough in the statement. Which of
the books in the Catalogue, or what proportion of them, may
safely be assumed to have belonged to Sir Thomas himself rather
than to his son Edward, who was also a distinguished physician
and the author of several books of travel?

Obviously, one begins by excluding from Sir Thomas's share of
the library the volumes published after his death [20]—that is to say,
about 400 lots out of a total approximating 2,400, or one-sixth of
the whole. Not a few of the remainder he definitely claims as his
own by mentioning them in one way or another; but what of the
considerable majority not so distinguished or distinguishable? Sir
Geoffrey Keynes, in his admirable bibliography of Browne,[21] remarks that "probably the greater part of the collection had been
formed by Sir Thomas himself," and this is certainly a safe estimate—for reasons not given by Keynes but worth noting here
even at the cost of delaying my long-promised evidence. The
extant correspondence between Sir Thomas and his son is full and
circumstantial on both sides. From it and from Browne's other
letters it is clear that as between father and son the former was
incomparably the better booklover and bookbuyer. For one
thing, he never tired of sending books to his sons, nor of endeavor-
ing to form or guide their taste.[22] He had young Edward Browne's
travel letters "writ out into a book" with a view to future publication, and later he provided illustrations, "hints," and moral
support to encourage his son to publish.[23] He urged the young
man to hold on to valuable books and manuscripts,[24] commissioned
him to buy books at home and abroad, and applauded his efforts
to obtain an important collection for the library of the College of
Physicians.[25] The letters, moreover, indicate that the elder

20. In 1682. (Accordingly, I eliminate from the discussion below all books dated after
1681. I count some 417 lots of these—almost all of which must have been added to the
collection by Edward Browne—out of the total of 2,377 in the S. C.)

21. See above, p. 237, n. 18.

22. See letters to Edward and Thomas Browne (the younger) in W, I, pp. 209, 211-212,
149, 119, 143, etc.

23. W, I, pp. 183, 202, 232.    24. W, I, pp. 214-215.    25. W, I, pp. 178 ff.

Browne remained, to the end of his life, not only a warm-hearted lover of books but a shrewd buyer thereof. Again and again he writes his son of some "prettie little book" [26] or other (a rare treasure finely printed or illustrated) which he has been able to purchase in London or Norwich.[27] But he also writes that he has refused to buy uninteresting offerings of the booksellers, and he complained, less than a year before his death, of the exorbitant price of certain new books.[28] He was twice blessed, nevertheless. He gave or lent numerous books and manuscripts to his sons and his friends, but they in turn gave him valuable gifts in kind.[29] And he bought books until he died. He complained of high prices in 1681, but he enumerates many books which he bought in Norwich thereafter; [30] and he ends by asking Edward Browne, in a letter dated March 1682, about six months before his death, to pay for him a bill of twenty-five shillings which he owed a London bookseller named Martyn, whom he had "always found . . . a very civill and honest person." [31]

My justification for lingering over these matters will be apparent as I return to this correspondence and to the Catalogue for confirmation of the conjectural list of Browne's Elizabethans with which I began: [32] Sidney and Spenser, Raleigh and Donne. As regards Sidney and Spenser, for example, I had previously been able to show only that these poets are mentioned in an exchange of letters between Browne and his friend Evelyn, the diarist.[33] This, however, does not end the matter. To begin with Sidney, the sale catalogue [34] definitely lists the 1622 edition of "*Sir Phil. Sidney's* Countess of *Pembroke's* Arcadia" among Browne's possessions, perhaps among his treasures. Browne, to be sure, does

26. "Dr. Love's book, which is a pretty book . . ." "A pretty opteck book . . . with figures" (W, I, pp. 281, 263, etc.); on his fine copies of Daniel and of North's Plutarch, and concerning his fine prints, see below, pp. 248, 244, and W, I, p. 117.

27. Some of his most interesting books seem to have been dispersed, for they are not in the S. C. (cf. p. 241 and n. 41, below).

28. W, I, pp. 251, 314, 321 ff.     29. W, I, pp. 409, 463 ff., 352, 393 ff., 413 ff.

30. W, I, pp. 342, 347 ff., 321 ff.     31. W, I, p. 337.

32. See above, p. 236.     33. W, I, p. 379; cf. above, p. 233, n. 2.     34. P. 46.

not name Sidney in his writings, but he evidently did not teach his sons to scorn the poet's memory. Edward Browne does mention Sidney, though he obviously did not know him well enough to know also the name of his greatest friend. In 1662 he set down in the journal he kept for his father's perusal the inscription he had read upon "a very handsome tombe" at Warwick: "Here lies—" (he could not make out Fulke Greville's name) "servant to Queen Elizabeth, counsellour to King James, and friend to Sir Philip Sidney." [35]

Mr. Letts has noted that the Catalogue names Sir Philip's humbler friend, Edmund Spenser. It is worth while to add, however, that Spenser is there represented by two editions of *The Fairie Queene* plus one of the complete works,[36] and that Browne himself [37] mentions him. He does so in a statement which puts Spenser in excellent company and incidentally suggests something of the range and quality of Browne's own taste, though his purpose was merely to supply a severe intelligence test for a remarkable young schoolboy. In 1672 Sir Thomas certified that he had heard

> Wm. Wotton,[38] son to Mr. Henry Wotton [39] of Wrentham, at the age of six years, read *a stanza in Spencer* very distinctly, and pronounce it properly, as also some verses in . . . Virgil, *which I purposely chose out.* . . . Also some verses in Homer and . . . Pythagoras . . . as . . . also the 1st verse of the 4th ch. of Genesis in Hebrew. . . .[40]

Browne's interest in Raleigh and Donne, again, may not have been overwhelming; but it was not negligible. Neither of these writers appears in the sale catalogue, but one cannot safely draw

35. W, I, p. 40; see above, p. 227, n. 9.
36. *F. Q.*, eds. 1609, 1687; *Works*, 1679 (S. C., pp. 45, 53, 46, 58).
37. As I am reminded by Professor A. C. Howell, who has kindly furnished me with several notes in this connection.
38. Who later became Bentley's friend.
39. *Sir* Henry Wotton (whose chief prose work, *The State of Christendom*, appears in the S. C., p. 44) was related to this family by name only.
40. Cf. Henry Wotton, *Education of Children*, and W, I, xcv.

negative conclusions from such omissions, for omitted also are many important books which Browne certainly read and owned.[41] Certainly he knew both Raleigh's *History* and his travels. In the *Vulgar Errors* [42] he speaks of Raleigh's personal "observations" upon the redness of the Red Sea, and in one of his commonplace books he queried a passage [43] in Book III of the *History*. Raleigh, finally, is represented also in Browne's manuscript collections, for one of his manuscripts [44] includes three of Raleigh's discourses: "Of . . . Shippes . . . and the sea force of England," "Of the . . . fundamental cause of Warre," and his "Apologie at his re-turne from . . . Guiana." If vast distances would seem to stretch between these voyages and the work of Donne, it may well be recalled that Donne, too, was a representative Elizabethan who wrote out of the storm and the calm of spacious voyagings. There can be no doubt, in any case, that Browne admired Donne's work early and late—the poems and the sermons. In Browne's youth the "strange fire" of the poems moved him to express the generous "envie" of his commendatory verses of 1633,[45] and a year before his death he wrote to his son, "Dr. Donnes sermon is a very good one." [46]

As it happens, we have from Browne's own pen another note about his reading which is especially in point here. In it he cheer-fully admits that he had read "some hundreds of Sermons," [47] thereby justifying the conjecture that at least a few more of Donne's may have been among the lot. The document which contains this note was discovered by Keynes not long ago, and

41. *E.g.*, North's Plutarch, Foxe's *Book of Martyrs*, Purchas, and others discussed below.

42. VI, ix; W, III, p. 261.

43. Concerning "a town . . . belonging of old to the state of Italy . . . which . . . an oracle had foretold . . . the Athenians should build . . . anew. . . ." "What city this was . . . ?" (W, IV, p. 420).

44. See also p. 258, n. 122, under item (7).

45. Apparently Browne's first published work (cf. H. J. C. Grierson, *Donne's Poetical Works*, Oxford, 1912, I, 372 ff.; II, p. 255).

46. W, I, p. 307.

47. Another document, an undated and unpublished letter to Browne from a certain William Oliver, promises him "some sermons w^ch this son of mine shalle bringe ye to-mor-row" (Sloan. MS. 1843, f. 39).

deserves to be widely known.[48]  Its chief importance for us lies in the fact that it contains further information concerning Browne's readings in several Elizabethans other than the group discussed above.  Into the Commonplace Book of his daughter, Elizabeth Lyttleton, Sir Thomas wrote a formidable list of "The books which my daughter . . . hath read unto me at nights till she read y$^m$ all out."  From it I quote the following items, representative of his interest in history, travel, and divinity:

> all Plutarks liues, folio . . .
> all the History of Josephus, fol.
> all fox his book of Martyrs, fol. . . .
> all the historie of Queen Elizabeth by Camden, fol. . . .
> all Sands his Travels . . .
> all Suetoneus of the twelve Caesars . . .
> some parts of Purchas his Relations
> some hundreds of Sermons
> many other Books . . .

It goes almost without saying that some of these books, originals and translations, are Elizabethan classics; but certain implications and connotations of the list require further comment. Foxe's *Book of Martyrs* [49] speaks for itself, but whose, besides Donne's, and of what quality, were the hundreds of sermons Browne had read to him?  One or two of his favorite divines are readily identified.  Archbishop Tillotson, for instance, did him the honor of alluding to the *Religio Medici* in a sermon, and a letter of Browne's shows that he repaid the compliment by reading the Archbishop's sermons.[50]  The sale catalogue, again, proves — if proof were needed — that he possessed miscellaneous sermons and the complete *Works* [51] of a divine who was also a notable controversialist and a writer of vigorous satire, a literary species

48. *Commonplace Book of Elizabeth Lyttleton*, ed. Keynes (privately printed, 54 copies only), Cambridge, 1919; see pp. 13-15.  Browne gives the titles of 28 works, of which 17 (including Foxe) are historical, and the rest travel books.

49. Twice mentioned in Browne's *Antiquities of Norwich* (W, IV, pp. 16, 31) but not in S. C. (see above, p. 241, and n. 41).

50. W, I, xliii ff.; I, p. 237.          51. S. C., pp. 54, 44.

which always interested Browne.[52]   That Browne *read* Bishop Joseph Hall appears from the fact that he describes him in *The Antiquities of Norwich* [53] as "my honoured friend . . . a person of singular . . . piety" whose "own works are the best monument and character of himself."   I cannot with equal assurance identify the authors of all the sermons still to be accounted for, but Browne's friend Whitefoot supplies a useful hint.   Browne, he writes, "read *the best* English sermons he could hear of." [54]   Among them must have been the work of such masters as Richard Baxter, Thomas Fuller, and Jeremy Taylor, all of whom are well represented in the Catalogue.[55]

Of considerable interest also, with regard to Browne's Elizabethan background, is his enumeration of some of the historians which his daughter read "all out" to him, many of them probably in translation.   We have already seen that he read closely in Raleigh's *History*.   The Catalogue,[56] once more, shows that in addition to Camden's *History of Queen Elizabeth* he possessed the same writer's *Britannia* (the 1637 edition, Englished by Philemon Holland).   It is worth observing, incidentally, that Holland's versions of Plutarch, Suetonius,[57] and Pliny were also among the many English translations of the classics in Browne's library.   His daughter would naturally have used these rather than the originals in reading to him.   For, however great or small her proficiency in Greek and Latin may have been, we shall see that Sir Thomas, for all his scholarly attainments, by no means disdained certain of the great Elizabethan translations.   It is therefore interesting to find that when Elizabeth Lyttleton read her father "all the History of Josephus, fol." she was, in all probability, using the folio listed in

52. Cf. *Rel. Med.*, II, iv; *Christian Morals*, I, iii; *Vulgar Errors*, I, vi (W, II, p. 95; IV, p. 61; II, p. 215); and below, p. 247, and n. 81.

53. W, IV, p. 18.        54. W, I, xlv.        55. S. C., pp. 48, 45, 47, 46.

56. P. 45.   Besides Camden (see text following) Browne read such antiquaries as Leland and Lambarde (W, I, p. 388; IV, p. 457).

57. "Of the 12 Caesars," S. C., p. 49; Plutarch and Pliny, *Id.*, pp. 45, 44.   Other translations listed include Homer, Juvenal, Tacitus, Persius and Lucan (*Id.*, pp. 46, 55, 50), and Boccaccio, Tasso, and Machiavelli (pp. 45-46).   Browne mentions Sir John Harington in *The Ant. of Norwich*, W, IV, p. 16.

the sale catalogue as *"Josephus's* Works, translated by Tho. Lodge, 1640," [58] that is to say, by the author of *Rosalynde* metamorphosed into the learned physician and translator, Doctor Thomas Lodge.

I am less certain as to which translation of "all Plutarks liues" she may have read to him. The Catalogue lists only Philemon Holland's, but one of Browne's letters proves that this was not his own favorite. Plutarch was one of Browne's first loves, and almost his last. A few months before his death, therefore, when Edward Browne had been invited to take part in a fresh translation of the *Lives*, Sir Thomas, obviously pleased, wrote as follows: [59]

> You write of a designe of translating Plutarch . . . agayne. . . . It was first translated by Amyot . . . *Sir Thomas North* translated his out of the French . . . *which was that you and your brother Thomas vsed to read at my howse*, reprinted 1612, of a fayre and legible print. . . . If the disused words and some other faults had been altered [in later reprints] North's translation might have sufficed and still passed, especially with gentlemen. . . .

A passage in the *Vulgar Errors*,[60] further, proves that Browne also read North's almost equally famous *Dial of Princes*, translated from "Antonius Guevara, that elegant Spaniard."

Browne's notes upon his *private* reading supply most of the information still to be presented in the first part of this study, except for one item more out of the list of his daughter's nocturnal ministrations. She read him divinity, biography, history, and also many books of travel. The outstanding work of this kind on the list is, of course, that of Samuel Purchas, to whom Browne refers also in *Vulgar Errors*.[61] Purchas, however, was but one of many. Browne never ceased reading the travellers, because travel and observation were with him, as with his sons, a passion second to none. Most of his readings in this kind, however, do not concern

58. P. 44.  59. February 13, 1682 (W, I, p. 332). My italics.
60. I, vi; W, II, p. 223.  61. III, p. xxvi; W, II, p. 515.

us here because they are not particularly significant to the student of literature. To the roll of those which are, one or two besides Raleigh and Purchas should be added. Sir Thomas as well as his son must have liked the zestful downrightness of Coryat's *Crudities*, even though this work of "Heroical Tom Coriat" (as Edward Browne described him to his father) [62] is not in the Catalogue. By the same token both of them must have enjoyed Fynes Moryson's spirited *Itinerary*, which is named in the Catalogue [63] but apparently not in their writings.

I have yet to notice three or four significant utterances of Browne's upon poets and poetry; supplementary references must suffice for still other poets, critics, and philosophers whose works were in his library. A word may be in order, first, concerning his supposed lack of sympathy with the literature "of the modern vernaculars" [64] other than English. Having already shown that he wrote appreciatively of such "great poets" as Petrarch, Dante, and Ariosto,[65] and of such prose masters as Boccaccio, Machiavelli, and Rabelais,[66] I need merely add that the works of all these writers, and those of Tasso, Guarini, Du Bellay, and Boileau to boot, were in his library.[67] That he read some of them closely appears from his frequent allusions to Dante and from the fact [68] that he fitted a portion of one of Du Bellay's sonnets into the *Religio Medici*.[69] I shall not undertake to guess how much or how little Browne may have read of his contemporary Boileau, for I know only that among his books was a copy of the Frenchman's *Oeuvres* (1675).[70] As regards his immediate English contemporaries, however, his famous reference to Butler is *not* the only one, for it is to be noted that in 1669 he mentioned to his son the death

62. W, I, p. 37; cf. Edward Browne's *Journal of a Visit to Paris, 1664,* ed. Keynes (1923), p. 16.

63. P. 57.    64. See above, p. 236.    65. See above, p. 234.

66. Cf. Thaler, *Shakspere's Silences*, p. 101.    67. S. C., pp. 34-40, 68, 13, 53.

68. Proved conclusively by Mr. H. G. Ward, *Review of English Studies*, V (1929), pp. 59 ff.

69. II, iv (W, II, p. 93); sonnet 68 of Du Bellay's *Les Regrets*.    70. S. C., p. 38.

of Sir John Denham.[71]  Others of his contemporaries whose volumes (all dated before his death) made part of his library, include [72] scholars and philosophers such as Lord Herbert, John Barclay, Robert Boyle, and Thomas Hobbes,[73] and critics and minor poets such as D'Avenant and Thomas Rymer, Alexander Brome, John Quarles, and John Oldham.[74]  To complete this part of my roll-call and to prove again that in all his reading Browne looked before as well as after, I may add that he also possessed a commentary upon Chaucer,[75] together with Lydgate's rendering of Boccaccio's *De Casibus Virorum* [76] and a manuscript of Occleve's *De Regimine Principis.*[77]

Something remains to be said concerning Browne and the greater English poets.  It is true that he himself did not say much about any one of them and that—like Virgil, Chaucer, Shakespeare, and Milton—he did not enlarge upon certain of his most significant literary relationships.  Poets engaged in the high task of composition often seem too preoccupied to wonder whence came the raw materials of their visions, and not even scholars are in the habit of multiplying footnotes when *they* write poetry.  The poet-scholar Browne, I imagine, knew the great English poets better than anyone could hope to *prove* by the most painstaking study of his remarks about them, or of his silences.  I have already shown, however, that the record is not altogether blank.  So far as I know, he possessed only a commentary upon Chaucer, but this argues a foregone conclusion: some familiarity with the text. He had no commentary upon Spenser, but he owned several editions of his works, and of Milton, Beaumont and Fletcher, Drayton, and Ben Jonson.[78]  I think he did not scorn any of these

71.  W, I, p. 184.  (Edward Browne had the 1684 ed. of Denham's *Poems;* S. C., p. 53.)

72.  Besides those already mentioned (cf. above, p. 237 and n. 19).

73.  S. C., pp. 15-17, 30-32, 48-57.          74.  *Id.*, pp. 52-55.

75.  "Coment. upon the 2 Tales of Jeffrey Chaucer, 1665" (S. C., p. 52); not listed in Hammond's *Bibliographical Manual* nor in the British Museum catalogue.

76.  "*J. Bocha's* Tragedies, translated by *J. Lidgate*" (S. C., p. 45).

77.  Sloan. MS. 1825; cf. W, IV, p. 466.

78.  See above, p. 240, n. 36, and S. C., pp. 45 ff., p. 52, etc.

poets, nor Shakespeare either. This in spite of the fact that no copy of Shakespeare appears in the sale catalogue, and that of the others he actually *names* in his writings only Spenser, Drayton, and Jonson. Perhaps he had read his Shakespeare "all out," as also his Raleigh and Purchas, Foxe and Sir Thomas North, all of which are conspicuously missing from the Catalogue. For the rest, I have shown elsewhere that in lieu of Shakespeare himself Browne does mention "the tale of Oberon [79] — somewhat as we shall see him alluding to *The Advancement of Learning* without naming Francis Bacon. [80]

Browne's mention of Spenser, already noted, is brief but to the point. Brief also but more expressive are his remarks upon Jonson and Drayton, which I have saved for the last because in them Browne sets forth unequivocally his admiration of these representative Elizabethans. For Ben Jonson he had a word of praise such as one reserves for a man who is not only witty in himself but the cause of wit in others. He lauded Ben *for the salt wit with which he had scoured the city*, and he did it in a form which would certainly have pleased the learned compiler of *Timber or Discoveries*. Like him, Sir Thomas culled many a line for comment and remembrance from Horace and Plautus and Catullus, and, like Jonson again, he admirably illuminated old saws by modern instances — especially in one of his commonplacebook excerpts from Horace, [81] after which he wrote the name of the great Elizabethan:

> [Quod] sale multo
> Urbem defricuit. — Ben Johnson [82]

Elsewhere, I might add, Browne paid his respects also to Ben's fellow-worker, Inigo Jones. [83] More important here is the fact that Wilkin, [82] who printed Browne's lines in praise of Jonson, failed

79. *Vulgar Errors*, IV, p. xi; cf. *Shakspere's Silences*, p. 113.
80. See below, p. 254, n. 106.     81. Satires, I, x.
82. The excerpt is printed (not quite accurately) in W, IV, p. 456, from MS. Sloan. 1866, p. 54 ff.
83. W, I, p. 388.

to print certain additional entries in the same manuscript which should not remain unknown.  In this commonplace book Browne jotted down English captions for many other Horatian mottoes, "To be prefixed unto a satyre or sharpe poem," "On a sober good poem," "Upon a . . . booke of bad verses," "On any unskillfull . . . person preferred before an artist," "Upon a good poem contemned by the populace," "Upon a loftie butt . . . dry poem," "Upon a smooth & easie poem," "On a poem writt without paynes or carelessly," and upon many similar topics which attracted him, I take it, because he was vitally interested in poets and poetry.

The memory of at least one good poem, sober and painstaking and lofty withal, certainly remained with Browne to the end.  In 1681, a year before his death, he recalled to his son

> a prettie book,[84] writ 1612, by Michael Drayton, a learned poet, in smooth verse, called Polyolbion; and Mr. Selden writt a learned comment upon it. . . .  It describeth many rivers and hills in England and Wales, with figures of nymphs or shephards at them.[85]

In view of what has gone before, I am not "tempted to believe," with Mr. Letts,[86] "that it was 'Mr. Selden's learned comment' " only which attracted Browne to Drayton's *Polyolbion*.  I am tempted, rather, to call attention to the fact that young Edward Browne liked Drayton well enough for himself to copy long extracts from this poem into one of his notebooks,[87] and to the fact that Sir Thomas did not require Selden's good offices to attract him to Spenser, Donne, and Jonson.

How much of them he absorbed, and what he learned from the Elizabethans at large, is, of course, another question.  It is no more than one would expect that the influence of some of them —

---

84. Browne possessed another pretty book which he probably read with pleasure, though I find it mentioned only in the S. C. (p. 48).  It is one of the earliest editions of another smooth and learned poet, "*Sam. Daniel's* Poetical Essays — 1599." (See p. 239, n. 26, above.)

85. W, I, 315.        86. *N. & Q.*, 11 Ser., X, 362.        87. Sloan. MS. 1865, f. 145.

of Shakespeare, for instance, and, as we shall see, of Francis Bacon — appears to have been more fruitful or more readily traceable than that of others. Personally I have little doubt that other traces remain to be uncovered, but the record as it stands is not negligible, even without more curious inquiry. Certainly Browne read many of the great Elizabethans, some of them with keen enjoyment. Being himself, therefore, he could scarcely have failed to profit by the experience. His Shakespearean reminiscence alone proves that he had eyes that saw and ears that heard. John Milton was not the only scholarly poet of his time who, whether he would or no, heard the enchanting music of Dame Memory and her siren daughters. Browne, we are assured by a contemporary,[88] "remembered all that was remarkable in any book that he had read." There was much in him "not pick'd from the leaves of any author," yet he constantly sought [89] facts, ideas, words, all things remarkable, from all sources near and far. And he himself seems to have realized more clearly than some of his critics that the study of literature is likely to exert strong influence upon a man of letters. "Our first and literary apprehensions," he writes, "being commonly instructed in authors, our inventions . . . cannot avoid their allusions"; and the "fictions of poets" settle "impressions in our tender memories" which even time and experience "generally neglect to expunge." [90] Who shall say that the unforgettable fictions of the Elizabethans (of Shakespeare, say, or Spenser), the noble rhythms and high exaltations of their prose and verse, did not play their part in training the ear of this their younger son, or in fanning to brighter flame the strange fires of *his* imagination?

## II

A passage in one of Sir Leslie Stephen's essays [91] epitomizes admirably the curiously contradictory state of critical opinion

88. His friend Whitefoot (W, I, xxviii).     89. Cf. Gosse, *op. cit.*, pp. 193 ff.
90. *Vulgar Errors*, I, ix; W, II, p. 247.
91. "Sir Thomas Browne," *Hours in a Library*, 2nd Ser. (1876), p. 7 (my italics).

concerning the relations between Francis Bacon and Sir Thomas Browne. Browne, says Stephen,

> *persuaded himself and has persuaded some of his critics* that he was *a genuine disciple of Bacon*, by one of whose suggestions the [*Enquiries into Vulgar Errors*] is supposed to have been prompted. Accordingly, as Bacon describes the idols by which the human mind is misled, Sir Thomas sets out with investigating the causes of error, but . . . his introductory remarks immediately diverge into strange paths, from which it is obvious that the discovery of true scientific method was a very subordinate object in his mind —

and that Bacon, presumably, could have meant little or nothing to him. The outstanding fact here is that some critics of Browne believe him to have been genuinely influenced by Bacon in thought or in style.[92] Stephen's inferences are: (1) that Browne himself believed in his discipleship; (2) that he and his editors are mistaken in this belief; (3) that his poetic fondness for the very fabulosities he attacked proves that he could have had no serious concern for the scientific approach to truth; (4) in fine, that because in the long run he took his own line (as who that matters does not?) Bacon's influence upon him must have been negligible. I need scarcely add that only the first of these inferences seems justified to me. There is, however, much to be said on both sides — and the critics have said it. Since their findings have never been reviewed, I shall try to do so here, and thereby open the way for some items of new information and a fresh statement of the evidence. I must confess, however, that my own view was first conceived in all but complete ignorance of critical opinion, and has not been substantially altered by my subsequent en-

92. According to Francis Thompson (*Works*, London, 1913, III, 194), "It is only by comparison with the great writers of the seventeenth century that" Bacon "appears less a master of his art. But then, he preceded them; and perhaps even Sir Thomas Browne learned something from him."

lightenment. A rereading of *Vulgar Errors* when I happened to have *The Advancement of Learning* and the *Novum Organum* freshly in mind, convinced me, quite independently, that Browne's discussion of the causes of error, and, in general, his thought, and to a lesser extent his language, in the first book of *Vulgar Errors*, show distinct traces of Bacon's influence. To recognize this relationship one has only to read enough of Browne's own words side by side with Bacon's. The general resemblances, accordingly, have been more or less effectively *analyzed* before now, only to be, as a rule, more or less superficially dismissed.[93] The trouble has been, perhaps, that they have not been so clearly *exhibited* as they ought to be to enable the reader to judge fairly and conveniently for himself. I hope to make this possible, after summarizing the pros and cons of critical opinion.

I return, therefore, to Gosse, who, like Stephen and Walter Pater, stands curiously in betwixt and between, but, with them, helps to define the issue. Thus, Gosse agrees that in so far as Browne was "the champion of nature" he was

> *the disciple of Bacon, or would have been* if he had exactly comprehended what [Bacon] had designed to teach. . . . There is no doubt for us and *there was probably but little* . . . *for Browne* that the outline of all future interpretation of the facts of nature was divined by Bacon. . . . But it seems certain that Browne was rather dim in his perception of what Bacon's drift had been. [Bacon, though] far ahead of his time [was] scarcely a stimulating influence. . . .

Gosse, therefore, found "little profit in trying to compare Browne with Bacon."[94] Walter Pater, meanwhile, had also attempted the comparison. He thought Browne

> as seriously concerned as Bacon to dissipate the crude impressions of a false common sense, of false science, and a fictitious

---

93. See below, pp. 251 ff., 255 f., and notes.    94. *Op. cit.* (1905), pp. 71 ff.

authority. [And yet Browne] seems to have no true sense
of natural law [and] . . . immanent reason in the natural
world. . . .[95]

It is well known by now that most of this exception against
Browne (specifically, that he was as much an antiquary as a
scientist) [96] is valid only as it applies to virtually all thinking men
of his time, including, to some extent, Francis Bacon himself.[97]
Another aspect of Pater's finding against Browne, however, is of
more immediate import for us: in Pater's own phrase, it is primarily Browne's "half poetic . . . turn of mind" that differen-
tiates him from Bacon. This point is decidedly important. Obviously there are vital differences between Bacon and Browne (as
there are also, for instance, between Shakespeare and Milton) but
it surely need not follow, as more than one critic intimates,[98] that
therefore the thought and savour of the one, the sum total of his
inherent appeal to a man of letters, must have been lost upon the
other. To illustrate my point I need merely quote Pater once
more:

> We almost seem to hear Bacon when Browne discourses on the
> use of doubts and the advantages which might be derived from
> drawing up a calendar of . . . popular errors. . . .[99]  In
> Browne's chapter [100] on the 'Sources of Error' . . . we may
> trace much resemblance to Bacon's striking doctrine of the
> Idola, the shams men fall down and worship. Taking source,
> respectively, from 'the common infirmity of human nature,'
> from 'the erroneous disposition of the people,' from 'confident
> adherence to authority,' the errors which Browne chooses to
> deal with may be registered as identical with Bacon's *Idola
> Tribus, Fori, Theatri*, the idols of our common human nature, of

95. *Macmillan's Magazine*, 1886, and *Appreciations* (1889), pp. 152 ff.

96. And, besides, "a believer in . . . pagan oracles and a cruel judge [?] of supposed
witches."

97. He shared Browne's interest in antiquarian "curiosities," alchemy, etc., and his
conservative views on the Ptolemaic System, etc. (Cf. Kittredge, *Witchcraft in Old and
New England*, and A. C. Howell, "Browne and . . . Scientific Thought," *Studies in Philology*, XXII (1925), pp. 61 ff.)

98. See below, p. 256, nn. 117 and 118.         99. See below, p. 254, n. 105.

100. Pater means Browne's *book* (I, of *Vulgar Errors*).

the vulgar when they get together, and of the learned when they get together.

Yet Pater had his doubts, first and last. "That there was any actual connexion," he writes, "between Browne's work and Bacon's is but a surmise."

It is high time for us to note that this surmise is now over a hundred years old; and to emphasize the distinction between it — Wilkin's suggestion in his edition of Browne,[101] that Browne may have owed to Bacon the original "impulse" that led to the "conception and plan" of *Vulgar Errors* — and the larger supposition, hinted at by Pater and others, that Bacon's influence is traceable also in the texture of the work. Both suggestions, I think, are sound; but it is desirable to deal with one at a time, for the reason among others, that only the first has been generally noticed by the critics. Nor shall I continue the tale of their denials and affirmations until I have reproduced, in justice to the reader, the evidence, somewhat augmented and rearranged, which supports Wilkin's suggestion. I print below the passages from Bacon[102] in which he points out the advantages that may accrue to the cause of truth from a study of the causes of error, together with various passages to the same purpose from Browne's address "To the Reader" of *Vulgar Errors.*

| Browne (W, II, 177 ff.).[103] | Bacon, *Advancement of Learning* (Spedding, III, 293.).[104] |
|---|---|
| *To purchase a clear and warrantable body of truth*, we must forget and part with much we know, our tender *inquiries* taking up learning at large, and, together with *true and assured notions*, receiving many wherein our *reviewing judgments* find no satisfaction. | The *two ways of contemplation* are . . . the one plain and smooth in the beginning and in the end impassible; the other rough and troublesome in the entrance, but after a while fair and even; if a man . . . be content to *begin with doubts*, he shall *end with certainties*. (W) |

101. 1835 (W, II, pp. 161-163).    102. A final "W" marks Wilkin's citations.
103. All italics mine.
104. "Sp.", hereafter = *Works of Francis Bacon*, ed. Spedding, Ellis, and Heath (London, 1857); "A. of L." = *Advancement of Learning.*

And therefore in this . . . round of knowledge, like the great . . . wheels of heaven we must observe *two circles;* that while we are daily . . . whirled on by the swing . . . of the one, we may maintain a . . . proper course in the *slow and sober* wheel of the other. And this we shall more readily perform if we timely *survey our knowledge,* impartially *singling out those encroachments which . . . popular credulity* hath admitted. Whereof at present we have endeavored *a . . . copious list.*

*De Augmentis* (Sp., IV, 357 ff.)
*The registering of doubts has a double use:* first, it guards philosophy when upon a point not clearly proved . . . *judgment is suspended;* . . . secondly, doubts once registered are so many . . . spunges which continually draw . . . *increase of knowledge* . . . Wherefore I . . . wish . . . that a *calendar of doubts or problems* in nature . . . be taken in hand . . . and . . . *a calendar of popular errors* . . . that the sciences may be no longer troubled with them. (W) [105]

[This may be welcome to] those honored worthies who endeavor *the advancement of learning;* [106] as being likely to find a *clearer progression* when so many *rubs are levelled* and many untruths are taken off which disturb the tranquillity of axioms which otherwise might be raised. And *wise men cannot but know that arts and learning want this expurgation;* [107] and if the course of truth be permitted unto itself . . . it cannot escape many *errors,* which duration still enlargeth.

*Novum Organum* (Sp. IV, 92.)
If . . . men had kept *the true road* . . . bold doubtless and rash would be the opinion that *further progress* is possible. But if the road itself has been *mistaken* . . . it follows that the difficulty has its rise not in things themselves . . . but in the . . . use . . . of . . . the human understanding, which *admits of remedy and medicine.* It will be of great use, therefore, to set forth . . . these *errors* . . . for as many *impediments* as there have been in times past from this cause, so many arguments are there of hope for the time to come.

---

105. For the corresponding passage in the *A. of L.* ("The registering of doubts hath two excellent uses . . .") see Bk. II (Sp. III, p. 364).

106. Concerning this allusion to Bacon's work cf. Howell (see above p. 252, n. 97).

107. With this phrase compare Bacon's concerning the "purgation" of "the human understanding" (*Nov. Org.,* LXI, Sp. IV, p. 63).

One or two comments may be in order here. Wilkin did not set Browne's text side by side with Bacon's, and therefore failed to indicate that besides these resemblances in thought there appears to be some similarity in language. Next, Browne's allusion to *The Advancement of Learning* seems unmistakable, especially as he alludes to the "advancers" again elsewhere in the Address and in the first book.[108] Again, to anticipate a little, if he remembered Bacon's proposal for a study of vulgar errors, could he possibly have forgotten Bacon's trenchant *analyses* of the errors of the learned in the *Advancement*, and of the idols that beset all men, in the *Novum Organum?* Finally, however much Browne pleased his fancy and troubled the critics by the way, his primary and consistent purpose in the *Vulgar Errors* was, like Bacon's, to serve truth in the large. Most of his first book, in particular, is no mere museum of curiosities but a studied and eloquent analysis of the causes of error unprecedented in earlier works of this sort [109] except in Bacon's. In short, Browne's work as a whole, however obsolete his science has grown, never loses sight of his stated method — of testing opinion by dispassionate observation and inquiry; nor of the purpose, "the sober promotion of learning," announced in his prefatory Address, of which virtually the first and literally the last word is a dedication to the service of truth.[110]

Some critics (to have done with them!) besides those already mentioned have been willing to entertain Wilkin's suggestion, within limits. Mr. A. H. Bullen,[111] for instance, admits that "the subject" of the *Inquiry* "may have been suggested" by Bacon, and Mr. Charles Whibley[112] thinks it "not unlikely" — with the unobjectionable reservation (substantially like another by Keynes) [113] that "if he accepted Bacon's hint, he interprets it after his own fashion." Meanwhile an able French critic, M. Milsand,[114] found

---

108. Cf. W, II, p. 178, and my notes 106, 131.     109. See below, p. 256, n. 119.
110. He begins, "Would truth dispense . . . ." and reiterates at the last that his "end" is "truth."
111. Cf. *D. N. B.* on Browne.     112. *Essays in Biography* (London, 1913), p. 299.
113. *Bibliography*, p. 48.     114. *Revue des Deux Mondes*, XIV (1858), pp. 646 ff.

in Browne "l'esprit de Bacon," but his observations end upon the familiar note, "quoi qu'il soit . . ."! This is happily lacking in Howell's effective analysis, already referred to.[115] Opinions, however, have always differed. Thus, the *Quarterly's* reviewer of Wilkin did not "think it necessary to suppose" that Browne owed anything to Bacon. On the contrary, he felt with Sir Hamon L'Estrange that "naturalists readily follow one another as wild geese flye." [116] And recent opinion, on the whole, supports him rather than the affirmative. One critic, while urging that Browne "needs to be studied in connection with Bacon," asserts that "the two men were utterly unlike," [117] and another sees only "profound differences between Browne's loose indications of the sources of error and Bacon's penetrating analysis." [118]

The evidence must speak for itself. Before presenting it I have only to call the reader's attention, summarily, to certain external circumstances, not all of them known hitherto, which should be given such weight as they deserve in deciding whether Browne is likely to have remembered Francis Bacon.

(1) If we may assume with Wilkin that in undertaking the *Inquiry* Browne "might have been in some degree impelled . . . by the suggestions of another," Bacon would certainly seem to be the most likely impeller. Wilkin, of course, knew of the three or four books of vulgar errors "in physick" only, anterior to Browne's compendious study of the whole subject. In his Address, Browne rightly says that he got from these books [119] little or nothing con-

---

115. See above, p. 252, n. 97.    116. *Quarterly Review*, LXXXIX (1851), pp. 379 ff.
117. W. P. Dunn, *Sir Thomas Browne* (1925), pp. 83, 46.
118. Cf. *Year's Work in English Studies*, 1925, p. 189.
119. By Dr. James Primrose, *De Vulgi Erroribus* (1639); Scipione Mercurius, *De gli Errori Popolari* (1603); Laurent Joubert, *Erreurs Populaires* (1579). (Browne also mentions a lost work by Andreas.) These books, unlike Browne's, limit themselves specifically to the folklore of quackery. One or two of the earliest editions apparently antedated Bacon's suggestion for the larger catalogue of errors in philosophy and science, and it is possible (but not probable, I think) that Browne may have seen one or another of these books as a young medical student before he had read Bacon. His mention of them in the Address has every appearance of being a scholarly afterthought. In any case, there is in them nothing of Bacon's challenge toward larger inquiry.

ducive "unto the generality" of "his doctrine." He might have added that there is little or no "impelling" virtue in them, and that none of them has anything even remotely resembling a substantial introductory inquiry into the philosophy of the causes of error. Bacon, as indicated, repeatedly urged a fresh and adequate inquiry, and provided several unforgettable analyses of its conditions.

(2) Browne does not *name* Francis Bacon any more than he does Shakespeare, but he makes handsome acknowledgement of the light and leading of the great family whose bright particular star was Francis Bacon. He dedicated his *Garden of Cyrus* to his "worthy and honoured friend," Sir Nicholas Bacon, grandson of Francis Bacon's half-brother. The dedication salutes the younger Bacon not only as a "serious student in the highest arcana of nature," but as "a flourishing branch *of that noble family unto whom we owe so much observance.*" [120]

(3) If anyone still thinks that Browne's allusion to *The Advancement of Learning* [121] is insignificant or accidental, he may be interested to learn of another fact which seems to have escaped notice; namely that Browne had this book, and many another of Bacon's, where his contacts with it would have been least likely to be accidental — that is to say, in his library. I reproduce in the note below [122] the Bacon entries from the sale catalogue so

120. Epistle Dedicatory, *Garden of Cyrus* (W, III, pp. 381 ff.). Sir Nicholas, incidentally, was, like Francis Bacon, an eminent gardener; and Browne, if he followed his usual habit, had probably read everything in print on the subject of gardens (cf. W, I, 379, and above, note 119). It is not impossible, therefore, that Browne's somewhat oblique remark, in the same dedication, concerning "the example of old and new plantations wherein noble spirits contented . . . themselves . . . with all variety [that] made their gardens the epitome of the earth," may have been intended as a complimentary allusion to Bacon's essay "Of Gardens."

121. See above, p. 254, n. 106.

122. (1) "*Franc. Baconi*, Opuscula Philosophica . . . Lond. 1658" (S. C., p. 15).
(2) "*Franc. Baconi*, Scripta in Naturali Philosophia [Amsterdam] 1653" (p. 17).
(3) ". . . Historia Naturalis & Novus Atlas. L. B. 1648" (p. 17).
(4) "*Franc. Ld Bacon's* Natural Hist. . . . 1628.
. . . Of the Advancement of Learning" (p. 45).
(5) "Ld *Bacon's* Relation of the Sweating Sickness . . . 1671" (p. 47).

frequently referred to in the first part of this chapter. These comprise at least seven separate lots of volumes (probably a good many in all) including some of the outstanding philosophical and scientific works in Latin and English, among others, the *Natural History*, *The History of Life and Death*, the *New Atlantis*, and *The Advancement of Learning*.

In the following pages I print (1) in sequence, many extracts from the first seven chapters [123] of *Vulgar Errors*, Book I, together with many others from *The Advancement of Learning* and *Novum Organum* which challenge comparison increasingly and progressively, point by point. I think that as a whole, even if exception be taken to details, and due allowance made for "coincidence," they demonstrate that Browne's analysis of the causes of error was substantially influenced by his memories of Bacon. (2) I have inserted a few cognate passages from other works of Browne and Bacon, to show that traces of the relationship between them would seem to appear also in some works besides the three (*Vulgar Errors, Novum Organum, Advancement of Learning*) which show it most clearly. My purpose has been to illustrate *with reasonable fullness* the resemblances between Bacon's thought (sometimes also between his words or imagery) and Browne's, even at the risk of inviting the criticism that such and such a "parallel" taken by itself is not "convincing." The differences between Bacon and Browne require no illustration here, nor do they necessarily make the resemblances [124] less significant. Let the reader glance at Browne's own words, chapter by chapter, and Bacon's. He will

---

(6) "Ld *Bacon's* Genuine Remains . . . 1679" (p. 52).

(7) "Ld *Bacon's* Hist. of Life and Death [London] 1638" (p. 56).

Bacon may have been represented also in two collections, comprising 50 vols., of "tracts" and "transactions" in "Physick, Philosophy, Politicks &c." (pp. 47-48). Browne also possessed an Elizabethan MS. (Sloan. 1856) containing—in addition to various tracts by Raleigh, on which see p. 241, n. 44, above—a speech by Bacon, his testimony in the Essex case, and the letters of his brother Anthony (cf. W, IV, 470).

123. Thereafter, Browne goes from the general to the specific, and, in discoursing of "the endeavours of Satan," takes decidedly his own line.

124. For there can be no exact "parallels" in such a case as this.

scarcely escape the conclusion that the likenesses, however unconsciously wrought and however incapable of exact definition or final analysis, are too progressive and cumulative to be accidental.

(1) Browne, *Vulgar Errors*, Bk. I, Ch. I (W, II, pp. 183 ff.)

"Of the first Cause of Common Errors."
The *first . . . cause* of common error is *the common infirmity of human nature* . . . [witness] our . . . forefathers . . . but once removed from God. Who, notwithstanding . . . were *grossly deceived* in their perfection and . . . weakly deluded in the clarity of their *understanding* . . . They were deceived through the conduct of their *senses*. . . .

Bacon, *Novum Organum*, XXXVIII-XLI (Sp. IV, pp. 53-54).

[The first of the four] classes of idols . . . now in possession of the human understanding . . . the *idols of the Tribe, . . . have their foundation in human nature itself.* [They thrive upon our innate tendency to error] for it is a false assertion that the *sense of man* . . . the human *understanding* . . . a false mirror . . . which . . . *distorts and discolors* . . . is the measure of things.

(2) *Id.*, Ch. III [125] (W, II, pp. 193 ff.)

"The second Cause . . . the erroneous Disposition of the People." [126]

(a) [Second only to] *the fallible*

*Nov. Org.* (cf. (1) above) XLVI-XLVIII, XLII-XLIII (Sp. IV, pp. 54-57).

(a) *Superstition* . . . delight in

125. Ch. II supplies "a further illustration" of "the first cause," but no fresh principle.
126. Bacon gives less formal prominence to this subject than Browne. Three of his idols touch upon it, but none deals with it exclusively, as does Browne's chapter. For analogous denunciations of popular ignorance, superstition, and aversion to truth, compare also:

Browne, *Id.*
[The people] illiterate in . . . intellect . . . are daily mocked into . . . incredible conceits [of] soothsaying, oblique idolatries . . . [by] priests . . . charlatans . . . impostors . . .

A confusion of knaves and fools . . . inconsistent with truth . . . How little of truth there is in the ways of the multitude . . . indisposed ever to attain to truth.

Bacon (*A. of L.*, I, Sp. III, pp. 283-291).
False miracles [gain credence through] the ignorance of the people . . . superstitious simplicity . . . and . . . politick toleration. . . . The multitude . . . ('the wretched crowd') . . . give[s] passage rather to that which is popular and superficial than to that which is substantial and profound. *Of Superstition.*—The master of superstition is the people, and in all superstition wise men follow fools.

Many another writer, of course, shared these sentiments.

*nature of man* [is the] erroneous inclination of [that] most *deceptable* part of mankind . . . *the people* . . .

(b) Their *individual* imperfections being great, and erroneous in their single numbers, once

(c) *huddled together*, they will be error itself . . .

(3) *Id.*, Ch. IV (W, II, pp. 202 ff.) "Of the more immediate causes of Common Errors, both in the wiser [127] and common sort; and first, of Misapprehension and Fallacy."

The fallacies whereby men deceive others and are deceived themselves are . . . *verbal* and real. Of . . . such as conclude from *mistakes of the word* . . . but *two* [are] worthy of our notation . . . that is, the fallacy of equivocation and amphibology, which conclude from the ambiguity of some one word or the ambiguous syntax of many . . .[128] The circle of this fallacy . . . is very large . . . *Whereby have arisen . . . popular errors in philosophy* [and] *vulgar heresies*.

vanities . . . unquietness, . . . *common to human nature* [are fostered also by,

(b)] the idols of the cave, the *individual,* . . . discolor[ing] . . . the light of nature [by] his own proper nature . . . or [by] his *conversation* with others; [i. e., by] the idols of the market-place . . .

(c) formed by the intercourse and *association of men* with each other.

*Nov. Org.*, LIX (Sp. IV, pp. 60-62).
The most troublesome of all, . . . the Idols of the Market-place, . . . have crept into the understanding through the alliance of *words* and names. . . . *This* it is that *has rendered philosophy* and the sciences *sophistical* and inactive. . . . *The idols imposed by words* . . . are of *two kinds* . . . names of things which do not exist . . . or names of things . . . *confused and ill defined* and irregularly derived.

*A. of L.*, I (Sp. III, pp. 283 ff.). [On vain affectations of the learned: [129] the Renaissance] did bring in an affectionate study of eloquence and . . . speech. . . . Then grew . . . the first distemper of learning, when men study *words and not matter*.

127. Cf. n. 129 and text.
128. Browne's illustrations differ from Bacon's, but their analyses of the principle are analogous.
129. Cf. n. 127 and text.

(4) *Id.*, Ch. IV (W, II, pp. 205 ff.).
Of "extradictionary" [not "verbal" but] "real" fallacies.
Other ways . . . of deceit . . . consist . . . not in false apprehension of words . . . but *fraudulent* . . . or inconsequent *deductions*, or . . . a false conception of things. [Then follow illustrations of current fallacies in divinity, medicine, oratory, etc.] [130]

*Nov. Org.*, XLIV, LXI (Sp. IV, pp. 55, 62 ff.)
[The fourth class of Idols—of the Theatre] have immigrated into men's minds from the various *dogmas of philosophies* and also from *wrong laws of demonstration* . . . entire systems [and] many principles . . . in science which by tradition, credulity and negligence have come to be received. . . .

(5) *Id.*, Ch. V (W, II, pp. 208 ff.) "Of Credulity and Supinity."
Another cause of common errors is . . . *credulity* . . . believing at first ear what is delivered by others . . . *without examination assenting unto things which . . . carry no persuasion;* whereby men oft swallow falsities . . . dubiosities . . . and things impossible. . . . *Which . . . weakness* [though] most discoverable in vulgar heads, . . . *hath . . . sometimes fallen upon wiser brains* and great *advancers* [131] *of truth.*

*A. of L.*, I (Sp. III, pp. 287, 292 ff.).
The third *vice . . . of learning* . . . is . . . the foulest: delight in deceiving and aptness to be deceived, imposture and *credulity* . . . the ready *accepting* or admitting *things weakly authorized* or warranted . . .

[One cause of this vice is] impatience of doubt and haste to assertion without due and mature suspension of judgment. . . . [See also above, quotation p. 253, after n. 104.]

[Another cause] is a *supinity* or *neglect of enquiry* . . . rather believing than going to see, or doubting with ease . . . than believing with difficulty. . . . *Some* . . . although they cannot but doubt, yet *neither make experiment* by sense *nor enquiry by reason.* . . . Had our forefathers [done so, or those] who pursued the knowledge of

*Men have withdrawn themselves too much from the contemplation of nature* and *the observations of experience.* . . . They disdain to spell, and so by degrees to read, in the volume of God's works. . . . Whereby they are deservedly deluded.

130. These, again, are decidedly Browne's own.
131. Cf. above, pp. 254-55, nn. 106, 108.

things through all the corners of *nature*, the face of truth had been obscure to us. . . .

[See also below, n. [132].]

(6) *Id.*, Ch. VI (W, II, pp. 214 ff.).
"Another . . . Cause: . . . obstinate Adherence unto Antiquity."
*The mortallest enemy unto knowledge* and . . . *truth hath been a peremptory adhesion unto authority and* [to] *the dictates of antiquity.*[133]

*Nov. Org.*, LXXXIV (Sp. IV, pp. 81-82.).

*Men have been kept back* as by a kind of enchantment *from progress* in the sciences *by reverence for antiquity* [and] *authority.*

132. For analogous passages also related to this subject: (a) upon the evil of easy despair; (b) on the false and the true end of knowledge — compare:

(a) *Christian Morals*, II, vi, v (W, IV, pp. 82-84).
*Despise not . . . younger ways, nor despair of better things* whereof there is yet no prospect. . . . *Many things happen, not likely to ensue* from any promise of antecedencies. . . . Men are not the same through all . . . their ages; time, experience, self-reflections, and God's mercies make in some well-tempered minds a kind of translation before death. . . . *Let thy studies be free as thy thoughts* . . . join sense unto reason, and experiment unto speculation, and so give life to embryon truths . . . yet in their chaos.

*Nov. Org.*, XCII (Sp. IV, pp. 90 ff.).
By far *the greatest obstacle to* the *progress* of science and to the undertaking of new tasks *is . . . that men despair and think things impossible.* For wise and serious men are wont in these matters to be altogether distrustful, considering with themselves the obscurity of nature, the shortness of life, the deceitfulness of the senses . . . and the like. . . . We must take good heed that we be not led away by . . . the lighter breezes of hope. . . . Nevertheless, *to give hope is no unimportant part. . . . Hope . . . is reasonable.*

(b) *Religio Medici*, I, xiii (W, II, p. 18).
The world was made to be inhabited by beasts but studied and contemplated by man: '*tis the debt of our reason we owe unto God,* and the homage we pay for not being beasts. The wisdom of *God receives small honour from* . . . *vulgar heads that rudely stare about.* . . . Those highly magnify him whose judicious inquiry into his acts and deliberate research into his creatures return *the duty of a devout and learned admiration.*

*A. of L.*, I (Sp. III, p. 294).
Men have . . . seldom . . . entered into a desire of . . . *knowledge* . . . sincerely *to give a true account of their gift of reason,* to the benefit and use of men: as if there were sought in knowledge . . . *a terrace* . . . *with a fair prospect* . . . or a shop for profit and sale, and not a rich store-house, *for the glory of the Creator* and the relief of man's estate. *But this is that which will indeed dignify and exalt knowledge.*

133. Cf. note 132(a).

*Most men*, of ages present, so *superstitiously* do *look upon ages past*, that the authorities of the one exceed the reason of the other, [and] their works . . . the farther removed from present times, are conceived to approach the nearer unto truth itself. Hereby . . . we . . . widely walk out of the track of truth.[134]

Men that adore times past, consider not that those *times* were once *present* . . . as *our own* are at this instant; . . . as we rely on them, even so will . . . the gray heads of [our] posterity . . . on us, and magnify us hereafter who at present condemn ourselves.

We applaud many things delivered by *the ancients* which . . . *come short of our conceptions.* Thus we extol . . . the . . . wise men of Greece . . . the apothegms of . . . Laertius . . . Macrobius, Cicero . . . and *the comical wits of those times* . . . most whereof *are* . . . *exceeded* [by the] wise men . . . and [the] *urbanities of our times* . . . of more unlearned nations, and many of our own.

*As for antiquity, the opinion touching it* which men entertain is . . . *scarcely consonant with the word itself.* For the old age of the world is to be accounted the true antiquity; and this is the attribute of *our own times*, not of that earlier age of the . . . ancients. . . . Truly, as we look for . . . riper judgment in the old man than in the young, because of his experience, so . . . from *our age*, if it but knew its own strength and chose to essay . . . it, much more might fairly be expected than from the ancient times, inasmuch as it is a more advanced age of the world.

Surely, when I set before me *the condition of these times*, in which learning hath made her third visitation or circuit, in all the qualities thereof; as *the excellency and vivacity of the wits of this age* . . . I cannot but be raised to this persuasion, that *this* third period of *time will far surpass that of the Graecian and Roman learning.*

(7) *Id.*, Ch. VII (W, II, pp. 225 ff.) "Another . . . Adherence unto Authority." [135]

*Nov. Org.*, LXXXIV (Sp. III, p. 82).

134. He adds, like Bacon (and Emerson) that Aristotle and others criticized their predecessors without claiming infallibility for themselves; they too being, in short, but "young men in libraries."

135. For analogous discussion of other aspects of this subject—(a) on the erroneous "authority" of the poets; (b) on the "magisterial" manner—compare:

Nor is only resolved prostration unto antiquity a *powerful enemy unto knowledge*, but any *confident adherence unto authority*, or *resignation of our judgments* upon the testimony of any age or author whatsoever.

Cf. *Christian Morals*, II, v (W, IV, p. 83):

Men disparage not antiquity who prudently exalt new enquiries; and *make not them the judges of truth* who were but the fellow enquirers of it. Who can but magnify the endeavours of Aristotle, and *the noble start* which learning had under him; or less than pity *the slender progression* made upon such advantages, while *many centuries were lost in repetitions*, sealing up the book of knowledge.

(a) *Vulgar Errors*, I, Ch. IX, (W, II, p. 247).

[Among those who promoted error, the *painters and* especially the *poets*] have exceeded others, trimly advancing the Egyptian notions of harpies, [the] phoenix . . . and many more. Now [though] *fictions apologues, and fables* . . . might point at laudable ends, yet do they *afford* . . . *frequent occasion of error*. . . . This way the *vain and idle fictions* of the Gentiles did first insinuate into the heads of Christians.

(b) *Id.*, "To the Reader" (W, II, p. 181).

Lastly, *we are not magisterial in opinions*, nor have we dictator-like obtruded our conceptions; but in the humility of enquiries or disquisitions have only proposed them unto more ocular discerners. And therefore opinions are free, and open it is for any to think or declare the contrary.

*With regard to authority, it shows a feeble mind to grant so much to authors* and yet deny time his rights, who is the author of . . . authority. . . . Those *enchantments of . . . authority have . . . made . . . men's powers . . . impotent.*

*A. of L.*, I (Sp. III, p. 289).

The overmuch credit that hath been given unto authors . . . *in making them dictators . . . and not counsels* [is] the principal cause that hath kept [the sciences] *without growth*. . . . Hence . . . *in . . . sciences the first author goeth furthest*. . . . So . . . the philosophies and sciences of Aristotle, Plato, Democritus [were] *of most vigour at the first and by time degenerated and imbased.*

*A. of L.*, II (Sp. III, pp. 343 ff.).

'*Painters and poets* have always been allowed to take . . . liberties.' But there remaineth . . . another use of *Poesy Parabolical . . . which tendeth to retire and obscure . . . that which is taught* . . . when the secrets and mysteries of religion are involved in *fables or parables*. . . . It was an ancient vanity . . . to fasten the assertions of the Stoics upon the fictions of ancient poets. But yet that all the *fables and fictions* of poets were but pleasure and not figure, I interpose no opinion.

*A. of L.*, I (Sp. III, p. 293).

Another error is in the . . . *magistral* and peremptory . . . *delivery of knowledge*. . . . In the true handling of knowledge men ought not to [fear] seeming to be in doubt about anything nor [fall] into the ironical doubting of all things . . . but to propound things sincerely . . . as they stand in a man's own judgment.

These likenesses, as I have said, must speak for themselves or not at all. A final question, however, may be in order. Did Bacon really, as Gosse asserts,[136] fail to exert "a stimulating influence" upon the thought of his aftertimes? Once more, opinion differs. Of course he did not found a school, either in science or philosophy. "And yet," writes a professional philosopher,[137] "the leading thinkers — such men as Leibnitz and Hume and Kant — acknowledge most fully the greatness of Bacon." Opinions are free, but on the face of the evidence it would seem that Browne honored his great predecessor by making him his own.

136. See p. 251, above.
137. Professor W. R. Sorley, *Cambridge History of English Literature*, IV, 335.

# XII

## BEN JONSON, RICHARD BROME, AND MINOR ACTORS

THE STROLLERS, as we have seen, loomed large in the humbler ranks of the Elizabethan players. But there were others. I shall have something to say here of the humblest of the humble—but first I wish to touch upon two dramatists, one of whom was among the most distinguished of them all. Both, I think, were actors to boot, even though neither one of them seriously rivalled Richard Burbage or Edward Alleyn. I refer to Ben Jonson and to "his man," Master Richard Brome, author of *The Antipodes*.

### 1. BEN JONSON'S "SHARE" [1]

The entry of the 28th of July, 1597, in *Henslowe's Diary*,[2] whereby Henslowe acknowledges that he had received "of Bengemenes Johnsones Share" the sum of 3*s.* 9*d.*, has never, I think, been satisfactorily explained, though it has frequently been dealt with. At any rate, no less an authority than Dr. Greg considers that the meaning of the entry is still an open question.[3] What exactly was the nature of Jonson's "share"? I propose an answer which suggests itself to me after a study of certain analogous entries in the *Diary*. To present my point adequately it will be necessary to say a preliminary word about Elizabethan theatrical "shares" and "sharers," and to review the explanations of the entry that have hitherto been offered.

In the Elizabethan theatre there were at least two types of

1. Reprinted from *Modern Language Review*, XVI (1921), 61 ff.
2. Edition W. W. Greg, I, 47.   3. See below, p. 269, n. 18.

sharers: first, the "actor-sharers," that is to say, the eight or ten mature players who had passed beyond the "hireling" stage. Each actor-sharer's income consisted of his part of the company's share in the daily takings. That share, at the time with which we are concerned, was made up of the general admission receipts at the door, plus one-half the extra money collected in the galleries — for it is well known that in those days each man paid his penny or twopence on entering the house, and additional sums if he desired a place in the galleries, the boxes, or on the stage.[4] The other half of the gallery money went to the second type of "sharer," — the "housekeepers," or proprietors of the playhouses. Here it should be noted — as Dr. Greg has shown [5] — that Henslowe frequently impounded his companies' share of the gallery receipts by way of security for the money he lent them to buy costumes and properties.[6] More significant for our purposes is a point which has not had the attention it deserves; namely, that Henslowe was in the habit of doing for individual actor-sharers just what he sometimes did for the companies at large. He repeatedly made loans to individual players, and recouped himself by attaching their part of the company's gallery money. Since the "gathering" was done by the housekeepers or their employees,[7] the process was simple. I shall try to show in a moment that the Jonson entry was but one of many which record similar liquidations of debts incurred by Henslowe's actor-sharers.

Let us look, meanwhile, at two other transactions between Jonson and Henslowe which are intimately connected with the entry in question. We have seen that on July 28, 1597, Jonson paid Henslowe 3s. 9d. upon a debt he owed him. Henslowe also notes that 'Bengemen Johnson Plaier' had borrowed 5s. from him

---

4. See the writer's *Shakspere to Sheridan*, pp. 27 ff. Shakespeare, and other exceptional actor-sharers, were also "housekeepers" and thus shared twice.

5. *Henslowe's Diary*, II, 124.

6. His 1613 contract with the Lady Elizabeth's Men specifically provided that this security be allowed him. See *Henslowe Papers*, ed. Greg, p. 24.

7. *Id.*, p. 3.

six months earlier,[8] and that, on the very day he paid the 3*s*. 9*d*., he borrowed another £4.[9] What is the meaning of these several transactions, and from what sort of a "share" of Jonson's did Henslowe draw the smaller amount? Fleay thought [10] it could "hardly have been a share in the Rose, much more likely in Paris Garden, where Jonson played Zulziman," according to "Horace's" admission in *Satiromastix* (acted 1601):

> *Tucca.*  Thou hast been at Parris garden, hast not?
> *Horace.*  Yes Captaine I ha plaide Zulziman there.[11]

"The smallness of the amount" Jonson paid Henslowe on July 28, 1597, leads Professor J. T. Murray to agree that the poet could not have been buying a share in the Rose, but, since Paris Garden — the Bear Garden, to be more exact — was an older and poorer house, Murray accepts as a plausible conjecture Fleay's view that Jonson held a proprietary share in that house.[12]

There are, however, many reasons for doubting this explanation. In the first place, the *Satiromastix* passage alludes to an early stage of Jonson's career,[13] and it seems clear that at the time he was acting at the Bear Garden he had but recently graduated from the ranks of the strollers and had yet to win his reputation as a playwright. It is well to recall, therefore, that the owners of proprietary shares in the theatres were at that time of two types only: either successful business men who were able to invest substantial sums of money, or actors and playwrights who stood at the very top of their profession.[14] Indeed, there is no real evidence to show that any actors or playwrights owned proprietary shares until the Burbages built the Globe in 1599, when, according to Cuthbert Burbage, they "joyned to ourselves those deserveing

8. January 5, 1597. See *H. D.*, I, p. 200.  9. *Id.*, I, 200.
10. *English Drama*, I, p. 342.  11. Scene 7. Ed. Scherer, p. 46.
12. *English Dramatic Companies*, II, 144.  13. *Id.*, II, 145.
14. Cf. the 1635 Globe and Blackfriars Share Papers, Halliwell-Phillipps, *Outlines*, I, p. 312 ff., and extant records of other theatrical litigation (bibliography in Sir Sidney Lee's 1916 ed. of the *Life of Shakespeare*, p. 310.)

men, Shakspere, Hemings . . . and others . . . partners in the proffittes of that they call the House." [15]   In any case, Alleyn and Henslowe and Jacob Meade, waterman, appear to have been the sole owners of the Bear Garden and the Hope, which replaced it later.[16]   Nor is there any other entry in the *Diary* which would justify the conclusion that Henslowe ever impounded a house-keeper's share.

He certainly did frequently lend money to individual actor-sharers, and then collected from their gallery money.   On September 4, 1602, for example, he lent half a crown to Thomas Heywood, then an actor-sharer in Worcester's Men, to "bye hime a payer of sylke garters," [17] and though in this case we have no record of a liquidation of the debt, there are a number of other cases where both loan and settlement are accounted for.   Before examining them, let us look at Dr. Greg's statement concerning the entry we are discussing.   "Jonson," he says,[18] "is . . . said to have acted himself, and, indeed, Henslowe describes him as 'player' in the *Diary*. *It is also possible that he may at one time have contemplated acquiring a share in the Admiral's Company.*" He then notes the payment of 3s. 9d., and adds, "*but no further payments seem to have been made.*   Of course the entry may refer to something quite different."   Dr. Greg, too, seems to have thought that Jonson may have been paying an instalment upon a share he had bought.   Here it should be said that if Jonson was then acquiring a share in the Admiral's Men (in the company, be it noted, as distinct from the playhouse) he would scarcely have paid an instalment upon the purchase to Henslowe, who was chief housekeeper, but not a member of the company.

The fact of the matter seems to be not that Jonson was paying for a share he expected to buy, but that he was an actor-sharer at the time, and that Henslowe was recouping himself for an earlier loan to the poet—from Bengemenes Johnsones share *of the gallery*

15. Halliwell-Phillipps, *op. cit.*, I, 317.
16. Greg, *H. D.*, II, 37-41; cf. *Henslowe Papers*, p. 19.
17. *H. D.*, I, 178.                    18. *H. D.*, II, 288-9.

*takings*. This was exactly what he did eight months later for another one of his actor-sharers, none other than Gabriel Spencer, whom Ben killed very shortly after.[19] From March 10 to April 5, 1598, Spencer obtained from Henslowe personal loans amounting to 46*s*.[20] A day later, on April 6, Henslowe was beginning to get his money back, for he notes that he had received "of gabrell spencer . . . of his share in the gallereyes," 5*s*. 6*d*.,—an entry almost identical with that "of Bengemenes Johnsones Share." [21] Probably just such another series of transactions was that between Henslowe and Humphrey Jeffes, another actor-sharer in the Admiral's Men. On April 6, 1598, once more, Jeffes borrowed from Henslowe 20*s*. "in Redy mony." [22] Probably there had been earlier borrowings, for, beginning with January 14, 1597, Henslowe was receiving regular weekly payments "of humfreye Jeaffes hallffe sheare." [23] At all events, the debt of April 6, 1598, seems to have been taken care of, for, beginning on April 29 and for several months after, Henslowe started to keep "A Juste acownte of all suche moneye as I dooe Receue for vmfrey Jeaffes and antoney Jeaffes" [24]—payments, usually, of half a crown each week. Three years later, when the Admiral's Men had moved to the Fortune, their actor-sharers apparently borrowed and paid in the old way. Between June 30 and September 5, 1601, Henslowe received from four of them, Richard Jones, Thomas Dowton, Robert Shaw, and William Bird, a number of weekly payments towards "ther privet deats wch. they owe vnto me." [25] *In any one week* the four paid identical amounts, but these amounts vary from one week to the next—a fact which suggests that the payments came from a common source: doubtless each man's part of

19. Cf. *Henslowe Papers*, p. 48.
20. *H. D.*, I, 75. He was also concerned, with one of his fellows, in another loan of 30*s*., on March 8, 1598. (*Id.*, I, 73.)
21. *Id.*, I, 63.          22. And further sums of 35*s*. later. *H. D.*, I, 64.
23. *Id.*, I, 67.
24. Another sharer in the Admiral's Men and perhaps a brother of Humphrey? (See *H. D.*, I, 64.)
25. *Id.*, I, 162.

the company's gallery takings. Henslowe, in short, regularly lent money to his actor-sharers, and as regularly collected from the earnings of their shares. It seems a fair inference, then, that Gabriel Spencer's share and Humphrey Jeffes's and Ben Jonson's were all of a kind, and that Jonson in 1597 was not a part owner of the Rose nor yet the Bear Garden, but an actor-sharer in the Admiral's Men. Like Shakespeare, Heywood, Nathaniel Field, and many another playwright, he apparently scored his first success as an actor, for the actor-sharers were players who had made their mark.

### 2. RICHARD BROME [26]

Of the early career of the author of *The Antipodes* and *A Jovial Crew* comparatively little is known. Andrews, whose study [27] of Brome is the most complete that has yet appeared, thinks the playwright was born about 1590. But few facts have come down to us concerning Brome's activities between that date and 1635, when, according to the contract discovered by Professor Wallace,[28] he agreed to deliver to the King's Revels Company at the Salisbury Court — and to this company only — three plays annually for a period of three years, at a salary of 15s. weekly, and with the understanding that he should not print any of his plays without the consent of the company. All that has hitherto been known concerning Brome's history before 1635 has been inferred from the commendatory verses prefixed to his plays, from references or allusions in the plays themselves, or from his relations with Ben Jonson. The latter's striking reference to "his man, Master Brome, behind the arras," in the Induction to *Bartholomew Fair* (1614), and his prefatory verses to Brome's *Northern Lass* (printed 1632):

26. Reprinted from *Modern Language Notes*, XXXVI (1921), 6 ff.
27. C. E. Andrews, *Richard Brome, A Study of His Life and Works*, Yale Studies in English, XLVI, 1913.
28. See his "Shakspere and the Blackfriars," *Century Magazine*, Sept., 1910, and Andrews, p. 13.

> I had you for a servant once, Dick Brome,
> And you performed a servant's faithful parts . . .

have been interpreted in various ways. Some have thought that
Brome was simply Ben's menial servant, and account for the
coarseness in his dramas by the assumption that he "describes
life from the groom's point of view." [29]  Professor Baker, [30] on the
other hand, concludes that he acted as a sort of amanuensis to
Jonson, while Fleay [31] speaks of him simply as Ben's "apprentice,"
without saying anything as to the nature of the apprenticeship.
Andrews, [32] finally, thinks that "Brome probably began his relations with Jonson as a witty young serving-man who interested
his master to such an extent that he undertook his education, as
he had already that of the young Nathaniel Field." The reference
to Field is significant here, since a strangely neglected bit of
evidence would seem to indicate that Brome, like Field, was an
actor before he became a playwright, and that, like Field, he may
have been indebted to Jonson in both capacities.

This evidence appears in the form of a royal warrant under
date of June 30, 1628, reprinted without comment by Mrs. Stopes
in the *Shakespeare Jahrbuch* for 1910.[33] The warrant is one of a
miscellaneous list of orders for payment of court performances,
allowances for actors' liveries, and the like. It reads as follows:

> "Warrant to swear the Queen of Bohemia's players [34]
> groomes of his Majesties chamber without fee,
> viz. Joseph Moore, Alexander Foster, Robert Gylman
> *Richard Brome*, John Lillie, William Rogers,
> George Lillie, Abel Swinnerton, George Gibbes,
> Oliver Howes; June 30, 1628." [35]

29. Compare *Cambridge History of English Literature*, VI, 225.
30. See Gayley's *Representative English Comedies*, III, 417.
31. See p. 273, n. 37.          32. P. 4.
33. See C. C. Stopes, "Shakespeare's Fellows and Followers," *Shakespeare Jahrbuch*,
XLVI, 94; printed from Warrant Book V, 93, 1628-1634, p. 26.
34. The Lady Elizabeth's Men.
35. Murray (*Elizabethan Dramatic Companies*, I, 259) did not know of the existence of
this warrant. In his sketch of the history of the Lady Elizabeth's Men between 1625 and

The chances are strongly in favor of the conclusion that the Richard Brome thus mentioned as an actor of some prominence [36] in the Lady Elizabeth's Company in 1628, was the playwright. If so, Fleay's conjecture [37] that Brome's "apprenticeship" to Jonson extended over the seven years 1623 to 1629, will have to be modified; incidentally some new light may be thrown upon the nature of that apprenticeship. "Bengemen Johnson, *player*," borrowed money from Henslowe in 1597 and 1598, and, as I have just indicated, he seems to have had a share in the Admiral's Men for a time. I see no reason, then, why at some later date Ben Jonson, actor-playwright, might not have taken on a theatrical apprentice, who would perhaps serve him as amanuensis, but also get a chance to act. Augustine Phillips, Shakespeare's colleague in the King's Men, had just such an apprentice. In his will [38] Phillips left 30s. to "my servaunte Christopher Beeston," who later became an actor-sharer and business manager of the Cockpit company. John Heminges, business manager of Shakespeare's company, also had his theatrical apprentice, Alexander Cooke,[39] who later became an actor-sharer in his "master's" company. Similarly, Brome may have been "made free o' th' Trade" of acting (as well as of playwriting) by Jonson. The apprentices of Jones and Downton ("Jones' boy" and "Downton's boy") of the Admiral's Men are known to have acted in the plays of that company given in 1599 and 1600.[40] And so I think it not unlikely that Jonson put "his man, Master Brome, behind the arras" in

---

June, 1629, he gives but one partial list of actors. This list (based on an incomplete document recorded in the *Calendar of State Papers, Domestic*, 1628-9) is dated December 9, 1628, and names but four actors: "Joseph Moore, Alexander Foster, Robert Gylman, Joseph Townsend, with the rest of their company."

36. Only the more prominent actors, not the "hirelings," are listed among those who received royal liveries or other court grants. The Richard Brome here mentioned must have been an actor-sharer.

37. *Drama*, I, 37; compare *Camb. Hist. of Eng. Lit.*, VI, 224.

38. See J. P. Collier's *Actors*, p. xxxi.

39. "I do intreate my Master Heminges" (he writes in his will) to look out for the interests of his orphans. (See Malone-Boswell, *Shakspeare*, III, 482.)

40. *Henslowe Papers*, p. 154.

*Bartholomew Fair* because Master Brome was acting a small part in that play. It would have been a good-natured bit of advertising for the young actor, in keeping with the mention, later in the play, of Field, "your best actor," who played a part in the piece.[41] Perhaps Jonson, when he recalled how Brome had "performed a servant's faithful *parts*," had in mind the acting as well as the other services of his former apprentice.

When *Bartholomew Fair* was produced in 1614 Brome must have been somewhere between twenty and twenty-five years old; it was the time when he was undergoing his training for his later activities as an actor-sharer and playwright. In 1623 he collaborated in a play which is not extant; in 1629 his first independently written play was produced. It is impossible to say whether Brome continued long as an actor after 1628, but I think the evidence to which I have called attention indicates that he was one of "the quality" before that date. "I love the quality of playing," says Letoy in *The Antipodes;*[42] and I believe he is voicing Brome's sentiments towards his old profession. Indeed this play and many others of Brome are full of allusions which support the conclusion that Brome, like Shakespeare, Jonson, Heywood, Rowley, Field, Armin, and a host of other Elizabethan playwrights, passed his apprenticeship upon the stage, and that it was in this sense that Jonson called him his "servant."

### 3. Minor Actors and Playhouse Employees [43]

Much interesting information is available concerning the minor employees of the Elizabethan dramatic companies. I propose to deal with the subject here because not all of this information has hitherto been accessible, and because certain doubtful inferences,

---

41. See *Bartholomew Fair*, Act V, Sc. 3, and Fleay, *Drama*, I, 172. Similar bits of advertising of the actors appear in many Elizabethan plays. See, for example, the Induction to *The Malcontent*, and *Greene's Tu Quoque*.

42. See Act I, Scenes 5 and 6; Act II, Scenes 1 and 2, etc.

43. Reprinted from *Modern Philology*, XX (1922), 49 ff.

based upon fragmentary evidence, have long been permitted to pass current without challenge. Of first importance among the company subordinates were the "hirelings"—the inferior players or novices who did not share in the takings [44] but were paid out of the company funds. I shall deal with them first, and then add brief notes on other employees—the boys, who did the female rôles and made themselves useful in other ways, the prompters or "book-keepers," tiremen and tirewomen, the "gatherers," stage hands, and musicians.

In a familiar passage of his *School of Abuse* (1579),[45] Stephen Gosson attacks the prevailing extravagance in dress, and incidentally throws some light upon the current wages for hirelings. "Overlashing in apparel is so common a fault," he writes, *"that the verye hyerlings of some of our plaiers,* which stand at reversion of VIs. by the weeke, jet under gentlemen's noses in sutes of silke, exercising themselves to prating on the stage, and common scoffing when they come abrode." From another document,[46] dating so late as 1620, which speaks of "the twelvepenny hirelings" making "artificiall Lightning in their Heavens," it appears that the hirelings then had still to be content with their shilling a day and their hopes of promotion to shareholdership, though the income and status of the better players, and of the playwrights, had been improved appreciably by this time.[47] Even considerably after the Restoration, some of the inferior actors received no more than 10s. a week,[48] and so late as 1765 three subordinate players in Garrick's company got but 12s.[49] Some of the earlier hirelings, indeed, had even less than their daily shilling, though some earned a little more. In 1597, for example, Henslowe hired Thomas Hearne and William Kendall "to searve . . . in the qualetie of

44. See *Shakspere to Sheridan*, pp. 71 ff.   45. *Shakespeare Society* (1841), p. 29.

46. John Melton, *Astrologaster*, p. 31 (quoted by Percy Simpson in *Shakespeare's England*, II, 254).

47. See above, note 44.

48. Cf. Tom Brown, "Amusements Serious and Comical," *Works* (1720), III, 39: "the cringing Fraternity, from fifty down to ten shillings a week."

49. Cf. *Notes & Queries*, 6th ser., XI, 461.

playenge" for a year, at 5s. a week—the understanding being, however, that Hearne was to have an extra 1s. 8d. during his second year of service, whereas it was specifically stipulated that Kendall's pay was to be doubled when he played in London, the 5s. being "cuntrie" wages.[50]

With wages of 5, 6, or even 10s. a week, the hirelings could not have had a very easy time of it, and one wonders how they could have found the wherewithal to jet under gentlemen's noses in suits of silk—unless they borrowed them on occasion from a friendly wardrobe-keeper. Yet it must be remembered that a good carpenter, for example, and other artisans as well, did not earn any more than their shilling a day in Shakespeare's time.[51] Even so, however, it seems a bit hard that a twelvepenny hireling should have had to furnish bond to the amount of £40 to stay out his appointed two or three years.[52] Unfortunately, moreover, the hirelings could not count upon prompt and regular payment of their wages. In 1592 one Richard Jones wrote to Edward Alleyn to ask for a loan of three pounds, to enable him to get some of his clothes out of pawn, so that he might rise from a hireling's estate to the dignity of a sharer in a company then forming to travel in Germany, "for hear," writes Jones, "I get nothinge, some tymes I have a shillinge aday, and some tymes nothinge, so that I leve in great poverty." [53] Again, it appears from certain theatrical litigation of the year 1616,[54] that the Red Bull company at that time owed William Browne, one of its hirelings, back wages of over sixteen pounds— he had not been paid for more than a year.

Occasionally a kind-hearted actor-sharer remembered the poor—and the hirelings—in his will. Thus Augustine Phillips, one of Shakespeare's colleagues, left five pounds each to the poor of his

---

50. *Henslowe's Diary*, I, 201, xlix, 182: H. Child (*Camb. Hist. Eng. Lit.*, VI, 278), puts the hirelings' wages at from 5s. to 8s.

51. Cf. Nichols, *Progresses of Elizabeth*, III, 411; Feuillerat, *Revels Documents, Elizabeth*, p. 79.

52. *Henslowe's Diary*, I, 204, 208.          53. *Henslowe Papers*, p. 33.

54. Reprinted in Fleay's *Stage*, pp. 284 ff.

parish and "the hyred men of the company w^oh I am of."[55] And the public seems to have been well aware of the fact that the hirelings' purses were not always well lined. In the old play *Histrio-Mastix*[56] the hostess reckons "the sharers' dinner, sixpence a piece; the Hirelings, pence." On the other hand, it is worth while to recall that the hirelings whose work attracted favorable notice were frequently promoted into the ranks of the sharers after an apprenticeship of only two or three years.[57] Further, it is certain that the five or six hirelings each company employed, were by no means an unimportant part of its organization. Henslowe, on more occasions than one, was able to control his companies by the threat of "breaking" them through the dismissal of their hirelings, of whose appointment and disposition he seems to have had personal charge. And it is well to remember that among the obscure hirelings of the King's Men and Admiral's Men at one time were such men as Shakespeare, Jonson, and Heywood.

"When I see," wrote the author of *A Second and Third Blast of Retrait from Plaies and Theatres* (1580),[58] "yong boies, inclining of themselves vnto wickedness, trained vp in filthie speeches, vnnatural and vnseemelie gestures, to be brought vp by these Schoolemasters in bawderie, and in idleness, I cannot chuse but with teares and griefe of hart lament." The reference, of course, is to the training and employment of boy actors, and it is a well-known fact that the antagonists of the stage, from Gosson to Prynne, continued to lament the practice, and to object particularly because the boys were employed in female rôles.[59] A number of scholars have studied the activities of the children's companies,[60] but certain details as to the employment of boys by the adult companies have remained more or less obscure.

55. Malone-Boswell, *Shakspeare*, III, 471.      56. Act VI, l. 196.
57. On this point and the material immediately following, cf. p. 275, n. 44.
58. See W. C. Hazlitt, *English Drama and Stage*, p. 147.
59. Cf. Gosson, *Plays Confuted*; Hazlitt, p. 195; and Heywood's answer to the charge in his *Apology for Actors* (1612), *Shakespeare Society*, (1841), p. 28.
60. Cf. C. W. Wallace, *Children of the Chapel at Blackfriars* (Lincoln, Neb., 1908), and H. N. Hillebrand, *Child Actors* (Urbana, Ill., 1926).

It seems clear that really good young actors were not easy to find, and that the adult companies were willing to pay rather handsomely for their services. Apparently the demand was met in part by the managers of the children's companies, and that sometimes against the best interests of these companies — for in 1608 the manager of the Whitefriars Children was required to give a bond of forty pounds to reinforce his promise not to dispose of any of the boys in his charge without the consent of his fellow "housekeepers." [61] On the other hand, certain of "your great players" helped to meet the situation by training young apprentices of their own. A number of Shakespeare's colleagues did this; Augustine Phillips had his "servaunte, Christopher Beeston," later the business manager of the Cockpit company; Alexander Cooke, who became a sharer in Shakespeare's company, started as John Hemings' apprentice; and Nicholas Tooley, a particularly good female impersonator, as Richard Burbage's. And we have just seen that Richard Brome was probably apprenticed to the stage under Ben Jonson.

Doubtless it was no easy task to train these lads for the important parts intrusted to them. Henslowe, therefore, when the Admiral's Men needed a boy actor in 1597, "bowght my boye Jeames brystow of william agusten player the 18 of desemb^r." for £8.[62] Many years later, in the Globe and Blackfriars Share Papers of 1635, the old actor, John Shanks, stated that he "out of his owne purse" had supplied the King's Men "with boyes . . . as Thomas Pollard, John Thompson deceased (for whome hee payed 40 *li.*) your suppliant haveing payd his part of 200 *li.* for other boyes . . . and at this time maintaines three more for the sayd service." [63] The statement is interesting if only because of the fact that when it was made Thomas Pollard had achieved such success as to become one of those who sought to oust Shanks and his fellows from their control of the Globe and Blackfriars. For the rest, in

61. *Shakespeare Society Transactions* (1887-92), p. 276. There was also much "taking-up" or kidnapping of boys for the service of chapel and stage.
62. *Henslowe's Diary*, I, 203.          63. Halliwell-Phillipps, *Outlines* I, 316.

view of the fact that Henslowe had to pay but £8 for his boy
"Jeames," it would seem that Shanks may have exaggerated a
bit, for the benefit of the Lord Chamberlain, to whom he was
appealing at the time.   In any case, it is interesting to note the
implication of the last part of his statement.   Apparently, having
retired as an actor, he was then devoting part of his time to the
training of boys for the stage, doubtless not without profit.

On the basis of a passage from Chapman's *May Day* (1611),
"Afore heaven 'tis a sweete-fac't child, methinks he should show
well in woman's attire. . . . Ile helpe thee to three crownes [64] a
weeke for him an she can act well. . . ." Collier [65] argued that
"the performers of female characters were paid more than ordinary
actors." An entry of Henslowe's, under date of February 15, 1600,
goes far to disprove Collier's inference.   On that day Henslowe
noted that the Admiral's Men owed him "for my boye Jemes
bristos wages from the 23 of ap^rell 1600 vnto the XV of febreary
1600 next *after the Ratte of iij s. a wecke*," [66] a total of £6 9s.   At the
rate of 3s. a week, "Jemes" was receiving only half the wages
ordinarily paid to the hirelings—that is to say, Henslowe was
charging the company that much for the boy's service.   Whether
his master—who was, of course, responsible for his keep—allowed
him that much spending money, is another question.   As for the
*May Day* passage, that may mean only that Quintilliano would
have been willing to pay Lionel's guardian 15s. a week in lieu of
such a fee as Henslowe paid for his boy.   And even though the boys
did not have much spending money, those who excelled sometimes
had extra rewards, for Queen Elizabeth is known to have given
valuable presents to young Thomas ("Cambyses"?) Preston and
other child actors who pleased her.[67]

When they were not acting, the boys made themselves useful

64.  I.e., 15s.   The passage occurs in Act III (ed. Parrott, II, 207).
65.  *Annals* (ed. 1879), III, 236.
66.  *Henslowe's Diary*, I, 134.
67.  Cf. Nichols, *Progresses of Elizabeth*, I, 213; Wallace, *Evolution of the English Drama*
p. 114; Cunningham, *Accounts of the Revels*, pp. xix-xx.

in other ways.  Thus, when Oliver in the *Mayor of Queenborough* exclaims, "O, I shall swound," Simon reassures him:

> If thou dost, to spite thee,
> A player's boy shall bring thee aqua-vitae! [68]

That the boys made the most of their opportunities upon such occasions appears from a passage in *Bartholomew Fair:* [69]

> Have you none of your pretty, impudent boys now to bring stools, fill tobacco, fetch ale and beg money, as they have at other houses?

Percy Simpson [70] thinks they had still other duties.  To insure that each actor came pat, he writes, "and to jog his memory if he were 'out,' was the duty of an underling—*usually a boy*—called the 'book-holder' or the 'prompter,' who watched the cues, got the properties ready, and arranged for the music, alarums, and stage thunder."  That the important duties of a prompter in a repertory theatre should have been intrusted to a boy, and that this boy should have been property-man, prompter, and general stage-manager all in one, is incredible, and I do not know of any evidence to support such a view.  Certainly the "Stage-keeper" and "Book-holder" who exchange notes in the Induction to *Bartholomew Fair* are not exactly children!  And "the blue-coated stage-keepers" mentioned in another document [71] were not boys, but ordinary servants.

Provision for the employment of a "booke keeper, tyreman," and "tyrewoman" is made in the 1608 agreement of the house-keepers of the Whitefriars,[72] and all are mentioned again in

---

68. Middleton, *Mayor of Queenborough*, V, 1.  (It is possible, of course, that these "players' boys" were not actors.)
69. V, 3.          70. *Shakespeare's England*, II, 265.
71. See below, p. 286 and n. 105.  The blue coat was the recognized livery of the Elizabethan servingman.  (Cf. *Malone Society Collections*, I, 164.)
72. *New Shakespeare Society Transactions* (1887-92), pp. 275-76.

*The Actor's Remonstrance* (1644), and, together with "the Sweepers of the house," in the Salisbury Court Papers of 1639.[73] What their wages may have been we may gather from a passage in the *Articles of Oppression against Mr. Hinchlowe* promulgated by the Lady Elizabeth's Men in 1615.[74] In that document the actors refer to the appointment of a man to have charge "in bying of Clothes (he beinge to have VI$^s$ a weeke)." Doubtless the sweepers and stagehands did not fare so well; we know, at all events, that Garrick's "dressers," "doorkeepers," and attendants in general, got but 9*s*. a week in 1765.[75] It will appear in a moment that in the Elizabethan theatre the stage-keepers, tiremen, gatherers and all, besides attending to their regular work, were pressed into service as supers when occasion demanded.

Of the dishonesty of the "gatherers," who collected the entrance money at the theatres, Mr. W. J. Lawrence [76] has written at length, and he has noted also that women as well as men were employed for this work. A hint as to the number of these worthies employed at the Hope Theatre, and of the miserable wages they ordinarily received, is to be gathered from the complaint of the Lady Elizabeth's Men just referred to. The actors charge Henslowe with "havinge 9 gatherers more than his due, itt Comes to this yeare from the Companie . . . 10$^{11}$." The passage is puzzling, but we know from other documents that the housekeepers or owners had the privilege of appointing some of the gatherers,[77] though the actor-sharers appear to have paid the wages. Still, nine gatherers, plus those to which Henslowe was justly entitled, make rather a large number, and one almost suspects a misreading of the manu-

73. *Shakespeare Society Papers*, IV, 100.

74. *Henslowe Papers*, p. 89. In 1584 the Smiths Company at Coventry paid 2*s*. to one Robert Lawton "for kepynge of the booke" of *The Destruction of Jerusalem*, its pageant of that year (Halliwell-Phillipps, *Illustrations*, p. 57).

75. *Notes and Queries*, 6th. ser., XI, 461.     76. *Elizabethan Playhouse*, II, 95 ff.

77. In 1612 Robert Browne wrote to Edward Alleyn to ask a gatherer's place for the wife of a hireling named Rose, who was then playing with the Prince's Men (*Henslowe Papers*, pp. 63, 85). Condell bequeathed to his "old servant Elizabeth Wheaton that place or privilege which she now exerciseth in the houses of the Blackfryers . . . and the Globe" (Malone-Boswell, *op. cit.*, III, 205).

script. If the passage means that a gatherer's wage was only about one pound a year—perhaps to be supplemented by tips—the housekeepers and actor-sharers were not taking the best conceivable means to discourage dishonesty. Yet there seem to have been many candidates for gatherers' places.[78] Perhaps they sought the spoils of office rather than its legitimate rewards. Another interpretation is possible, but does not fully explain matters after all. A document discovered by Professor Wallace,[79] while it does not bring "the first hint of either the amount or method of pay" of the gatherers, as Wallace asserted, does raise an interesting question as to their remuneration at the Red Bull, about the year 1607. One of the papers in the Woodford-Holland suit—brought in that year by Woodford, to establish his title to a one-seventh holding in the Red Bull—states that with this share went the right to a gatherer's place, the gatherer being entitled to "the eighteenth penny and the eighteenth part of such moneys & other comodities as should bee collected or receaved for the profitts of the Galleries or other places in . . . the Red Bull." But another deposition in the same suit throws doubt upon the first. It speaks only of "the arrerages of eighteen pence a weeke due to the gatherer's place." Even if the first deposition is trustworthy, not many gatherers in any one theatre could have been entitled to so large a proportion of the total receipts. And the fact that we do not hear of any such arrangement in the dozens of extant suits concerning theatrical shares, would indicate either that the Red Bull case was exceptional, or that the gatherer's commission in the other theatres was smaller and not worth contending for in the courts.

"Stage-playes," writes Prynne,[80] "are alwayes accompanied with . . . lust-provoking . . . Musicke." Something might be said on the subject of his adjective, but my point here concerns only the musicians. Their part in the entertainment offered by

78. See the preceding note.
79. "Three London Theatres," *Nebraska University Studies*, IX, 11 ff.
80. *Histrio-Mastix*, p. 274.

the Elizabethan theatre was, as has long been recognized, of considerable importance. In the *Diary of the Duke of Stettin-Pomerania*,[81] who came to London in 1602, it is recorded that on the occasion of his visit to the Blackfriars there was music "for a whole hour preceding the play." Opinions still differ as to just how much, and how regularly, music was provided in the public theatres; [82] but it is clear that in the private houses music between the acts and at other times was a regular portion of the feast, from the days of *Gammer Gurton's Needle* (1566) down to the time of *The Actors' Remonstrance* (1644).[83] I wish to add a note concerning the musicians rather than the music.

G. H. Cowling, in writing his book on *Music on the Shakespearian Stage* (1913), appears to have been puzzled by the fact that in Henslowe's inventory of the properties of the Admiral's Men in 1598, a number of musical instruments are listed.[84] "It is not impossible," says Cowling,[85] "that Henslowe had them in pawn; but the simplest solution is that the musicians in regular employment at the Rose Theatre left their instruments there over night." In this case, however, the simplest solution is not the right one. If Cowling had read *Henslowe's Diary* more closely, he would have found that on several occasions in 1598 and 1599 the Admiral's Men purchased base viols "& other enstruments *for the companey*." [86] The entries in question are interesting because they prove that the company purchased and owned the musical instruments used for its plays. Mr. W. J. Lawrence has suggested that the playhouses were free to engage the services of the Waits of London and nearby towns,[87] but the Henslowe entries re-

---

81. Quoted by Wallace, *Children of the Chapel*, pp. 105-7; W. J. Lawrence, *Musical Quarterly*, VI, 193, etc. (cf. *Transactions Royal Historical Society*, New Ser., VI, 1-67).

82. Professor Graves, Mr. W. J. Lawrence, and Professor Wallace differ in their interpretations of the all-important passage on the subject in the Induction to *The Malcontent*. For a summary of their views, cf. *Musical Quarterly*, VI (1920), 192 ff.

83. See *Gammer Gurton's Needle*, Act II; W. C. Hazlitt, *op. cit.*, p. 262; Lawrence, *Elizabethan Playhouse*, I, 90.

84. *Henslowe Papers*, pp. 116-18.        85. P. 83.

86. *Henslowe Diary*, I, 100, 110.        87. *Musical Quarterly*, VI, 200.

emphasize the point that musicians could be had even nearer home. In many cases—particularly in the public theaters—the musicians were doubtless hirelings or actor-sharers, rather than a regular "noise" or band of instrumentalists. At a time when every tavern and barber-shop had "some instrumente of musicke . . . laide in sighte," [88] and every gallant could play "his part o' th' Violls," [89] the actors, naturally enough, were frequently able to find all the instrumentalists they needed among their own number. It is interesting to note that Edward Alleyn was known as a "musicion" before he gained his reputation as an actor.[90] Again, "Wilhelm Kempe, *instrumentalist*" and actor, seems to have been as popular in one capacity as in the other when he appeared at the Danish court in 1586; [91] and Augustine Phillips bequeathed to his late acting-apprentices, James Sands and Samuel Gilborne, "a Citterne a Bandore . . . a lute" and "a Base Viall." [92] Indeed, later theatrical memoirs and biographies [93] show clearly that throughout the seventeenth and eighteenth centuries the lesser players continued to discourse their own music.

In the later decades of the Elizabethan period, however, "the playhouse musick improved yearly," [94] and it is likely that many of the theatres employed regular bands of musicians. The Blackfriars orchestra, in particular, became famous, and the playhouse musicians found much profitable employment outside the theatre as well. The author of *The Actors' Remonstrance* [95] writes regretfully of their departed glory: "Our Musike that was held so delectable and precious *that they scorned to come to a Taverne under twentie shillings salary for two houres,* now wander with Instru-

88. Gosson, *School of Abuse, Shakespeare Society* (1841), p. 26.
89. Letoy in *The Antipodes* (i, 5) says of his servants:
      "The worst can sing or play his part o' th' Violls
      And act his part too in a comedy."
90. Warner, *Catalogue MSS. of Dulwich College*, p. xvii.
91. *New Shakespeariana*, I, 17.      92. Malone-Boswell, *op. cit.*, III, 472.
93. Cf. Thomas Dibdin, *Reminiscences*, I, 108; Thomas Holcroft, *Memoirs*, I, 241-42; cf. above, p. 210.
94. Wright, *Historia Histrionica* (Collier's *Dodley*, I, cxliii).
95. Hazlitt, *op. cit.*, p. 263.

ments under their cloaks . . . saluting every roome where there is company with, Will you have any Musike, Gentlemen?" And we learn that "some of the musicke" employed in the Inns of Court Masque to Charles I in 1633 — the playhouse musicians doubtless among them — "had one hundred Pounds a-piece." [96] So far as I know, there is no evidence to support H. B. Baker's assertion [97] that "the musicians . . . paid . . . an annual stipend for the privilege of playing" at the theatres; on the other hand, it is unlikely that their services ever required a very heavy outlay on the part of the managers. [98]

A word remains to be said as to certain additional services rendered on occasion by all the employees the company could muster. The average Elizabethan company appears not to have had more than twenty actors on its roll, [99] of which ten or twelve were sharers and the rest hirelings and boys. It is interesting to recall, therefore, that Shakespeare's plays average twenty-five speaking parts, and that this number rises to thirty-five in the historical plays. One is inclined, therefore, to echo the sentiment of Feliche in the Induction to the first part of *Antonio and Mellida:* "I fear it is not possible to limn so many persons in so small a tablet as the compass of our plays afford." Yet Shakespeare made less demands upon the numerical strength of his company than many other dramatists. The play of *Tamar Cam*, for example (acted by the Admiral's Men in 1596 and after), besides calling for a very large cast, required a closing "procession of 12 pairs representing a number of different races"; [100] the *dramatis personae* of Heywood's *Silver Age* number forty-one, not counting "seruing-men, swaines, Theban ladies, the seuen Planets and the Furies";

96. Burney's *History of Music*, III, 376.          97. *London Stage*, p. 22.

98. The contract between D'Avenant and his actors in 1660 provided for "a consort of musiciens" to be paid not more than 30s. a day. In the Restoration theatre, of course, music played a much more important part than in that of Shakespeare (cf. Malone-Boswell, *op. cit.*, III, 258).

99. See Malone-Boswell, *op. cit.*, III, 179; Murray, *English Dramatic Companies*, I, 123-24; Wallace, *Shakspere and His London Associates*, p. 90.

100. *Henslowe Papers*, p. 148; *Henslowe's Diary*, II, 155.

and over a hundred characters appear in the course of the six acts of the interesting old play *Histrio-Mastix*.[101] It must have been a somewhat difficult task to cast these plays, but we can readily understand how it was done. The evidence shows, among other things, that the hirelings in their time played many parts — sometimes, indeed, as many as three or four in a single performance. The wife of Blaze, an inferior actor in *The Antipodes*, complains that she did not see her husband act. "I did though, Bab," he assures her, "two [mutes], the sage man-midwife and the Basket-maker." [102] And possibly even the leading actors took on two or more parts when the play called for it.[103] Thus, when Feliche inquires of the hero of *Antonio and Mellida*,[104] "What must you play?" Antonio replies, "Faith, I know not what; an hermaphrodite, two parts in one . . . my true person being Antonio . . . I take this feigned presence of an Amazon." But not even half a dozen such men as the ubiquitous Mr. Blaze could suffice to make up a procession of all the nations at the close of a tragedy which had already sent most of the leading actors — temporarily — to a better world. At such a time, while "the blue-coated stage-keepers," [105] perhaps, were beating a dead march, or sounding a peal of ordinance somewhere in the rear, all available hands — boys, "attendaunts," and gatherers,[106] — all in appropriate costume, slowly marched to the back of the stage and brought the piece to an impressive close.

101. See Simpson, *School of Shakspere*, II, 16.        102. V, iv.

103. Dr. Greg and Mr. J. Dover Wilson hold strongly to the view that "doubling" by leading players was the established practice, but this view is not accepted by Mr. W. J. Lawrence (cf. *London Times Literary Review*, for August 21, 1919, January 29, and February 5 and 19, 1920).

104. Induction, Part I.

105.                    "The horrid noise . . .
                        By the blue-coated stage-keepers."
(Prologue of Nabbes's *Hannibal and Scipio*, quoted by Collier, *op. cit.*, III, 143.)

106. "Gibs his boy," "little wil Barne," "guards," "Attendaunts," and "gatherers," are mentioned in the stage-manager's directions for the processions in *Frederick and Basilea* and *Tamar Cam* (*Henslowe Papers*, pp. 136-38; cf. Collier, *Annals*, ed. 1879, III, 207).

# XIII

THREE NOTES: *MUCH ADO, RICHARD III, AS YOU LIKE IT.*

### 1. *Much Ado:* Queen Elizabeth and Benedick's "Partridge Wing" [1]

IN THE second act of *Much Ado About Nothing* Beatrice jokingly comments upon Benedick's manly appetite — his hunger for good red meat. My purpose here is to note that thereby Beatrice comes delightfully close to echoing a pleasantry directed by no less a personage than Queen Elizabeth against the great Lord Leicester. Elizabeth's little joke is recounted in Mr. Frederick Chamberlin's interesting book on *The Sayings of Queen Elizabeth* (1923).[2]

Beatrice must be heard first. It is the masque scene, and Benedick has refused to admit that he is the Benedick who has dubbed Beatrice 'My Lady Disdain.' This Benedick, she tells her masqued cavalier, is the prince's jester — a very dull fool! She wishes that she might have been able to tell him as much to his face. The masqued cavalier somewhat ruefully offers to convey the message (to himself), and this offer Beatrice gaily accepts. And thereby hangs the joke anent Benedick's appetite. "Do, do," she says, —

> "He'll but break a comparison or two on me: which, peradventure not marked or not laughed at, strikes him into melancholy; *and then there's a partridge wing saved, for the fool will eat no supper that night.*" [3]

1. Revised from *Modern Language Notes*, XLI (1926), 527 ff.
2. Pp. 35-37.
3. *Much Ado*, II, i, 151-156.

Queen Elizabeth's winged word to the same purpose appears in a letter [4] addressed by her to the Countess of Shrewsbury, who had entertained Leicester "when he went to the baths of Buxton for treatment for the gout." It is, says Chamberlin, one of the best extant specimens of Elizabeth's "lighter style," and he adds that to get its full flavor one must bear in mind the fact that Leicester was "an extremely hearty eater and drinker."

The Queen begins by thanking her right trusty cousin, the Countess, for her entertainment of Leicester, — especially for the liberal "diet" which had been provided for him. She considers that this good service has been done not "unto him, but to our own self," and she therefore means "to take upon us the debt and to acknowledge you . . . our creditors, so as you can be content to accept us for debtor." But this might grow to be a dangerous debt if the Countess indulged Leicester too much! Therefore she must "cut off some part of the large allowance of diet you give him, lest otherwise the debt thereby may grow to be so great as we shall not be able to discharge the same, and so become bankrupt." For the saving of her credit, therefore, the Queen prescribes "a proportion of diet which we mean in no case you shall exceed, and that is to allow him by the day for his meat two ounces of flesh . . . and for his drink the twentieth part of a pint of wine to comfort his stomach, and as much of St. Anne's sacred water as he listeth to drink. On festival days, as is meet for a man of his quality, we can be content you shall enlarge his diet *by allowing unto him for his dinner the shoulder of a wren*,[5] and for his supper a leg of the same, besides his ordinary ounces."

It is a bit anti-climactic to turn, after this, to the commentators' meditations upon Benedick's partridge wing. Indeed, a glance at the Variorum [6] suggests that good Queen Bess's shoulder of a wren would have been no less delectable than wholesome a

4. Chamberlin gives no date.
5. My italics. (Cf. *Cymbeline*, IV, ii, 303-305: "If there be/Yet left in heaven *as small* a drop of pity/As *a wren's eye* . . .")
6. Furness, *Much Ado*, p. 74.

morsel for the commentators. The good queen's flight of fancy (not to crack the wind of the poor phrase!) might have helped to clear the air.

In the first place, Elizabeth's joke would seem to indicate that Halliwell's contribution to the subject is not especially in point. That "the wing seems to have been formerly considered the most delicate part of the bird" is a conclusion which nobody would wish to deny; but it is surely not a matter of consequence here. Deighton saw this, and came nearer to putting the thing to rights. "The jest," he says, "turns not upon the saving of the best part of the bird, but upon the effeminacy of Benedick's appetite, for whose supper such a trifle was sufficient." If Deighton had put it the other way about, he might have avoided trouble, for it would seem that other commentators took him seriously, or literally. The jest turns, of course, upon the *hugeness* of Benedick's appetite. For, as Wright observed, Beatrice had previously described Benedick as "a very valiant trencher-man," one who "hath an excellent stomach," [7] and such an one would not have been likely to make a supper off a partridge wing! Wright's idea, then, would seem to be that in eating a partridge wing "Benedick . . . would eat what he would call no supper." Furness, who has the last word, may have been troubled by the apparent suggestion that this would have been a case of eating the wing and saving it too! "Nevertheless," he writes, "I am inclined to doubt that there is any hidden meaning in the words." Then follows a sentence in which Furness seems almost to have foreseen that Beatrice's mind and Queen Elizabeth's ran along the same line. "The jest," he says, "would have been equally pungent had Beatrice specified any other delicacy." But the point is not as Furness finally puts it, "that Benedick's appetite would be utterly gone." It is this:— Benedick, like Leicester, had so robustious an appetite that his abstemious lady laughingly suggests an allowance of diet such as Oberon might have fancied, but not Benedick or Leicester. When

7. I, i, 51-52.

Benedick grows melancholy because no one will laugh at the jokes
he has cracked about Beatrice—why then the valiant trencher-
man won't eat his supper, and thereby, forsooth, a whole partridge
wing will have been saved! And poor Benedick, unlike Leicester,
would have had not even the twentieth part of a pint of wine nor
yet a swallow of St. Anne's sacred water to comfort his stomach!

### 2. SHAKESPEARE, DANIEL, AND *Richard III*

Many of Shakespeare's verbal and figurative borrowings from
his predecessors and contemporaries are perfectly familiar to students, but not a few have remained unnoticed. I wish to call
attention, in this note and in the following,[8] to two cases in point,
the first of which seems to me a certainty, and the second at least
an interesting possibility.

It is certain that Shakespeare knew, and, in his plays and
poems, frequently drew upon Samuel Daniel's *Complaint of Rosamond* (1592). For example, Romeo's lament over the body of
Juliet:

> beauty's *ensign* yet
> Is crimson in thy lips and in thy cheeks,
> And *death's pale flag* is not advanced there—

is certainly reminiscent of the king's complaint in *Rosamond* concerning "nought-respecting *death*," who

> Plac'd his *pale colours* (th' *ensigne* of his might)
> Upon his new-got spoyle before his right.[9]

So far as I can learn, however, no commentator has noticed an almost equally close likeness between *Rosamond* and *Richard III*

8. Reprinted from *Philological Quarterly*, XV (1936), 4 ff.
9. Lines 773-75; cf. H. R. Anders, *Shakespeare's Books* (Berlin, 1904), p. 87; and
W. Ewig, "Shakespeare, and Daniel's . . . *Rosamond*," *Anglia*, XXII (1899), 436-448.

(probably written in 1593, the year after Daniel's poem). Rosamond's king "vapours out sighs that to the skies ascended," —

> Sighs, the *poor ease calamity* affords,
> Which serve for speech when sorrow wanteth *words*.[10]

With these calamitous sighs and heart-easing words compare those in the colloquy between the old Duchess of York and Queen Elizabeth in *Richard III:*

> *Duchess.* Why should *calamity* be full of *words?*
> *Queen.*   Let them have scope; though . . . they . . .
>            Help nothing else, yet do they *ease* the heart.[11]

### 3. *As You Like It* AND *Everyman*.

I am not aware that the good Duke's speech in Arden —

> Sweet are the uses of *adversity*,
> Which, like the toad, ugly and venomous,
> *Wears yet a precious jewel in* his head —

has ever been connected with the words of Confession to Everyman in the famous old morality play of that title:

> I wyll you comforte as well as I can
> And *a precyous iewell* I will gyve the[e],
> Called penaunce, voyder of *aduersyte*.[12]

Yet in the combination of ideas (adversity as a precious jewel) and in the turn of phrase there appears to be at least a superficial resemblance. The point must not be pressed too far. The popular superstition concerning the "foul toad" bearing "a fair stone in his head" is in *Euphues*, and it remained a favorite vulgar error of the poets. Adversity, again, had long been a favorite topic for many

10. Lines 636-37.     11. IV, iv, 126-131.     12. Lines 556-58.

writers, sacred and prophane. The Scriptures, however, do not describe it as "a precious jewel," and I have not found this particular combination elsewhere in Shakespeare's contemporaries. Now *Everyman* was extant in at least four separate editions published between 1508 and 1537.[13] Since Shakespeare, like Ancient Pistol, certainly had a voracious appetite for old plays—even for those which out-heroded Herod or exploited "the old Vice" of the moralities—it is at least possible that the famous lines in *As You Like It* may be in some measure indebted to Shakespeare's memory of *Everyman*.

13. Cf. J. Q. Adams, *Chief Pre-Shakespearean Dramas* (Boston, 1924), p. 288n.

# EPILOGUE:  ON READING OLD POETS [1]

Not long ago Carl Sandburg visited our campus.  One night he gave a stirring public reading, and after that I heard him tell, privately, a story about poets and poetry.  A teacher had given her class an assignment on the life of John Milton.  Later on, she turned to question a small boy on the lesson.  "Tommy," said she, "what was John Milton's affliction?"  The boy looked puzzled.  And so she repeated, "What was his affliction?—What was wrong with him?—What did he *suffer* from?"—"O," said the boy, "I know.—Poetry!"

Most of us do not suffer from an overplus of this divine ailment.  The best of us suffer, rather, from that affliction of Milton's which the small boy had forgotten: from blindness, and from deafness to boot.  That is why we ought to *hear* more poetry—even if we have to read it to one another.  To be sure, Mr. Sandburg demonstrated once again that poetry ought to be read by a poet.  But perhaps this is a counsel of perfection.  Happily, some of the poets we want to hear no longer live on Grub Street; and we can not always pay them to come to our town.  Meanwhile, we can try to give them a "hearing" for one another—just as we can and do try to act plays, and indeed to write plays, out of our region or locality and our experience of life.

Of course it is a difficult thing to do—this "reading aloud for the pleasure of others."  But it is a thing that needs to be done, however difficult.  "Heard melodies are sweet, but those unheard are sweeter."  Perhaps—in those rare moments when our inward eye and ear are perfectly in tune with the infinite.  But most of us, most of the time, cannot catch the subtle overtones and the delicate harmonies of great poetry by mere *silent* reading, any

1.  Extracts from a radio address of the University of Tennessee faculty series.

more than most of us can catch by mere reading the melody or the meaning of great music. We need to *hear* both. Better still to try—each in his own way and time—to make them effectively audible to others: to play the game rather than be everlastingly content to sit back in the stands as a mere spectator. Music and poetry, of course, are no mere games; but even the greatest arts are best appreciated by those who try, however humbly, to interpret some of their meanings for themselves, if not for others. Certainly, excellence in poetic interpretation is hard to attain. "No accomplishment," said De Quincey, "is more rare." De Quincey, incidentally, took pride in his own reading, but he adds that Mrs. Siddons failed dismally in attempting to read *Paradise Lost*, and that even the poets themselves sometimes fall short of the ideal. Wordsworth, for example, was the only poet De Quincey knew "who could read his own verses," whereas Southey and Coleridge "read as if crying, or at least wailing lugubriously." [2] And yet the secret of success here is surely not too hard to fathom, provided one has even the most modest aptitude. Practice is the word,—practice in listening and practice in making oneself heard, not without passion, but without overstepping the modesty of nature.

It is doubtless a piece of presumption, even so, for a mere student of poetry to appear before those who may have heard a poet's own cadences (no lugubrious wailing, but stirring music!) ringing in their ears. Yet there may be comfort for reader and listeners. "Mankind," said Thomas Carlyle, "needs heroes to govern it." "But," he added on second thought, "is not every man, God be thanked, a potential hero?" I will not urge that every man and woman is, strictly speaking, a potential poet. Indeed, I have heard of one or two respectable persons who are said to dislike poetry. We all have our blind spots. Theirs are morbidly developed in one direction. Their potential enjoyment of life and its meaning is, to that extent, impoverished. "Poetry,"

2. *Confessions of an English Opium-Eater*, Part III.

said William Hazlitt, "is not a branch of authorship; it is the stuff out of which our life is made." What does this imply? For one thing, that every normal human being will wish to cultivate the open eye and the loving heart. He who has eyes that see and ears that hear *will keep them open:* he will drink as deep as he may of the ancient melodies and graces, will give thanks for the undying loveliness of earth, the mellowed hopes and fears of the human spirit which are poetry. In the clash and speed and uproar of our day, we need all the more to take time out now and then to hear these quiet rhythms and this world-old music. That is one reason why we need to read the old poets *and* the new.

And now it may be asked, "Why go so far back as Shakespeare and the Elizabethans?" I answer, not only because they came before the modern, but also because they *are* modern, being not of an age but for all time. Another good reason, amply sufficient in itself, is that some of my fellow-students, in the University and out, asked me to include in this reading certain of Shakespeare's sonnets. The reading included also some songs, pastorals, and other kinds of poems; some poets other than Shakespeare; and some illustrations of recurring moods and themes which the Elizabethans loved and for which we love them — because these are also *our* moods and themes. With all this, mere program notes had, of course, to be kept to a minimum. What is art? What is poetry? What is a lyric? What is truth? My hearers or readers, like jesting Pilate, would not stay for an answer! The poems, indeed, answer for themselves.

Still, I should like to return for a moment to my point that the Elizabethans are modern. To illustrate, let anyone who would like to test the point for himself turn to a modern poem by Archibald Macleish. It is the poem in which Macleish boldly says (but does he mean it?) that they were "lies" — the proud vaunts of the old poets who boasted that their lovely loves would be forever remembered by virtue of their immortal verse. And then let him turn to Shakespeare's sonnet number 55:

> Not marble, nor the gilded monuments
> Of princes, shall outlive this powerful rime. . . .

For the first line of this sonnet is also the title of Macleish's poem.
Or, again, turn to a very recent sonnet by Edna St. Vincent
Millay [3] which bids brave defiance to the hungry grave:

> Thou famished grave, I will not fill thee yet,
> Roar though thou dost, I am too happy here;
> Gnaw thine own sides, fast on; I have no fear
> Of thy dark project, but my heart is set
> On living—I have heroes to beget
> Before I die; I will not come anear
> Thy dismal jaws for many a splendid year:
> Till I be old, I aim not to be eat.
>
> I cannot starve thee out; I am thy prey
> And thou shalt have me; but I dare defend
> That I can stave thee off; and I dare say
> What with the life I lead, the force I spend,
> I'll be but bones and jewels on that day,
> And leave thee hungry even in the end.

This language and these bold accents Shakespeare would have
understood.  Witness *his* defiance:

> Poor soul, the centre of my sinful earth,
> [Thrall to] these rebel powers that thee array,
> Why dost thou pine within and suffer dearth,
> Painting thy outward walls so costly gay?
> Why so large cost, having so short a lease
> Dost thou upon thy fading mansion spend?
> Shall worms, inheritors of this excess
> Eat up thy charge?  Is this thy body's end?
> Then, soul, live thou upon thy servant's loss,
> And let that pine to aggravate thy store;
> Buy terms divine in selling hours of dross;
> Within be fed, without be rich no more:

3. From *Huntsman, What Quarry?*, published by Harper & Brothers.  Copyright,
1933, 1934, 1936, 1937, 1938, 1939, by Edna St. Vincent Millay.  Quoted by permission of
the author and publisher.

So shalt thou feed on Death, that feeds on men,
And Death once dead, there's no more dying then.

Or, finally, turn to that unforgettable passage in Thomas Nashe's song of the long ago, "Adieu, Farewell Earth's Bliss" —

Beauty is but a flower
Which wrinkles will devour:
Brightness falls from the air;
Queens have died young and fair;
Dust hath closed Helen's eye:
I am sick, I must die.
*Lord, have mercy on us!*

After which, for our last modern instance, turn to John Masefield's poem beginning "Be with me, Beauty, for the fire is dying. . . ." But this is the undying fire, at once old and new, whereby the true poets of all ages have brought light to men's eyes and warmth to men's hearts. Coleridge, also, was one of them, and Coleridge shall say our last word for the old poets and the new, and for the reading of poetry: "To find no contradiction in the union of old and new, to contemplate the Ancient of days with feelings as fresh as if they then sprang forth at his own *fiat* — this characterizes the minds that feel the riddle of the world, and may help to unravel it."

# INDEX